POE DAMERON

STAR WARS

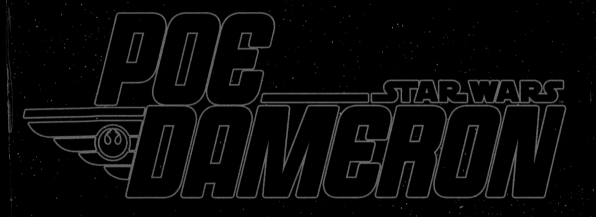

THE GATHERING STORM

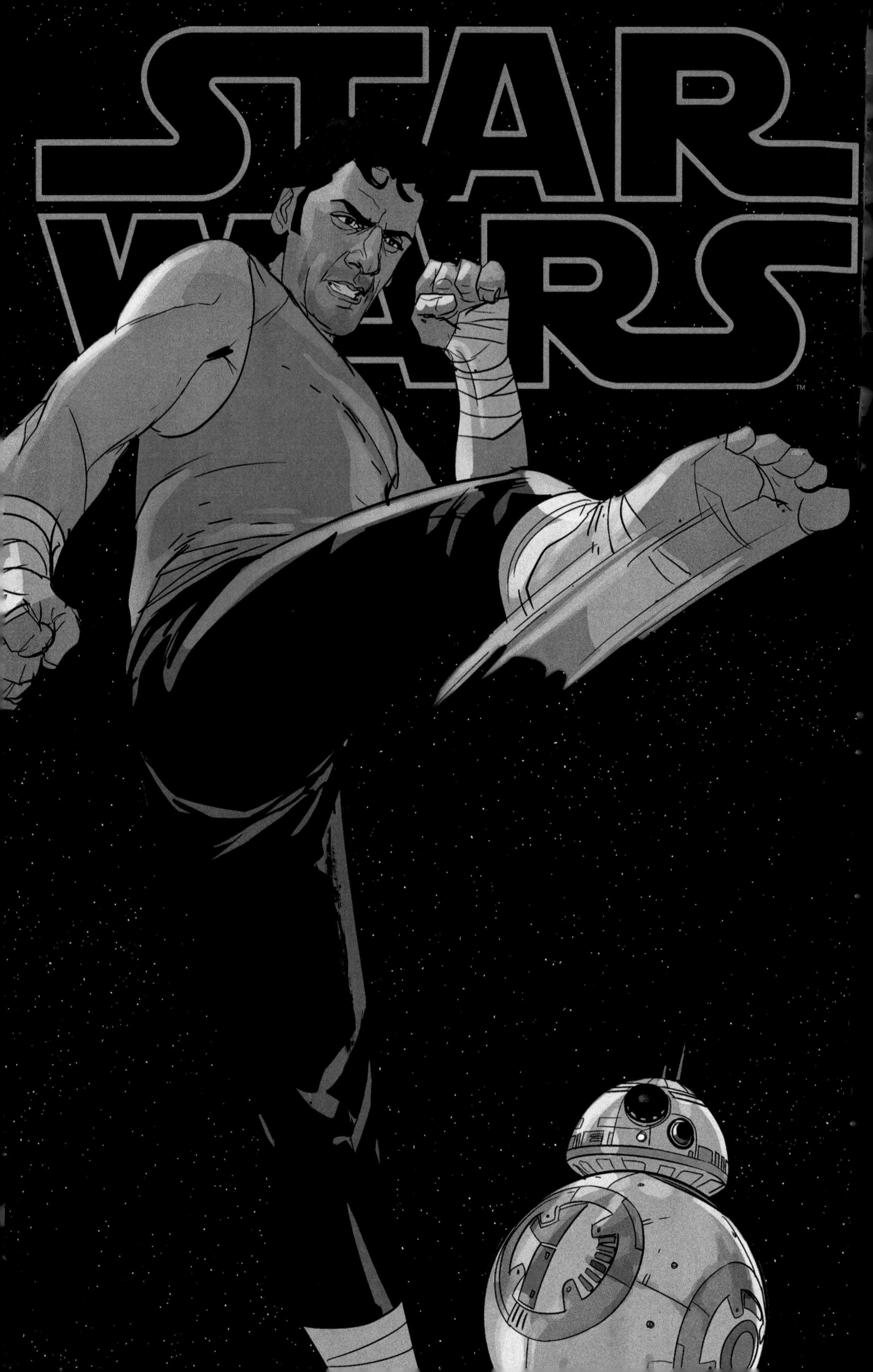
STAR WARS™

POE DAMERON

THE GATHERING STORM

Writer	**CHARLES SOULE**
Artist	**PHIL NOTO**
Letterer	**VC's JOE CARAMAGNA**
Cover Art	**PHIL NOTO**

Assistant Editor	**HEATHER ANTOS**
Editor	**JORDAN D. WHITE**
Executive Editor	**C.B. CEBULSKI**

Editor in Chief	**AXEL ALONSO**
Chief Creative Officer	**JOE QUESADA**
President	**DAN BUCKLEY**

For Lucasfilm:

Senior Editor	**FRANK PARISI**
Creative Director	**MICHAEL SIGLAIN**
Lucasfilm Story Group	**JAMES WAUGH, PABLO HIDALGO, LELAND CHEE, MATT MARTIN**

Collection Editor	**JENNIFER GRÜNWALD**
Assistant Editor	**CAITLIN O'CONNELL**
Associate Managing Editor	**KATERI WOODY**
Editor, Special Projects	**MARK D. BEAZLEY**
VP Production & Special Projects	**JEFF YOUNGQUIST**
SVP Print, Sales & Marketing	**DAVID GABRIEL**
Book Designer	**ADAM DEL RE**

STAR WARS: POE DAMERON VOL. 2 — THE GATHERING STORM. Contains material originally published in magazine form as STAR WARS: POE DAMERON #8-13. First printing 2017. ISBN# 978-1-302-90111-0. Published by MARVEL WORLDWIDE, INC., a subsidiary of MARVEL ENTERTAINMENT, LLC. OFFICE OF PUBLICATION: 135 West 50th Street, New York, NY 10020. STAR WARS and related text and illustrations are trademarks and/or copyrights, in the United States and other countries, of Lucasfilm Ltd. and/or its affiliates. © & TM Lucasfilm Ltd. No similarity between any of the names, characters, persons, and/or institutions in this magazine with those of any living or dead person or institution is intended, and any such similarity which may exist is purely coincidental. Marvel and its logos are TM Marvel Characters, Inc. Printed in the U.S.A. DAN BUCKLEY, President, Marvel Entertainment; JOE QUESADA, Chief Creative Officer; TOM BREVOORT, SVP of Publishing; DAVID BOGART, SVP of Business Affairs & Operations, Publishing & Partnership; C.B. CEBULSKI, VP of Brand Management & Development, Asia; DAVID GABRIEL, SVP of Sales & Marketing, Publishing; JEFF YOUNGQUIST, VP of Production & Special Projects; DAN CARR, Executive Director of Publishing Technology; ALEX MORALES, Director of Publishing Operations; SUSAN CRESPI, Production Manager; STAN LEE, Chairman Emeritus. For information regarding advertising in Marvel Comics or on Marvel.com, please contact Vit DeBellis, Integrated Sales Manager, at vdebellis@marvel.com. For Marvel subscription inquiries, please call 888-511-5480. Manufactured between 4/14/2017 and 5/16/2017 by QUAD/GRAPHICS WASECA, WASECA, MN, USA.

10 9 8 7 6 5 4 3 2 1

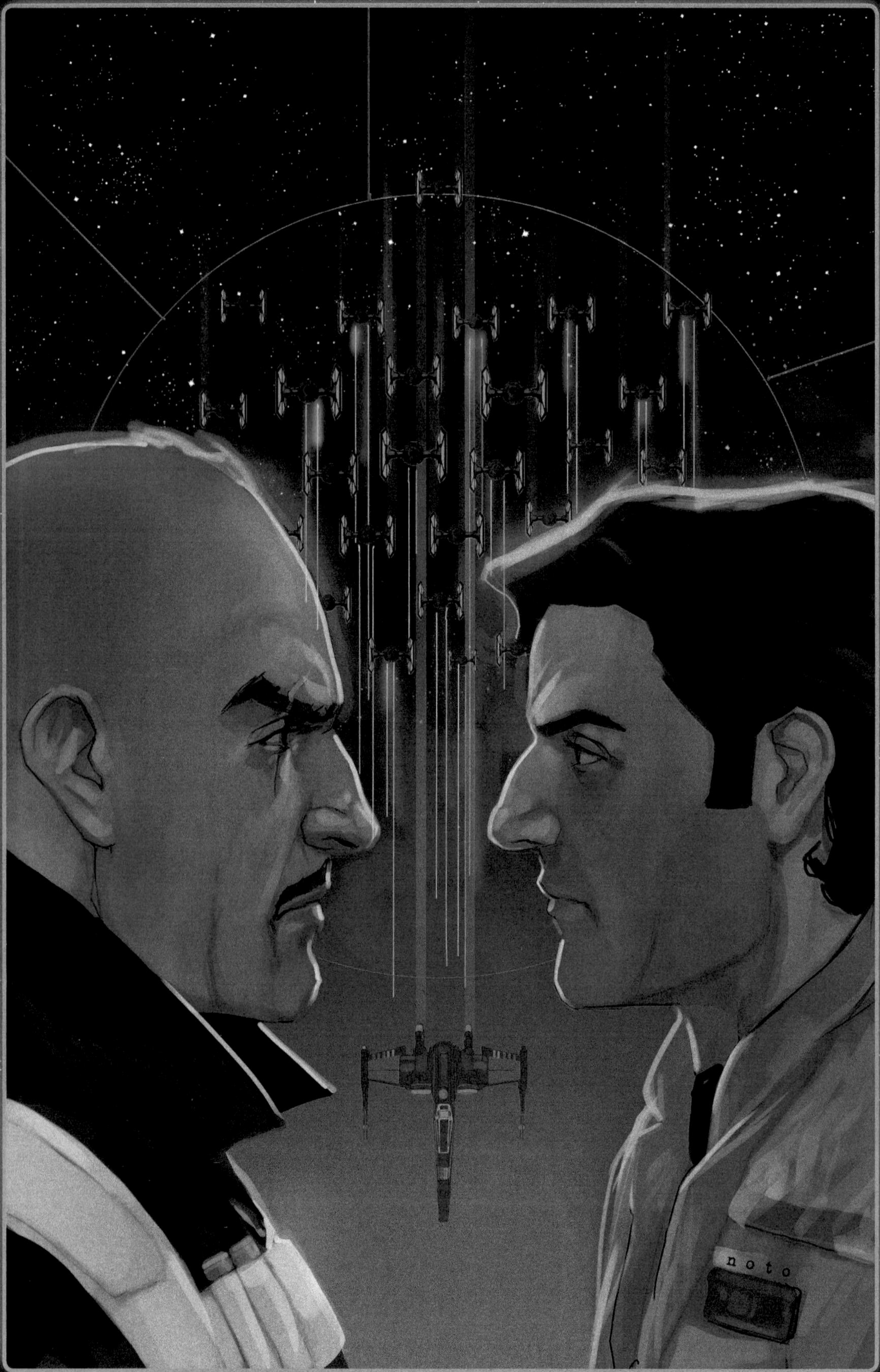
noto

8

THE GATHERING STORM

It is a time of uncertainty in the galaxy. Standing against the oppression of the First Order is General Organa's Resistance, including Poe Dameron and his team of ace pilots—Black Squadron.

After undertaking a mission to find the explorer Lor San Tekka, a new enemy has emerged: Terex, an officer of the First Order Security Bureau. Though Poe's crew of pilots has managed to survive multiple encounters, Terex has vowed to destroy them.

Meanwhile, shadows gather around Poe, as he has become increasingly certain that a member of Black Squadron is feeding information to the First Order about the Resistance and its allies, and darkness continues to spread across the galaxy....

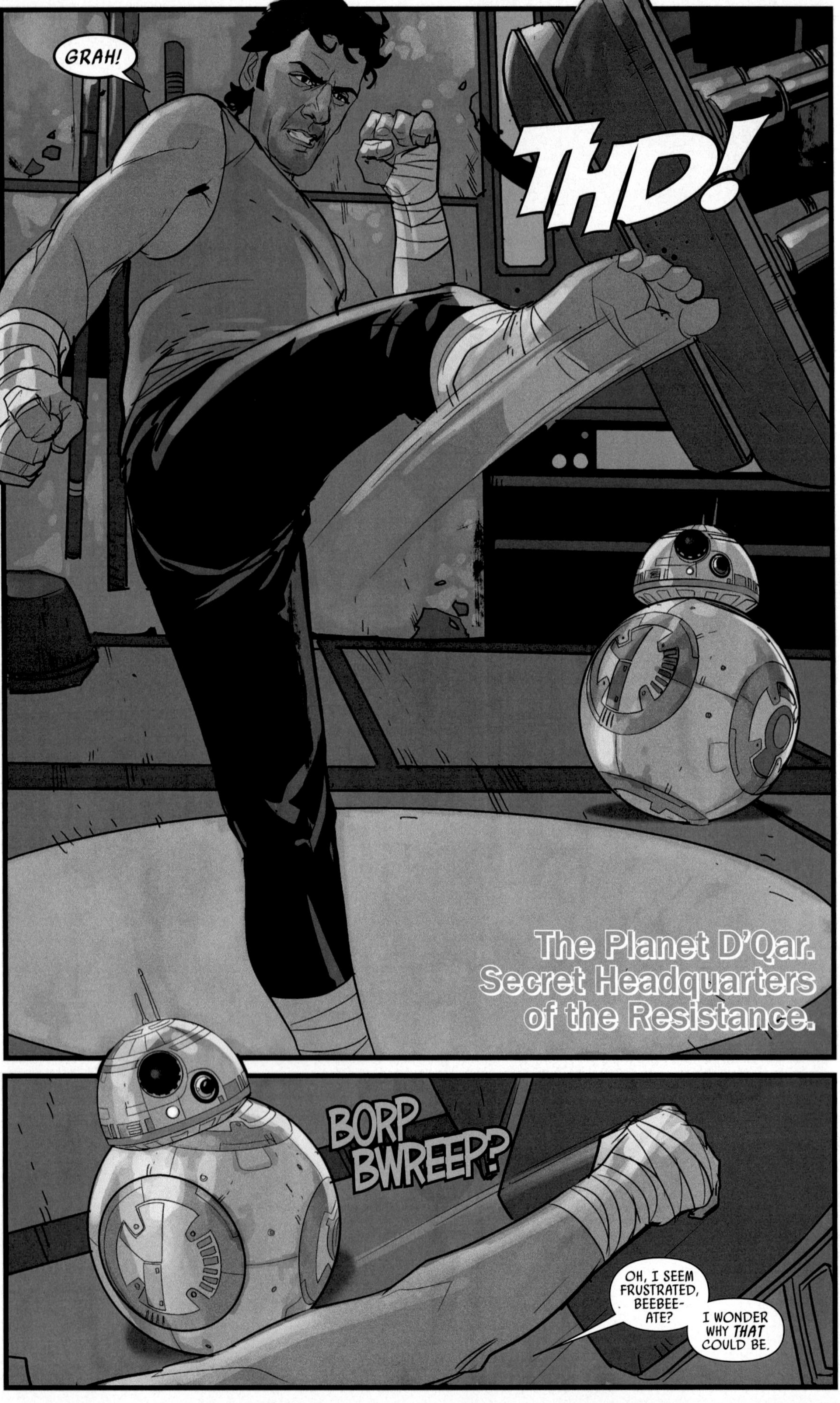
GRAH!
THD!
The Planet D'Qar. Secret Headquarters of the Resistance.
BORP BWREEP?
OH, I SEEM FRUSTRATED, BEEBEE-ATE?
I WONDER WHY THAT COULD BE.

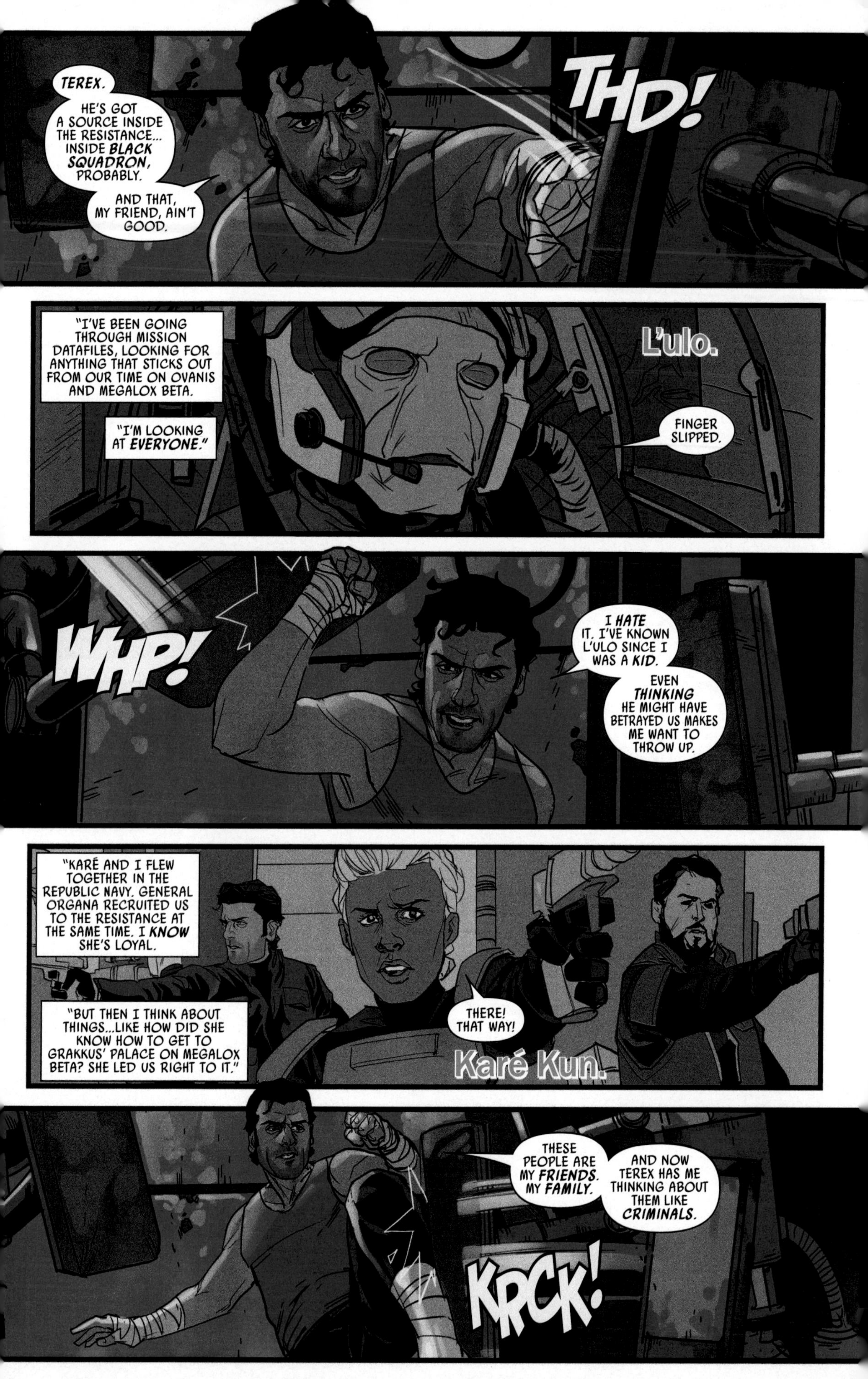

TEREX.
HE'S GOT A SOURCE INSIDE THE RESISTANCE... INSIDE BLACK SQUADRON, PROBABLY.
AND THAT, MY FRIEND, AIN'T GOOD.
THD!
"I'VE BEEN GOING THROUGH MISSION DATAFILES, LOOKING FOR ANYTHING THAT STICKS OUT FROM OUR TIME ON OVANIS AND MEGALOX BETA.
"I'M LOOKING AT EVERYONE."
L'ulo.
FINGER SLIPPED.
WHP!
I HATE IT. I'VE KNOWN L'ULO SINCE I WAS A KID.
EVEN THINKING HE MIGHT HAVE BETRAYED US MAKES ME WANT TO THROW UP.
"KARÉ AND I FLEW TOGETHER IN THE REPUBLIC NAVY. GENERAL ORGANA RECRUITED US TO THE RESISTANCE AT THE SAME TIME. I KNOW SHE'S LOYAL.
"BUT THEN I THINK ABOUT THINGS...LIKE HOW DID SHE KNOW HOW TO GET TO GRAKKUS' PALACE ON MEGALOX BETA? SHE LED US RIGHT TO IT."
THERE! THAT WAY!
Karé Kun.
THESE PEOPLE ARE MY FRIENDS. MY FAMILY.
AND NOW TEREX HAS ME THINKING ABOUT THEM LIKE CRIMINALS.
KRCK!

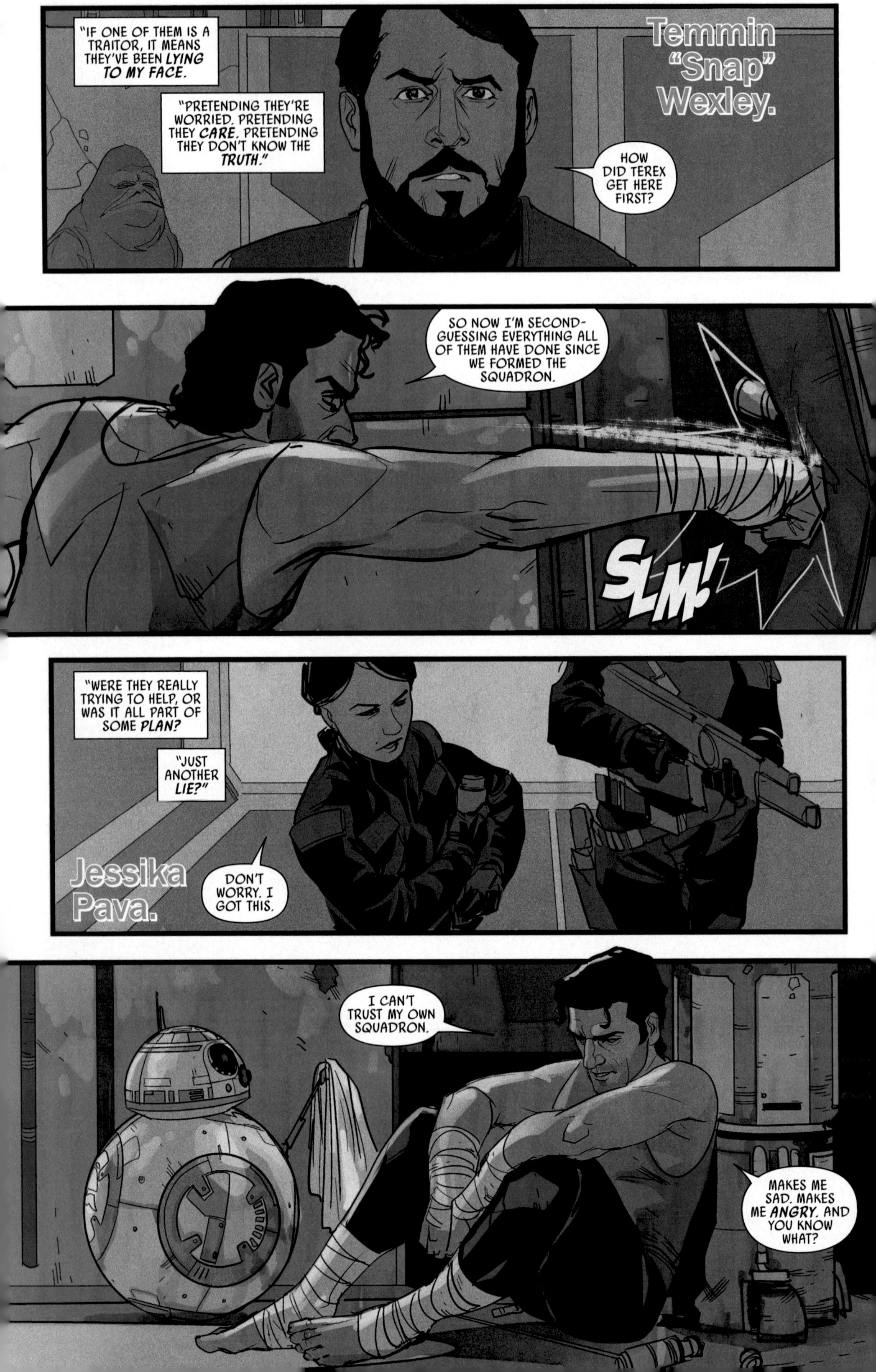

"IF ONE OF THEM IS A TRAITOR, IT MEANS THEY'VE BEEN LYING TO MY FACE.
"PRETENDING THEY'RE WORRIED. PRETENDING THEY CARE. PRETENDING THEY DON'T KNOW THE TRUTH."
Temmin "Snap" Wexley.
HOW DID TEREX GET HERE FIRST?
SO NOW I'M SECOND-GUESSING EVERYTHING ALL OF THEM HAVE DONE SINCE WE FORMED THE SQUADRON.
SLM!
"WERE THEY REALLY TRYING TO HELP, OR WAS IT ALL PART OF SOME PLAN?
"JUST ANOTHER LIE?"
Jessika Pava.
DON'T WORRY. I GOT THIS.
I CAN'T TRUST MY OWN SQUADRON.
MAKES ME SAD. MAKES ME ANGRY. AND YOU KNOW WHAT?

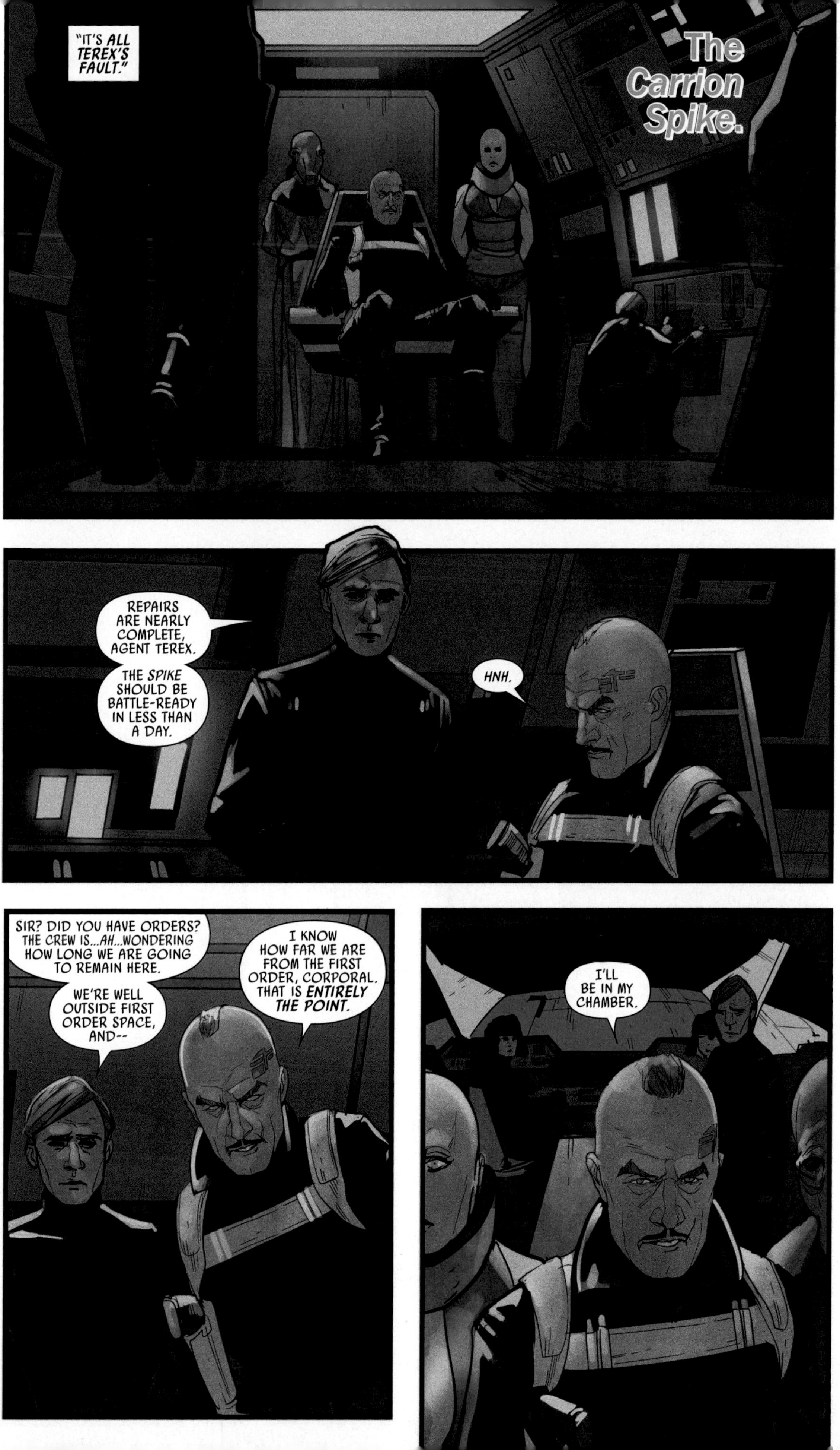
"IT'S ALL TEREX'S FAULT."
The Carrion Spike.
REPAIRS ARE NEARLY COMPLETE, AGENT TEREX.
THE SPIKE SHOULD BE BATTLE-READY IN LESS THAN A DAY.
HNH.
SIR? DID YOU HAVE ORDERS? THE CREW IS...AH...WONDERING HOW LONG WE ARE GOING TO REMAIN HERE.
WE'RE WELL OUTSIDE FIRST ORDER SPACE, AND--
I KNOW HOW FAR WE ARE FROM THE FIRST ORDER, CORPORAL. THAT IS ENTIRELY THE POINT.
I'LL BE IN MY CHAMBER.

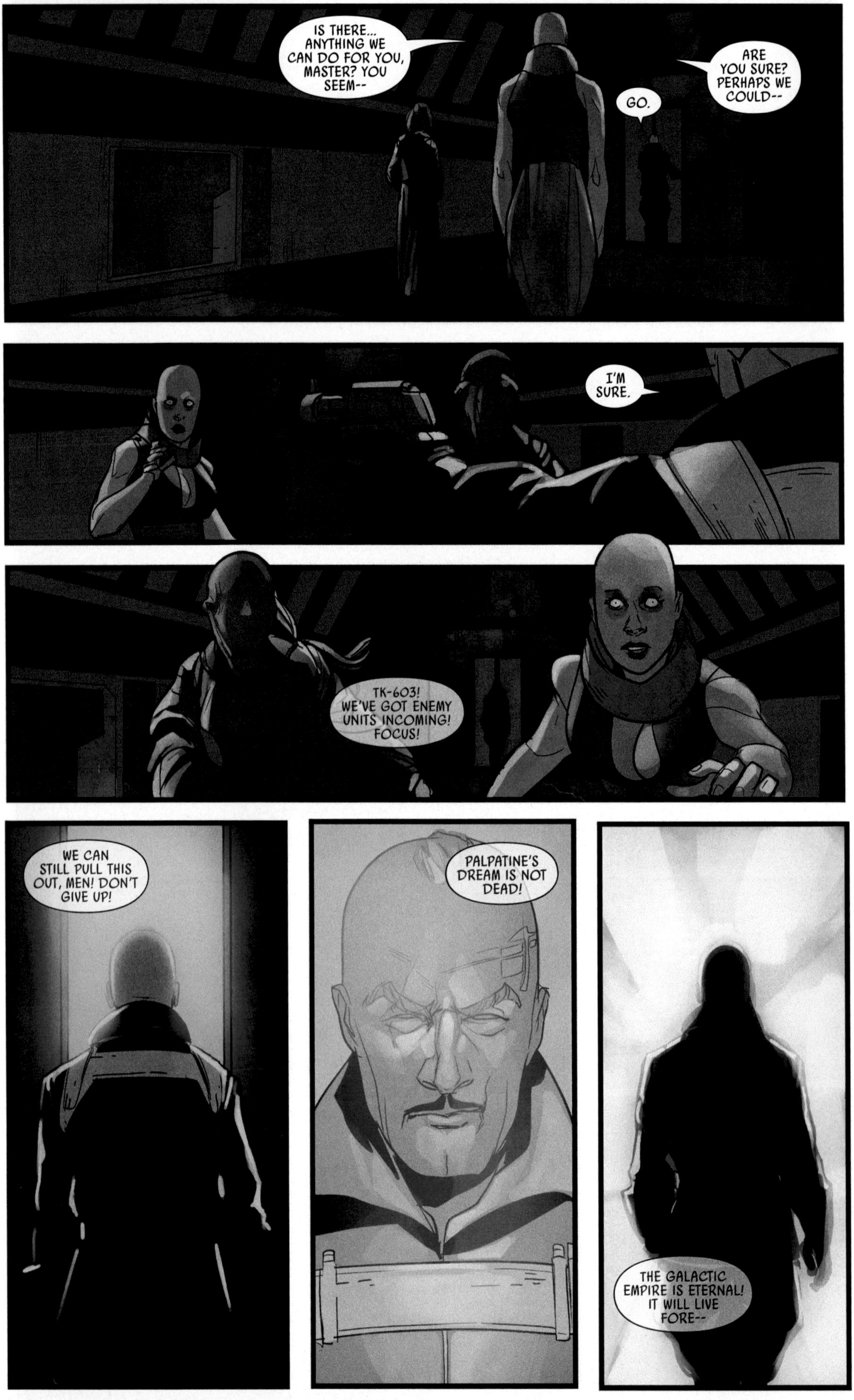
IS THERE... ANYTHING WE CAN DO FOR YOU, MASTER? YOU SEEM--
GO.
ARE YOU SURE? PERHAPS WE COULD--
I'M SURE.
TK-603! WE'VE GOT ENEMY UNITS INCOMING! FOCUS!
WE CAN STILL PULL THIS OUT, MEN! DON'T GIVE UP!
PALPATINE'S DREAM IS NOT DEAD!
THE GALACTIC EMPIRE IS ETERNAL! IT WILL LIVE FORE--

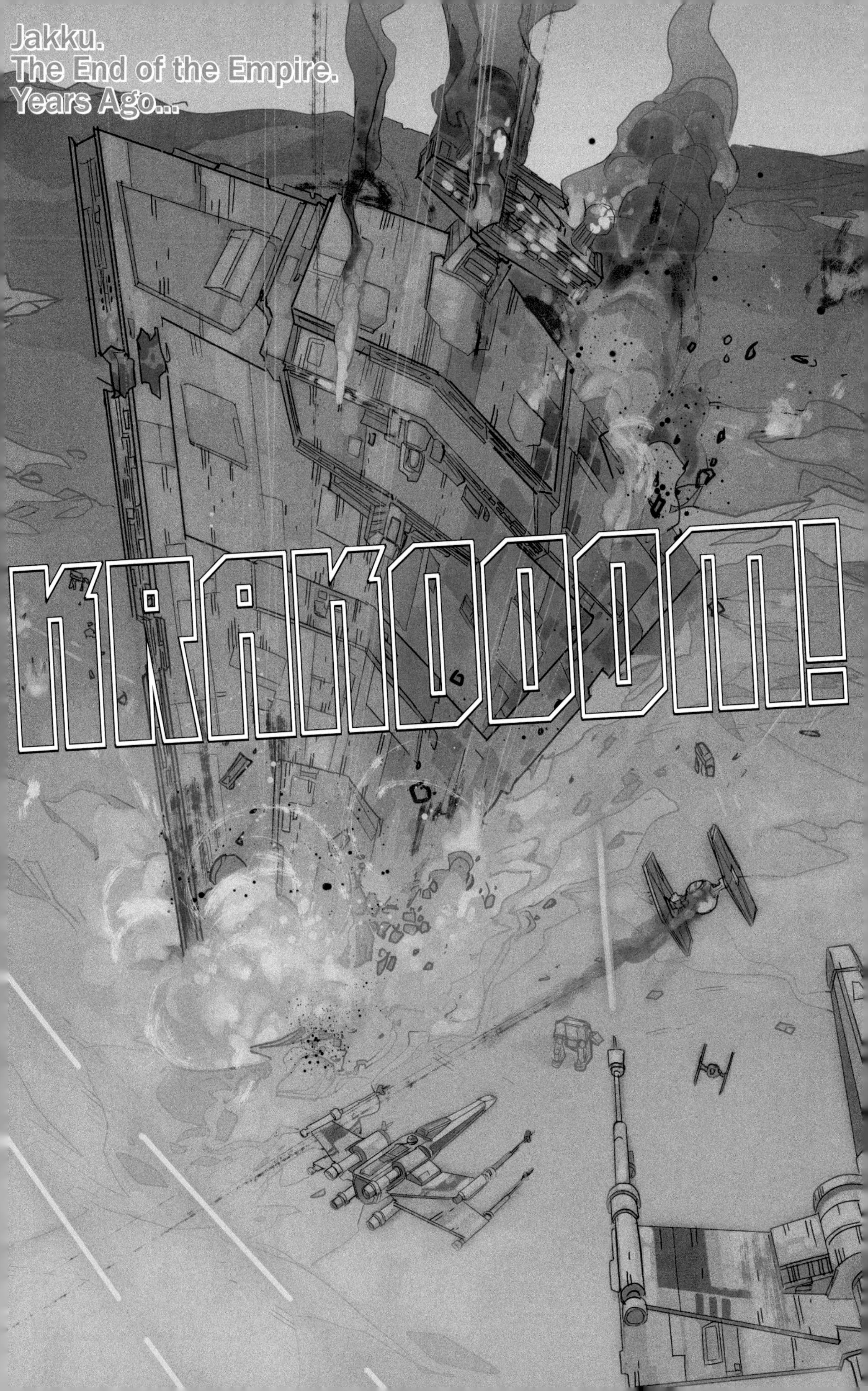
Jakku.
The End of the Empire.
Years Ago...
KRAKOOOM!

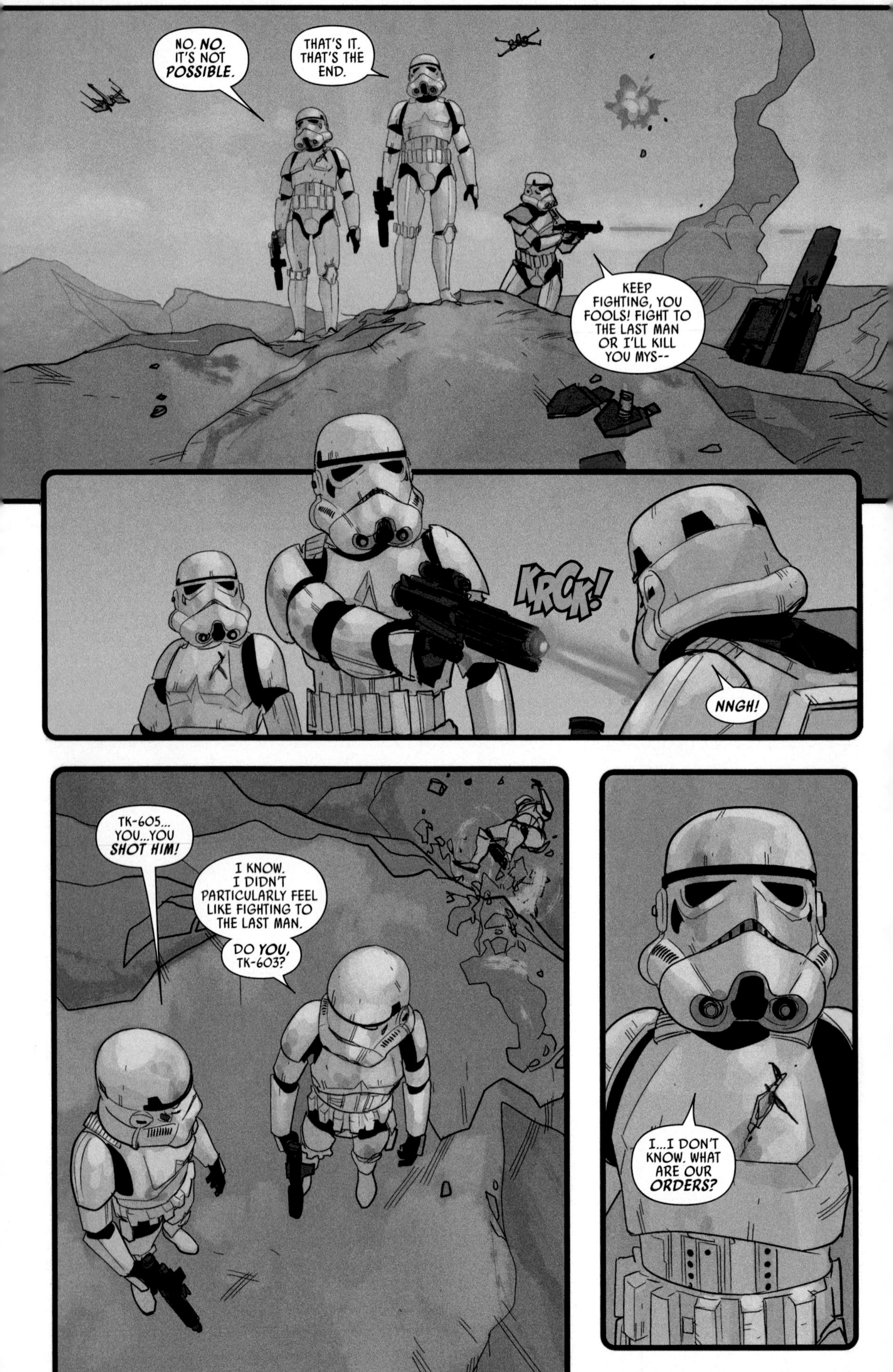
NO. NO. IT'S NOT POSSIBLE.
THAT'S IT. THAT'S THE END.
KEEP FIGHTING, YOU FOOLS! FIGHT TO THE LAST MAN OR I'LL KILL YOU MYS--
KRCK!
NNGH!
TK-605... YOU...YOU SHOT HIM!
I KNOW. I DIDN'T PARTICULARLY FEEL LIKE FIGHTING TO THE LAST MAN.
DO YOU, TK-603?
I...I DON'T KNOW. WHAT ARE OUR ORDERS?

YOU SEE THAT, YOU IDIOT? THAT MEANS THERE *ARE* NO MORE ORDERS!

THERE'S NO ONE LEFT TO *GIVE* THEM. THIS WAS THE EMPIRE'S LAST SHOT TO PUSH BACK THE REBELLION.

THEY COMMITTED *EVERYTHING THEY HAD* TO THIS ACTION, AND THEY *LOST*. THE EMPIRE IS *DEAD*.

AND WE DON'T WORK FOR THEM ANYMORE.

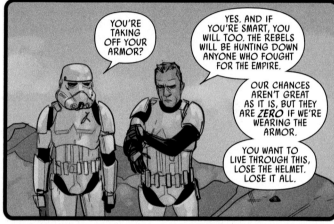

YOU'RE TAKING OFF YOUR ARMOR?

YES. AND IF YOU'RE SMART, YOU WILL TOO. THE REBELS WILL BE HUNTING DOWN ANYONE WHO FOUGHT FOR THE EMPIRE.

OUR CHANCES AREN'T GREAT AS IT IS, BUT THEY ARE *ZERO* IF WE'RE WEARING THE ARMOR.

YOU WANT TO LIVE THROUGH THIS, LOSE THE HELMET. LOSE IT ALL.

I...

ALL RIGHT.

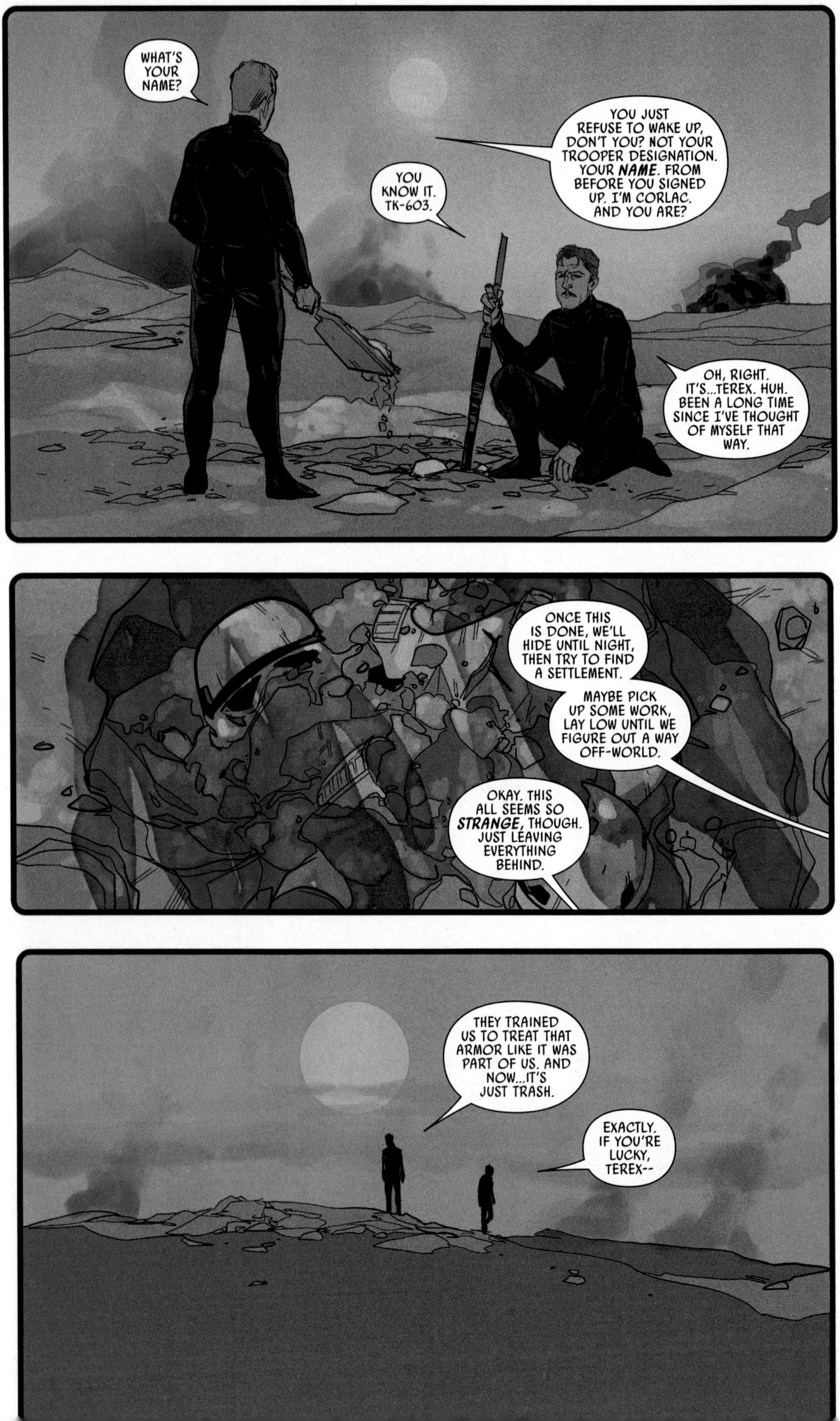
WHAT'S YOUR NAME?
YOU KNOW IT. TK-603.
YOU JUST REFUSE TO WAKE UP, DON'T YOU? NOT YOUR TROOPER DESIGNATION. YOUR NAME. FROM BEFORE YOU SIGNED UP. I'M CORLAC. AND YOU ARE?
OH, RIGHT. IT'S...TEREX. HUH. BEEN A LONG TIME SINCE I'VE THOUGHT OF MYSELF THAT WAY.
ONCE THIS IS DONE, WE'LL HIDE UNTIL NIGHT, THEN TRY TO FIND A SETTLEMENT.
MAYBE PICK UP SOME WORK, LAY LOW UNTIL WE FIGURE OUT A WAY OFF-WORLD.
OKAY. THIS ALL SEEMS SO STRANGE, THOUGH. JUST LEAVING EVERYTHING BEHIND.
THEY TRAINED US TO TREAT THAT ARMOR LIKE IT WAS PART OF US. AND NOW...IT'S JUST TRASH.
EXACTLY. IF YOU'RE LUCKY, TEREX--

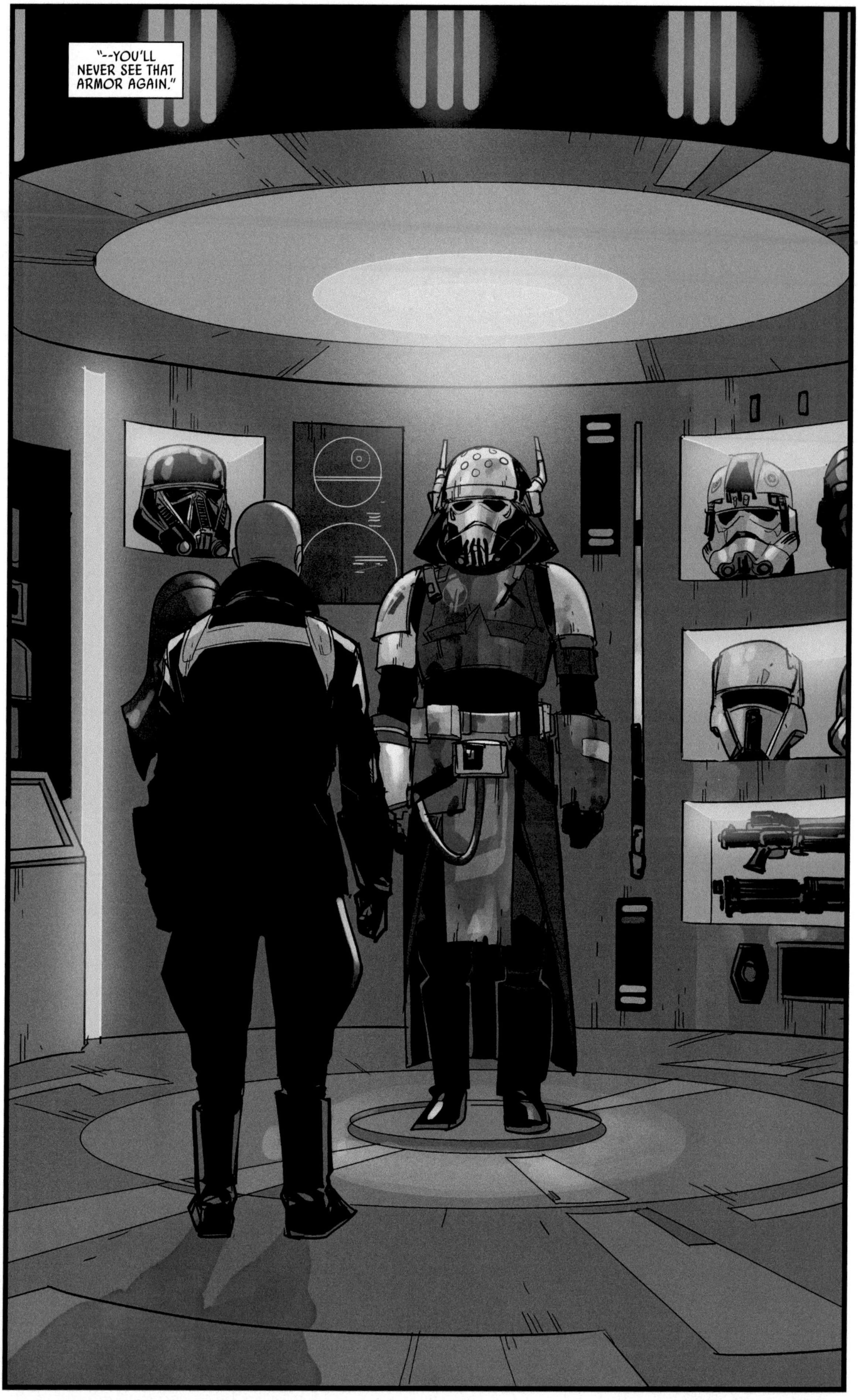
"--YOU'LL NEVER SEE THAT ARMOR AGAIN."

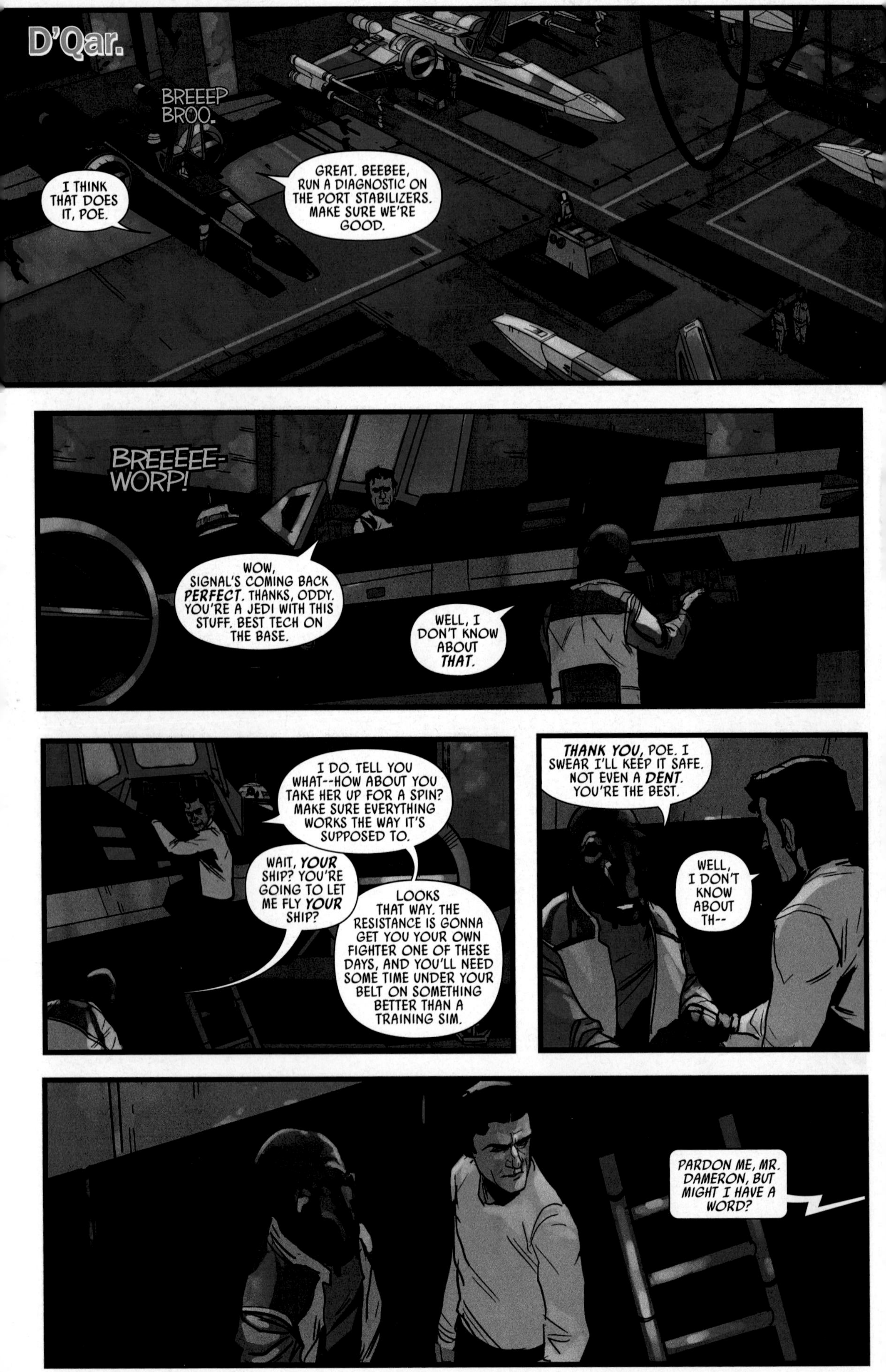
D'Qar.
BREEEP BROO.
I THINK THAT DOES IT, POE.
GREAT. BEEBEE, RUN A DIAGNOSTIC ON THE PORT STABILIZERS. MAKE SURE WE'RE GOOD.
BREEEEE-WORP!
WOW, SIGNAL'S COMING BACK *PERFECT*. THANKS, ODDY. YOU'RE A JEDI WITH THIS STUFF. BEST TECH ON THE BASE.
WELL, I DON'T KNOW ABOUT *THAT*.
I DO. TELL YOU WHAT--HOW ABOUT YOU TAKE HER UP FOR A SPIN? MAKE SURE EVERYTHING WORKS THE WAY IT'S SUPPOSED TO.
WAIT, *YOUR* SHIP? YOU'RE GOING TO LET ME FLY *YOUR* SHIP?
LOOKS THAT WAY. THE RESISTANCE IS GONNA GET YOU YOUR OWN FIGHTER ONE OF THESE DAYS, AND YOU'LL NEED SOME TIME UNDER YOUR BELT ON SOMETHING BETTER THAN A TRAINING SIM.
THANK YOU, POE. I SWEAR I'LL KEEP IT SAFE. NOT EVEN A *DENT*. YOU'RE THE BEST.
WELL, I DON'T KNOW ABOUT TH--
PARDON ME, MR. DAMERON, BUT MIGHT I HAVE A WORD?

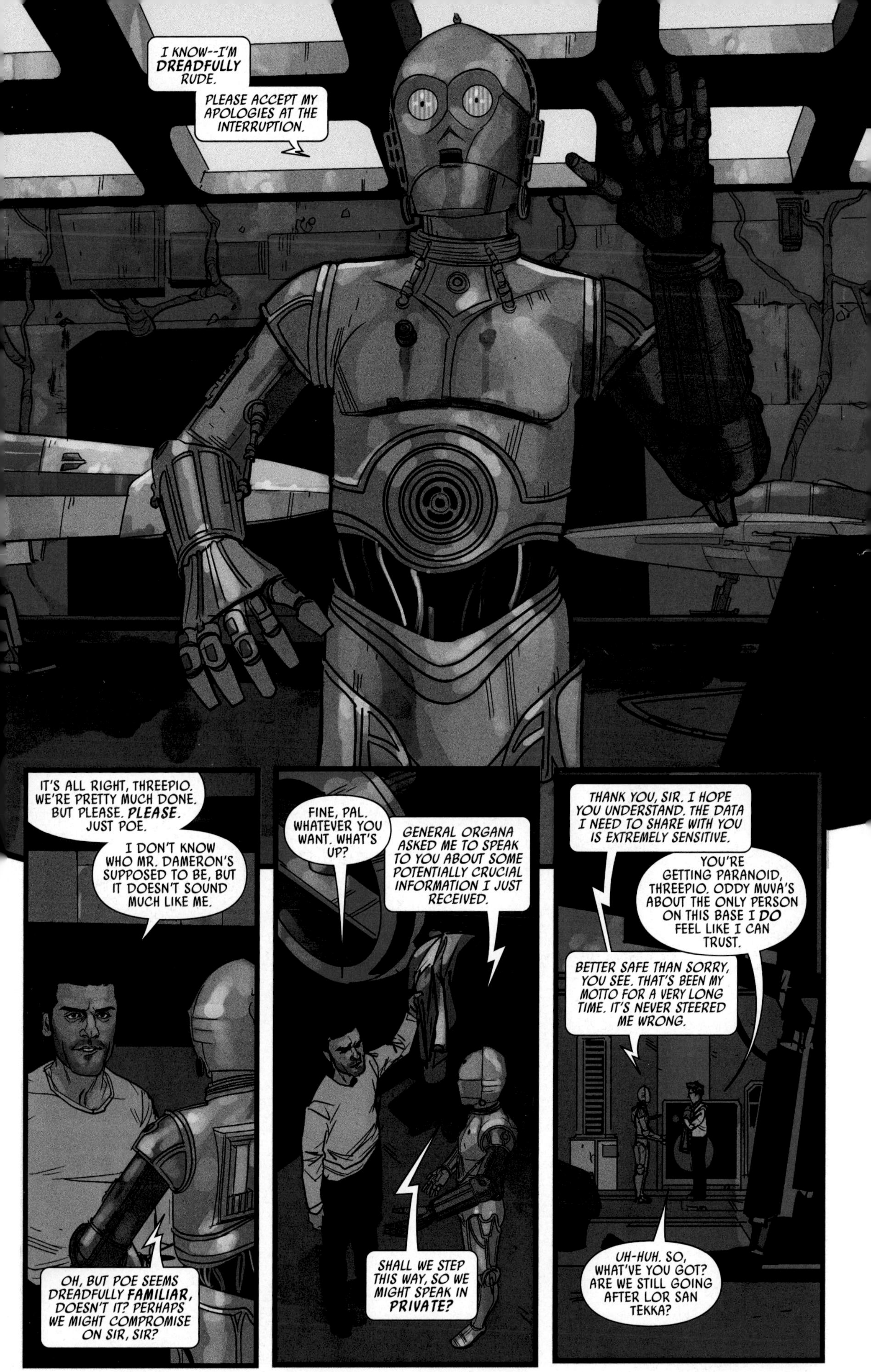
I KNOW--I'M DREADFULLY RUDE.
PLEASE ACCEPT MY APOLOGIES AT THE INTERRUPTION.
IT'S ALL RIGHT, THREEPIO. WE'RE PRETTY MUCH DONE. BUT PLEASE. PLEASE. JUST POE.
I DON'T KNOW WHO MR. DAMERON'S SUPPOSED TO BE, BUT IT DOESN'T SOUND MUCH LIKE ME.
OH, BUT POE SEEMS DREADFULLY FAMILIAR, DOESN'T IT? PERHAPS WE MIGHT COMPROMISE ON SIR, SIR?
FINE, PAL. WHATEVER YOU WANT. WHAT'S UP?
GENERAL ORGANA ASKED ME TO SPEAK TO YOU ABOUT SOME POTENTIALLY CRUCIAL INFORMATION I JUST RECEIVED.
SHALL WE STEP THIS WAY, SO WE MIGHT SPEAK IN PRIVATE?
THANK YOU, SIR. I HOPE YOU UNDERSTAND. THE DATA I NEED TO SHARE WITH YOU IS EXTREMELY SENSITIVE.
YOU'RE GETTING PARANOID, THREEPIO. ODDY MUVA'S ABOUT THE ONLY PERSON ON THIS BASE I DO FEEL LIKE I CAN TRUST.
BETTER SAFE THAN SORRY, YOU SEE. THAT'S BEEN MY MOTTO FOR A VERY LONG TIME. IT'S NEVER STEERED ME WRONG.
UH-HUH. SO, WHAT'VE YOU GOT? ARE WE STILL GOING AFTER LOR SAN TEKKA?

NO. THE GENERAL NEEDS TO SCAN THROUGH THE DATA YOU OBTAINED FROM GRAKKUS THE HUTT TO DETERMINE WHICH LEADS TO FOLLOW. THIS IS...SOMETHING ELSE.

YOU ARE AWARE THAT I MAINTAIN A NETWORK OF... WELL-PLACED INDIVIDUALS WHO SHARE INFORMATION WITH ME FROM TIME TO TIME THAT MIGHT AID THE RESISTANCE?

YOU MEAN YOUR DROID SPIES? YEAH, THREEPIO. I MIGHT HAVE HEARD SOMETHING ABOUT THAT.

SPIES? NO, SIR. THE WORD SPY IMPLIES SKULLDUGGERY, FALSE PRETENSES...NO, NO. THAT'S NOT WHAT MY PEOPLE DO AT ALL.

"YOU SEE, DROIDS ARE EVERYWHERE. WE DON'T HAVE TO SNEAK. OUR VERY EXISTENCE GRANTS US ACCESS TO SOME OF THE MOST SENSITIVE SPOTS IN THE GALAXY.

"THIS BASE, FOR EXAMPLE. NO ONE PAYS ATTENTION, NO ONE CARES, AS LONG AS WE DO OUR DUTY WITH DILIGENCE AND PRECISION. AND WHY WOULD THEY? AFTER ALL..."

...WE'RE JUST DROIDS.

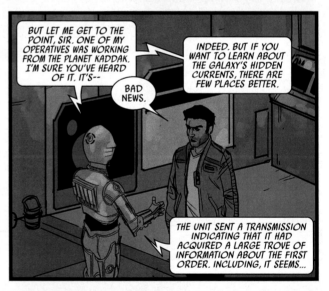

BUT LET ME GET TO THE POINT, SIR. ONE OF MY OPERATIVES WAS WORKING FROM THE PLANET KADDAK. I'M SURE YOU'VE HEARD OF IT. IT'S--

BAD NEWS.

INDEED. BUT IF YOU WANT TO LEARN ABOUT THE GALAXY'S HIDDEN CURRENTS, THERE ARE FEW PLACES BETTER.

THE UNIT SENT A TRANSMISSION INDICATING THAT IT HAD ACQUIRED A LARGE TROVE OF INFORMATION ABOUT THE FIRST ORDER. INCLUDING, IT SEEMS...

...THE CURRENT LOCATION OF SUPREME LEADER SNOKE.

WHOA.

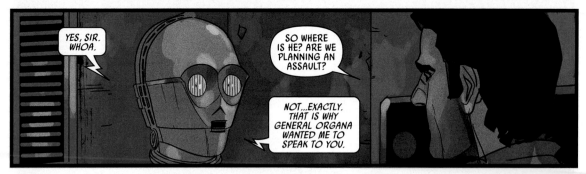

YES, SIR. WHOA.

SO WHERE IS HE? ARE WE PLANNING AN ASSAULT?

NOT...EXACTLY. THAT IS WHY GENERAL ORGANA WANTED ME TO SPEAK TO YOU.

YOU SEE, MY AGENT'S TRANSMISSION WAS INTERRUPTED BEFORE IT COULD SEND THE CRUCIAL DATA.

WE RECEIVED ENOUGH TO CONFIRM ITS LEGITIMACY, BUT THEN THE SIGNAL SIMPLY CEASED.

HMM. YOU THINK SOMEONE GOT TO YOUR DROID?

POSSIBLY. OR IT WAS DESTROYED, THE MAKER FORBID. WE JUST DON'T KNOW--BUT WE MUST DISCOVER THE TRUTH.

GENERAL ORGANA ORDERED ME TO TRAVEL TO KADDAK TO SEE WHAT WE MIGHT LEARN. IF POSSIBLE, WE ARE TO RETRIEVE MY OPERATIVE.

AND SHE WANTS BLACK SQUADRON TO TAKE YOU?

YEAH. THIS SOUNDS ABOUT AS SENSITIVE AS IT GETS. WE DON'T WANT TO DRAW ATTENTION, ESPECIALLY ON *THAT* PLANET.

NO. SHE WANTS *YOU* TO TAKE ME, AND ONE OTHER PILOT, FOR BACKUP, IN A SHUTTLE. SHE FEELS THAT A LARGER GROUP WOULD BE NOTICED, ESPECIALLY IN STARFIGHTERS.

WE SHOULD LEAVE IMMEDIATELY. WHICH OF YOUR BLACK SQUADRON PILOTS WILL ACCOMPANY US?

WELL...

...THAT'S COMPLICATED.

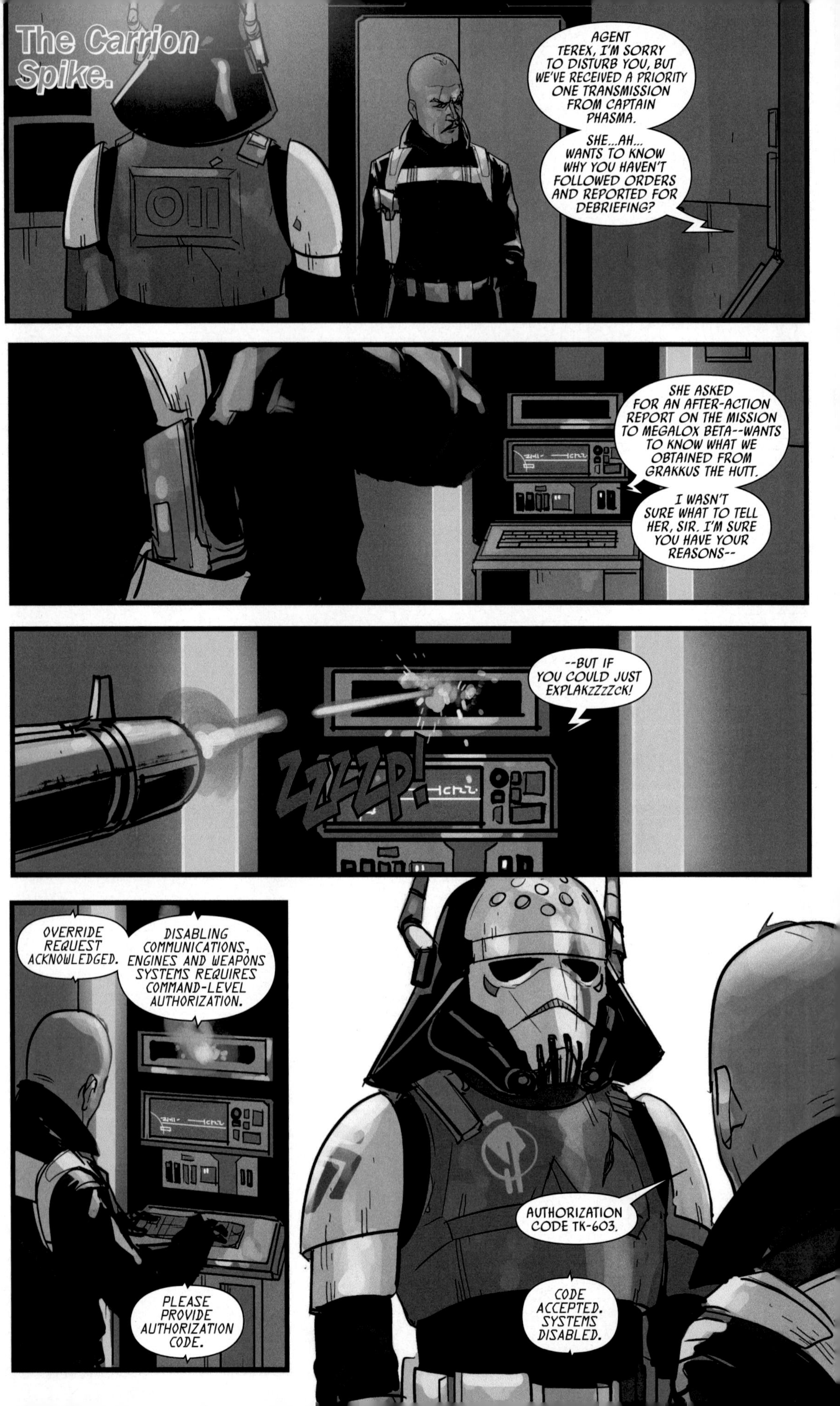
The Carrion Spike.
AGENT TEREX, I'M SORRY TO DISTURB YOU, BUT WE'VE RECEIVED A PRIORITY ONE TRANSMISSION FROM CAPTAIN PHASMA.
SHE...AH... WANTS TO KNOW WHY YOU HAVEN'T FOLLOWED ORDERS AND REPORTED FOR DEBRIEFING?
SHE ASKED FOR AN AFTER-ACTION REPORT ON THE MISSION TO MEGALOX BETA--WANTS TO KNOW WHAT WE OBTAINED FROM GRAKKUS THE HUTT.
I WASN'T SURE WHAT TO TELL HER, SIR. I'M SURE YOU HAVE YOUR REASONS--
--BUT IF YOU COULD JUST EXPLAKZZZZCK!
ZZZZP!
OVERRIDE REQUEST ACKNOWLEDGED.
DISABLING COMMUNICATIONS, ENGINES AND WEAPONS SYSTEMS REQUIRES COMMAND-LEVEL AUTHORIZATION.
PLEASE PROVIDE AUTHORIZATION CODE.
AUTHORIZATION CODE TK-603.
CODE ACCEPTED. SYSTEMS DISABLED.

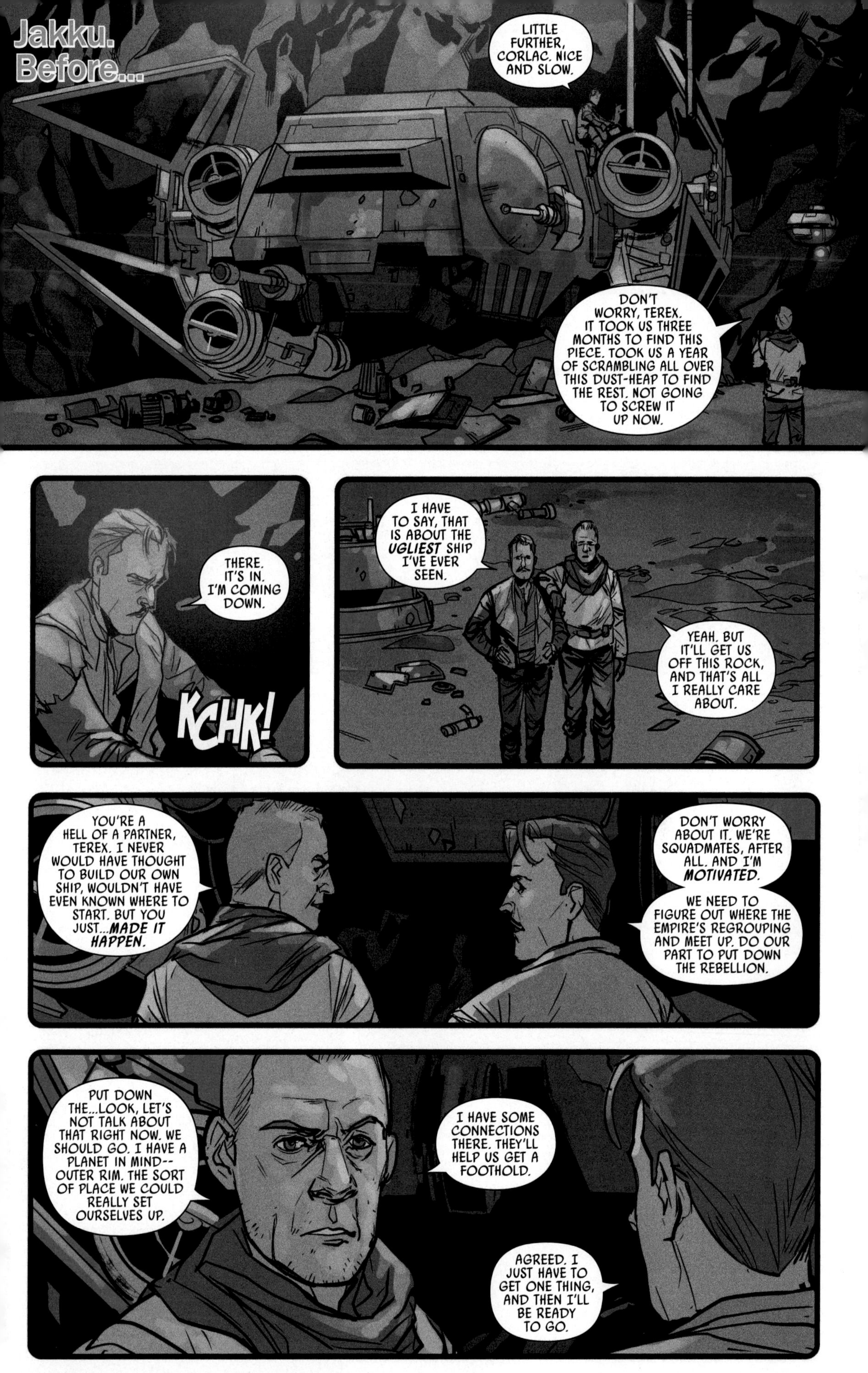
Jakku. Before...
LITTLE FURTHER, CORLAC. NICE AND SLOW.
DON'T WORRY, TEREX. IT TOOK US THREE MONTHS TO FIND THIS PIECE. TOOK US A YEAR OF SCRAMBLING ALL OVER THIS DUST-HEAP TO FIND THE REST. NOT GOING TO SCREW IT UP NOW.
THERE. IT'S IN. I'M COMING DOWN.
KCHK!
I HAVE TO SAY, THAT IS ABOUT THE UGLIEST SHIP I'VE EVER SEEN.
YEAH. BUT IT'LL GET US OFF THIS ROCK, AND THAT'S ALL I REALLY CARE ABOUT.
YOU'RE A HELL OF A PARTNER, TEREX. I NEVER WOULD HAVE THOUGHT TO BUILD OUR OWN SHIP, WOULDN'T HAVE EVEN KNOWN WHERE TO START. BUT YOU JUST...MADE IT HAPPEN.
DON'T WORRY ABOUT IT. WE'RE SQUADMATES, AFTER ALL. AND I'M MOTIVATED.
WE NEED TO FIGURE OUT WHERE THE EMPIRE'S REGROUPING AND MEET UP. DO OUR PART TO PUT DOWN THE REBELLION.
PUT DOWN THE...LOOK, LET'S NOT TALK ABOUT THAT RIGHT NOW. WE SHOULD GO. I HAVE A PLANET IN MIND-- OUTER RIM. THE SORT OF PLACE WE COULD REALLY SET OURSELVES UP.
I HAVE SOME CONNECTIONS THERE. THEY'LL HELP US GET A FOOTHOLD.
AGREED. I JUST HAVE TO GET ONE THING, AND THEN I'LL BE READY TO GO.

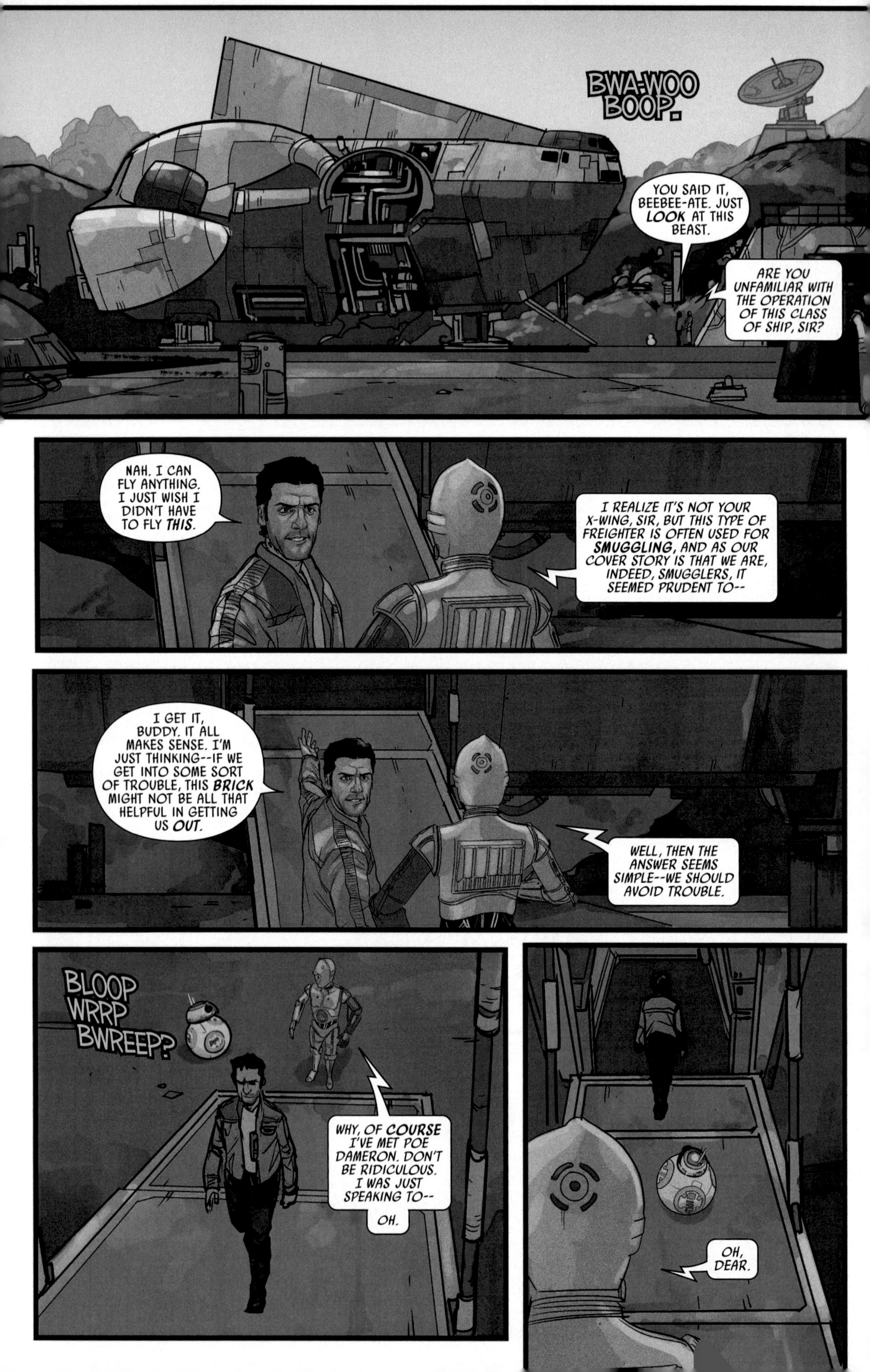
BWA-WOO BOOP.
YOU SAID IT, BEEBEE-ATE. JUST LOOK AT THIS BEAST.
ARE YOU UNFAMILIAR WITH THE OPERATION OF THIS CLASS OF SHIP, SIR?
NAH. I CAN FLY ANYTHING. I JUST WISH I DIDN'T HAVE TO FLY THIS.
I REALIZE IT'S NOT YOUR X-WING, SIR, BUT THIS TYPE OF FREIGHTER IS OFTEN USED FOR SMUGGLING, AND AS OUR COVER STORY IS THAT WE ARE, INDEED, SMUGGLERS, IT SEEMED PRUDENT TO--
I GET IT, BUDDY. IT ALL MAKES SENSE. I'M JUST THINKING--IF WE GET INTO SOME SORT OF TROUBLE, THIS BRICK MIGHT NOT BE ALL THAT HELPFUL IN GETTING US OUT.
WELL, THEN THE ANSWER SEEMS SIMPLE--WE SHOULD AVOID TROUBLE.
BLOOP WRRP BWREEP?
WHY, OF COURSE I'VE MET POE DAMERON. DON'T BE RIDICULOUS. I WAS JUST SPEAKING TO--
OH.
OH, DEAR.

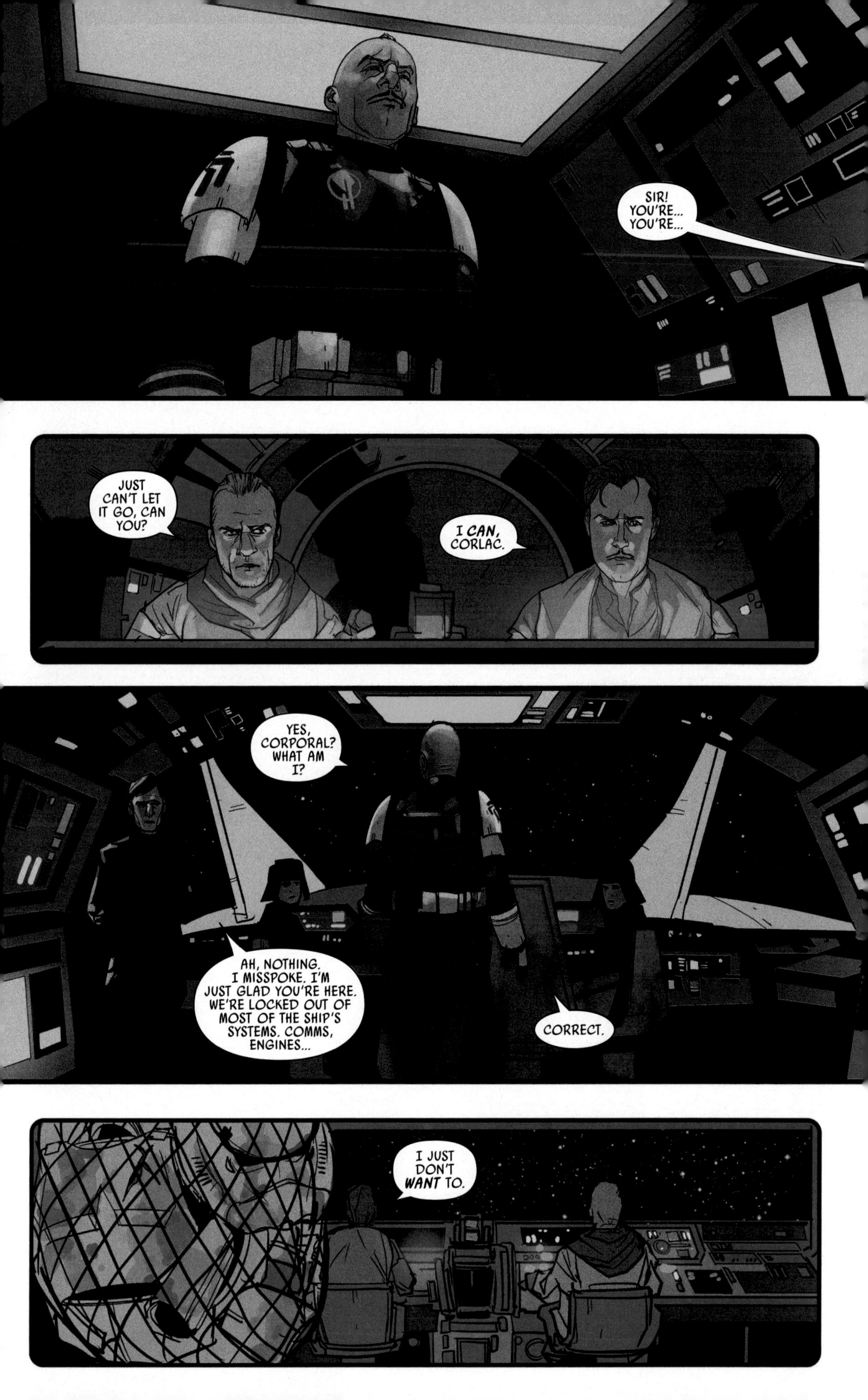
SIR! YOU'RE... YOU'RE...
JUST CAN'T LET IT GO, CAN YOU?
I CAN, CORLAC.
YES, CORPORAL? WHAT AM I?
AH, NOTHING. I MISSPOKE. I'M JUST GLAD YOU'RE HERE. WE'RE LOCKED OUT OF MOST OF THE SHIP'S SYSTEMS. COMMS, ENGINES...
CORRECT.
I JUST DON'T WANT TO.

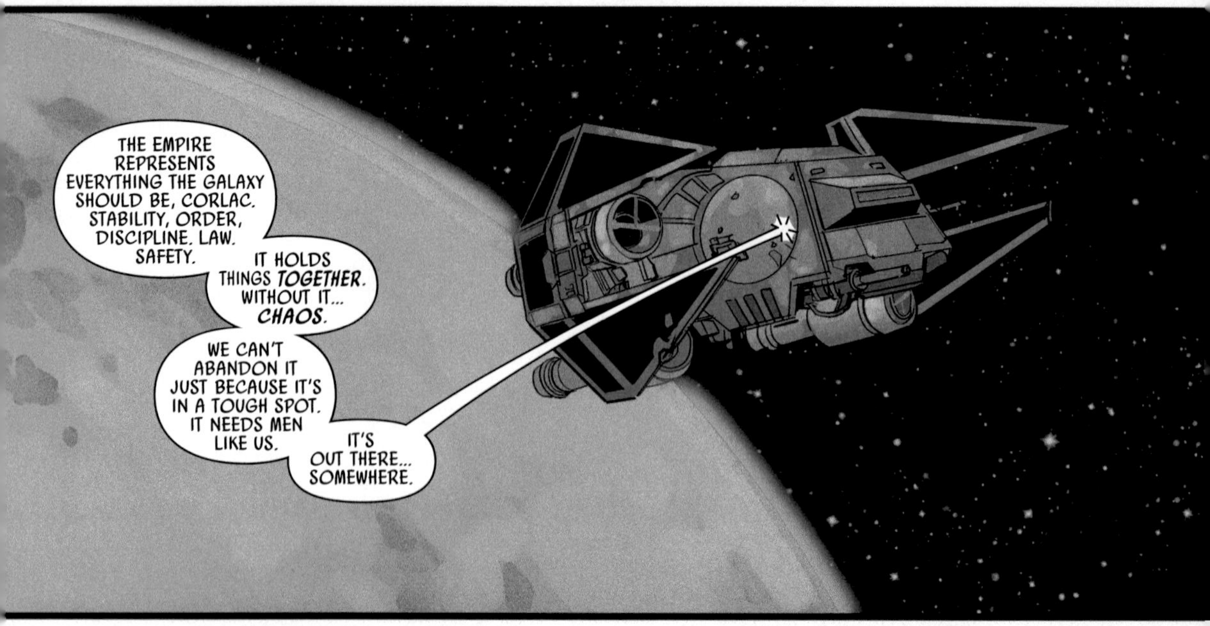
THE EMPIRE REPRESENTS EVERYTHING THE GALAXY SHOULD BE, CORLAC. STABILITY, ORDER, DISCIPLINE. LAW. SAFETY.
IT HOLDS THINGS TOGETHER. WITHOUT IT... CHAOS.
WE CAN'T ABANDON IT JUST BECAUSE IT'S IN A TOUGH SPOT. IT NEEDS MEN LIKE US.
IT'S OUT THERE... SOMEWHERE.

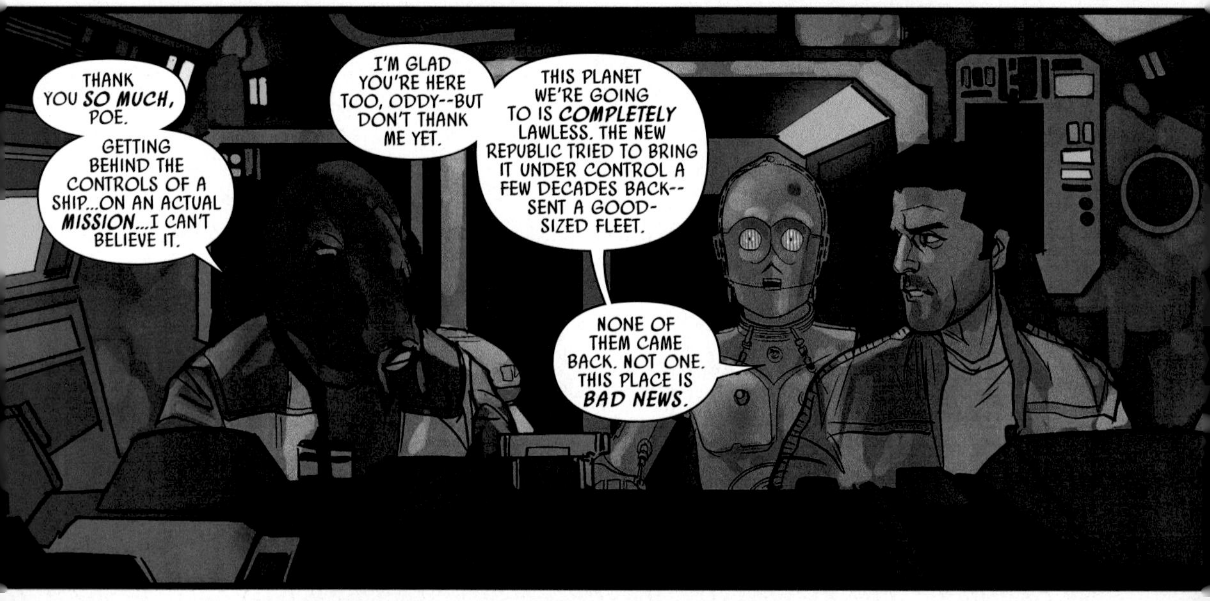
THANK YOU SO MUCH, POE.
GETTING BEHIND THE CONTROLS OF A SHIP...ON AN ACTUAL MISSION...I CAN'T BELIEVE IT.
I'M GLAD YOU'RE HERE TOO, ODDY--BUT DON'T THANK ME YET.
THIS PLANET WE'RE GOING TO IS COMPLETELY LAWLESS. THE NEW REPUBLIC TRIED TO BRING IT UNDER CONTROL A FEW DECADES BACK--SENT A GOOD-SIZED FLEET.
NONE OF THEM CAME BACK. NOT ONE. THIS PLACE IS BAD NEWS.

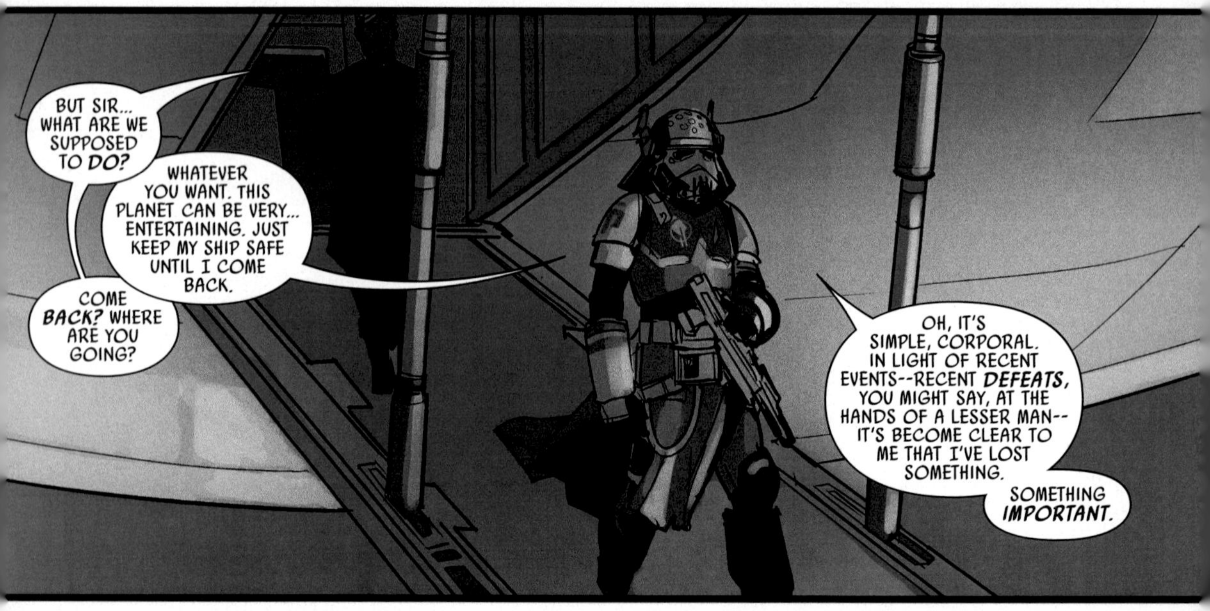
BUT SIR... WHAT ARE WE SUPPOSED TO DO?
WHATEVER YOU WANT. THIS PLANET CAN BE VERY... ENTERTAINING. JUST KEEP MY SHIP SAFE UNTIL I COME BACK.
COME BACK? WHERE ARE YOU GOING?
OH, IT'S SIMPLE, CORPORAL. IN LIGHT OF RECENT EVENTS--RECENT DEFEATS, YOU MIGHT SAY, AT THE HANDS OF A LESSER MAN--IT'S BECOME CLEAR TO ME THAT I'VE LOST SOMETHING.
SOMETHING IMPORTANT.

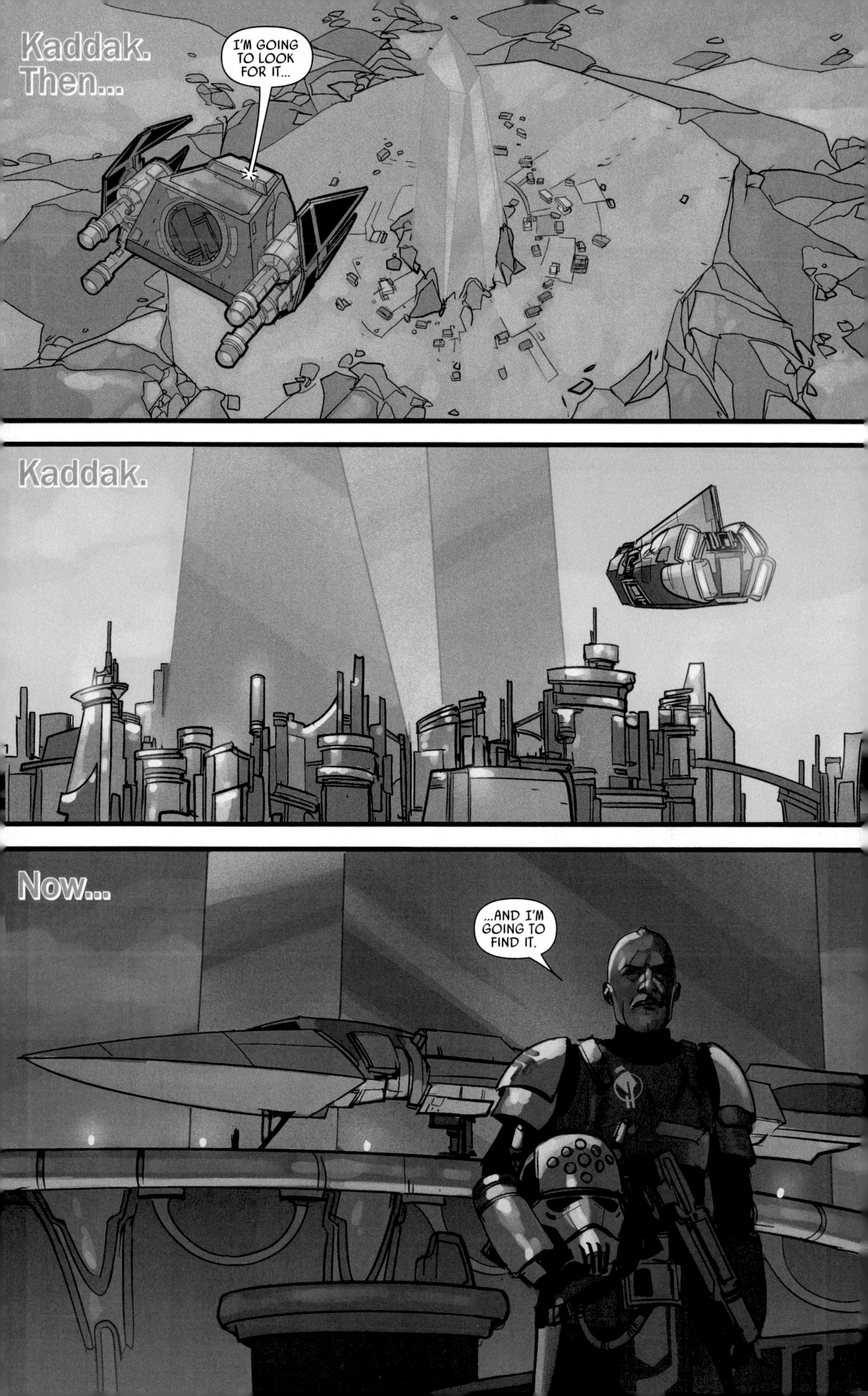
Kaddak. Then...
I'M GOING TO LOOK FOR IT...
Kaddak.
Now...
...AND I'M GOING TO FIND IT.

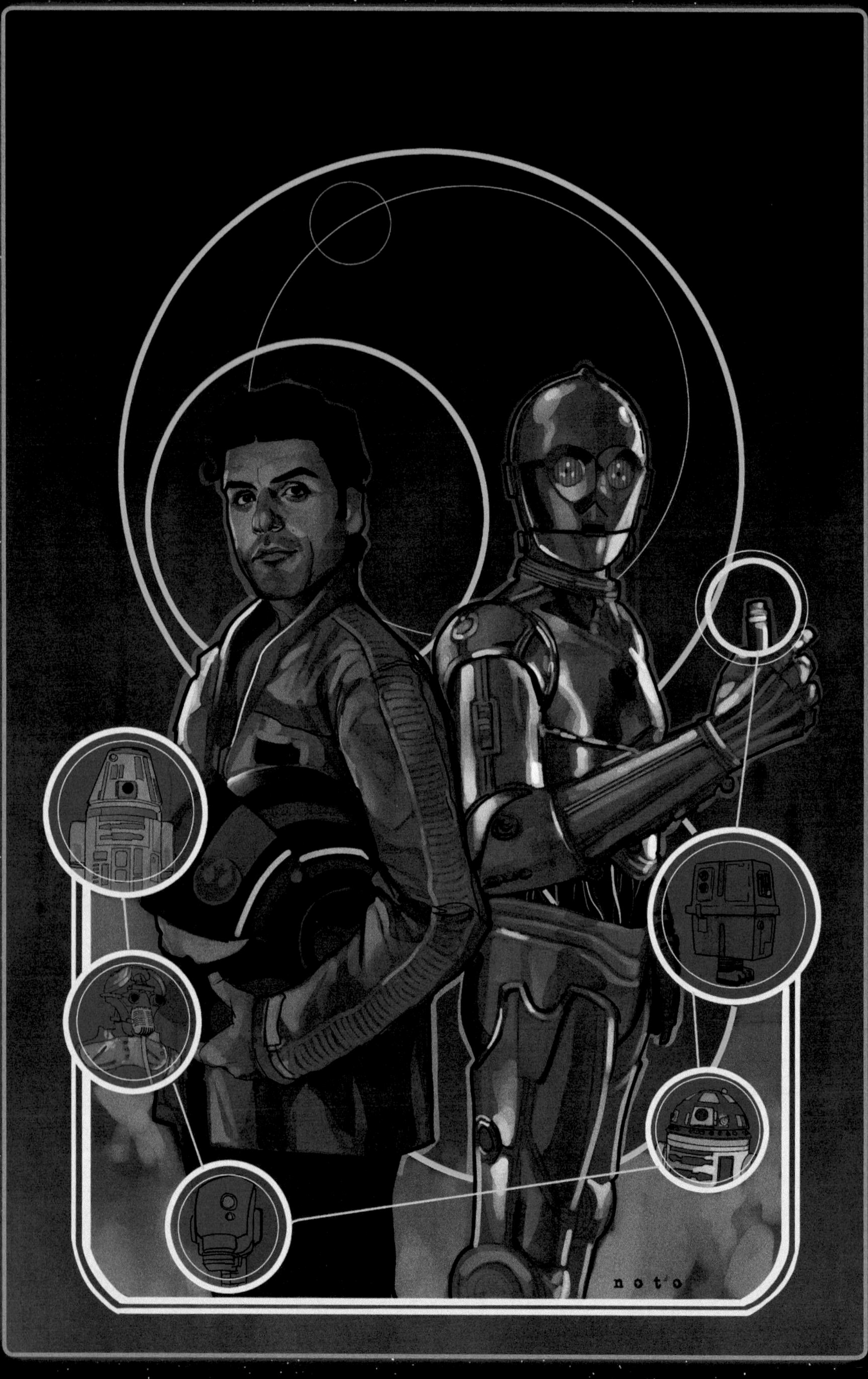
noto

9

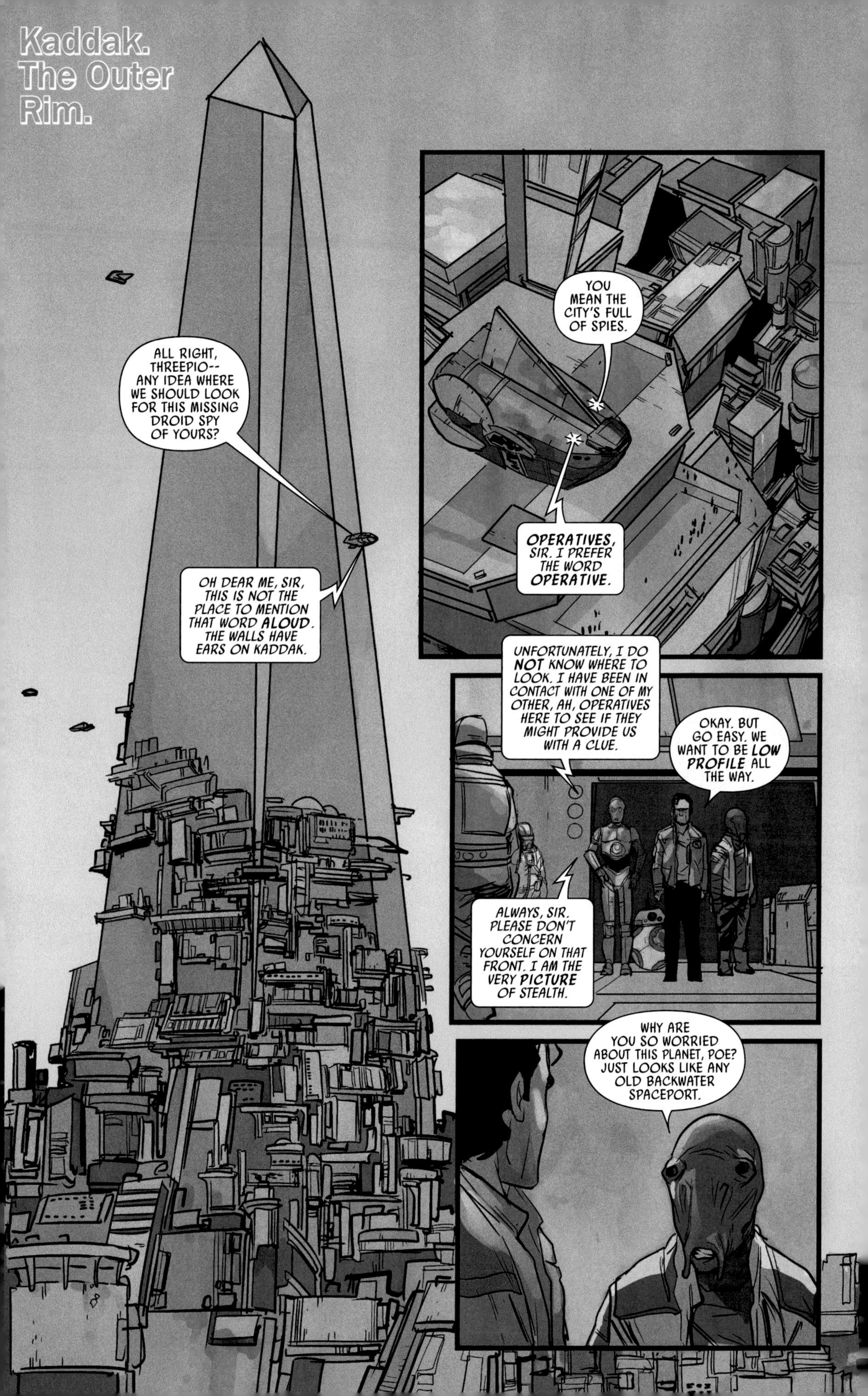
Kaddak. The Outer Rim.
ALL RIGHT, THREEPIO-- ANY IDEA WHERE WE SHOULD LOOK FOR THIS MISSING DROID SPY OF YOURS?
OH DEAR ME, SIR, THIS IS NOT THE PLACE TO MENTION THAT WORD ALOUD. THE WALLS HAVE EARS ON KADDAK.
YOU MEAN THE CITY'S FULL OF SPIES.
OPERATIVES, SIR. I PREFER THE WORD OPERATIVE.
UNFORTUNATELY, I DO NOT KNOW WHERE TO LOOK. I HAVE BEEN IN CONTACT WITH ONE OF MY OTHER, AH, OPERATIVES HERE TO SEE IF THEY MIGHT PROVIDE US WITH A CLUE.
OKAY. BUT GO EASY. WE WANT TO BE LOW PROFILE ALL THE WAY.
ALWAYS, SIR. PLEASE DON'T CONCERN YOURSELF ON THAT FRONT. I AM THE VERY PICTURE OF STEALTH.
WHY ARE YOU SO WORRIED ABOUT THIS PLANET, POE? JUST LOOKS LIKE ANY OLD BACKWATER SPACEPORT.

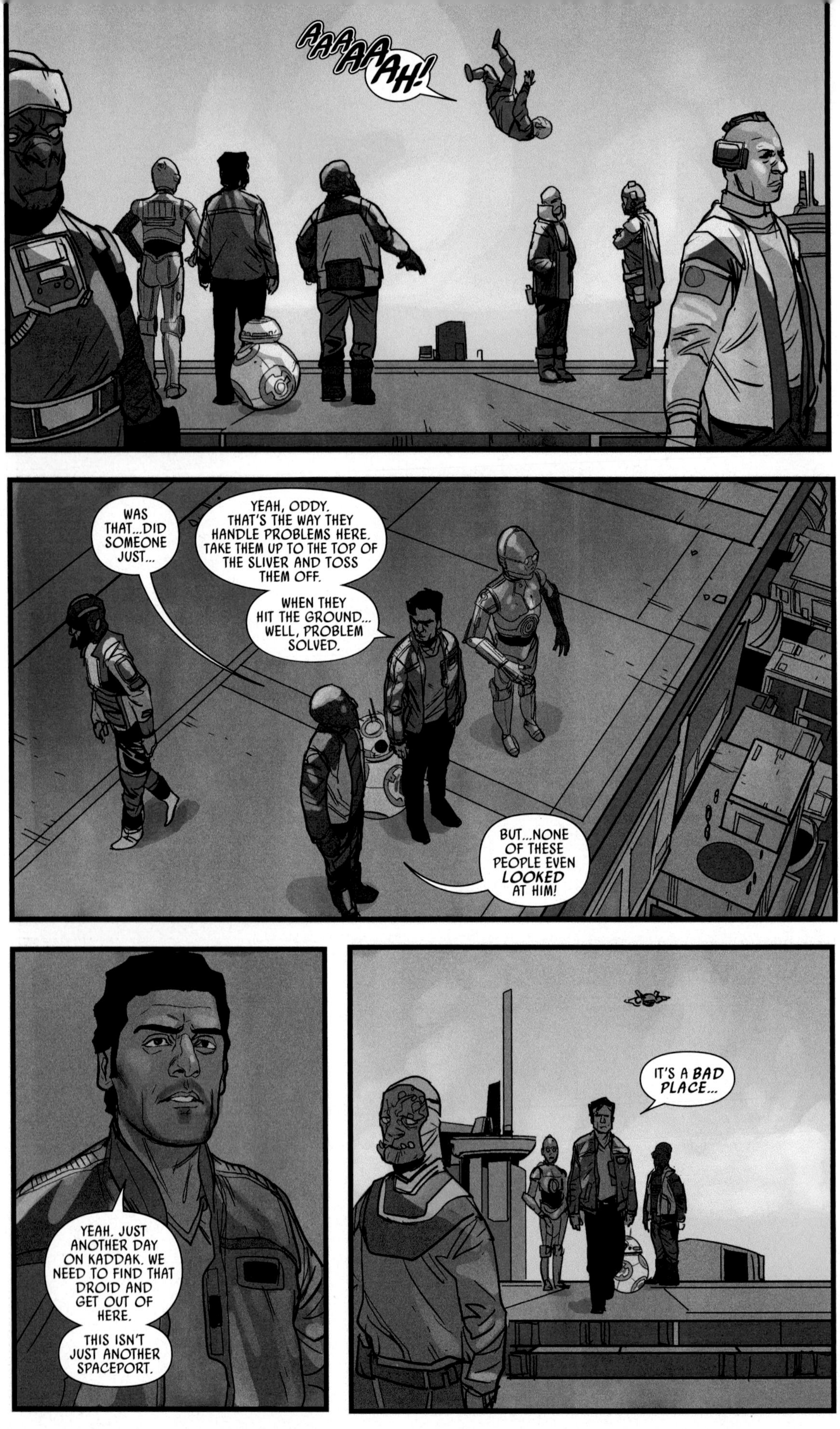
AAAAAAH!
WAS THAT...DID SOMEONE JUST...
YEAH, ODDY. THAT'S THE WAY THEY HANDLE PROBLEMS HERE. TAKE THEM UP TO THE TOP OF THE SLIVER AND TOSS THEM OFF.
WHEN THEY HIT THE GROUND... WELL, PROBLEM SOLVED.
BUT...NONE OF THESE PEOPLE EVEN LOOKED AT HIM!
YEAH. JUST ANOTHER DAY ON KADDAK. WE NEED TO FIND THAT DROID AND GET OUT OF HERE.
THIS ISN'T JUST ANOTHER SPACEPORT.
IT'S A BAD PLACE...

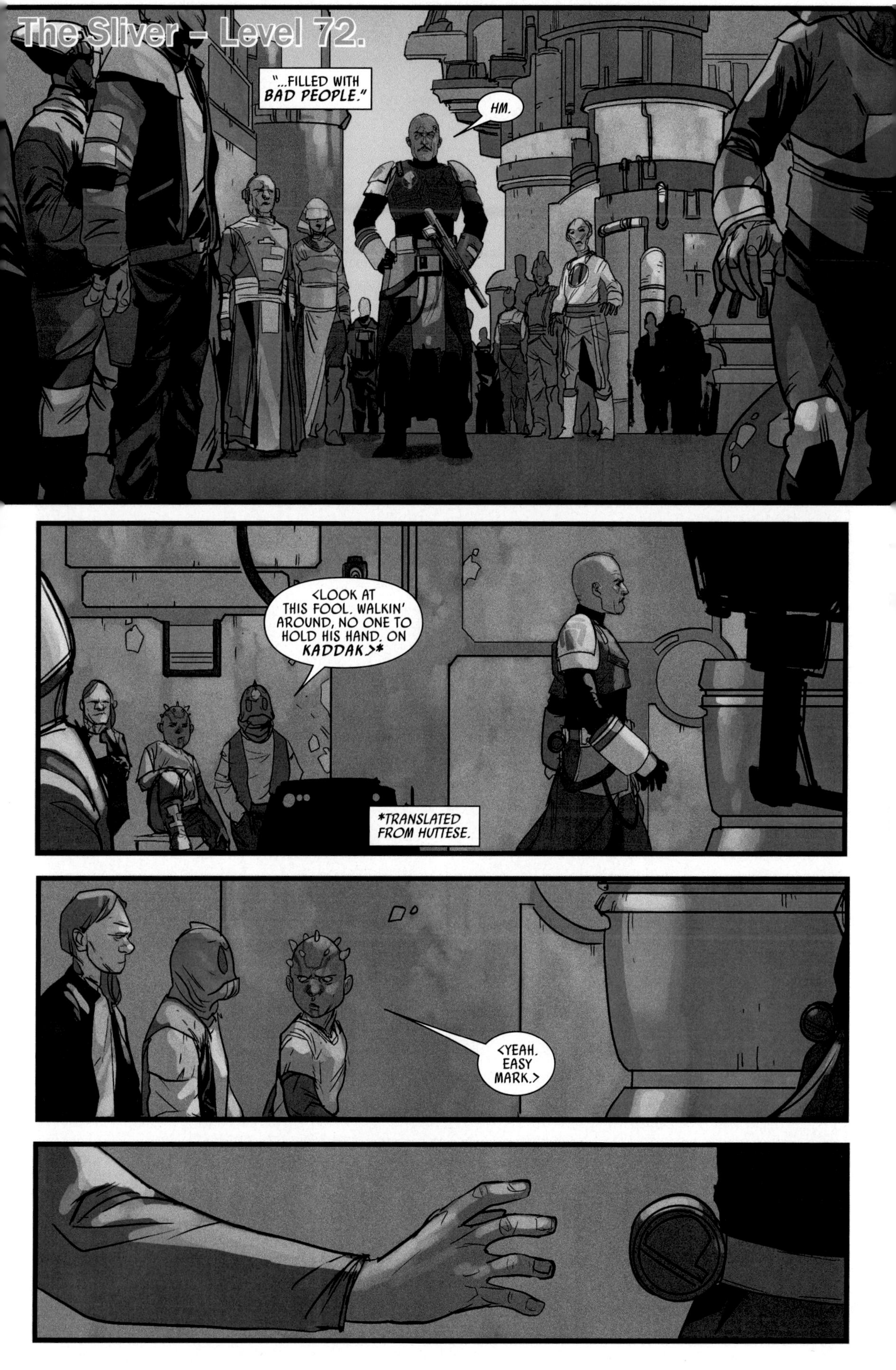
The Sliver – Level 72.
"...FILLED WITH BAD PEOPLE."
HM.
<LOOK AT THIS FOOL. WALKIN' AROUND, NO ONE TO HOLD HIS HAND. ON KADDAK.>*
*TRANSLATED FROM HUTTESE.
<YEAH. EASY MARK.>

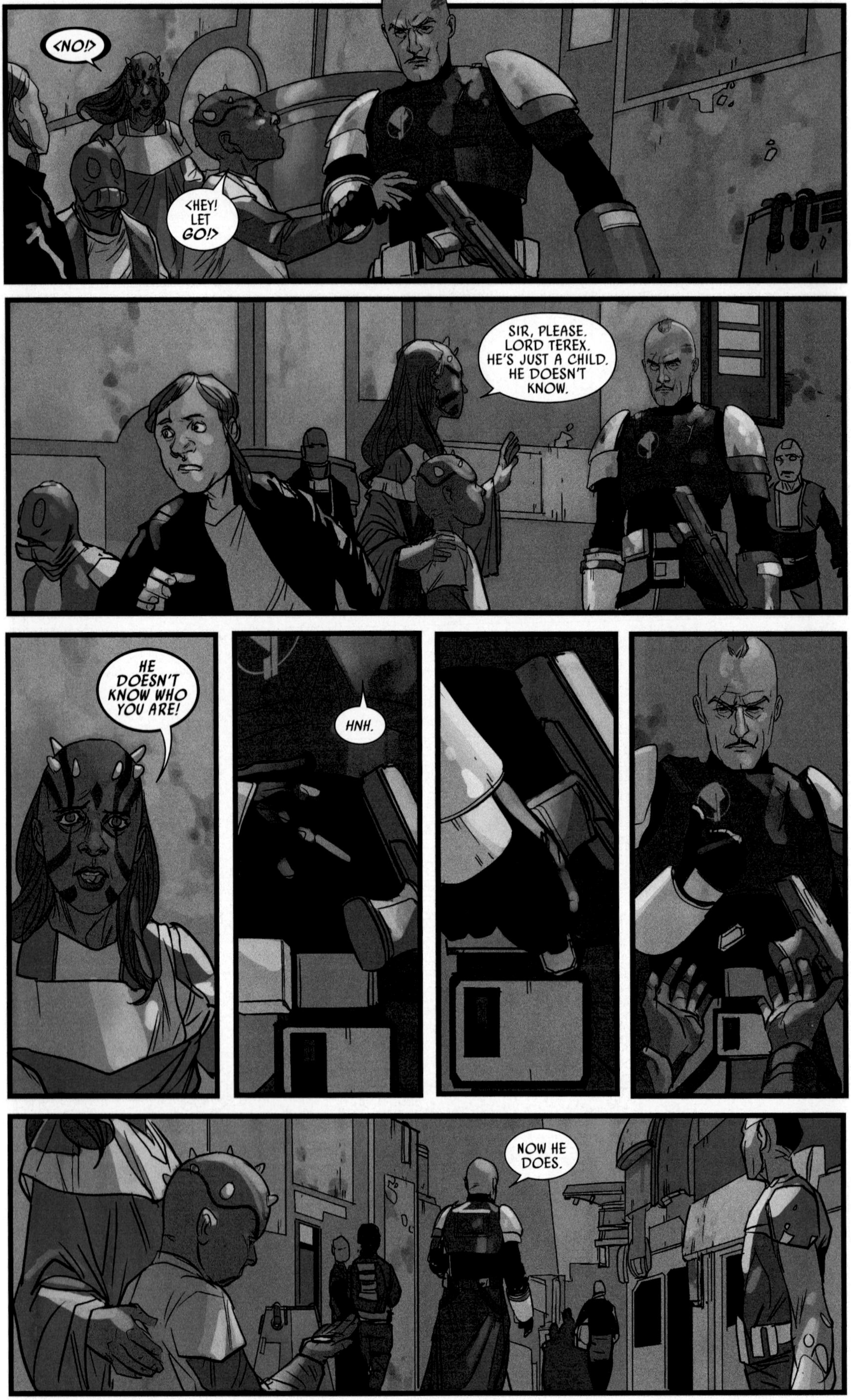
<NO!>
<HEY! LET GO!>
SIR, PLEASE. LORD TEREX. HE'S JUST A CHILD. HE DOESN'T KNOW.
HE DOESN'T KNOW WHO YOU ARE!
HNH.
NOW HE DOES.

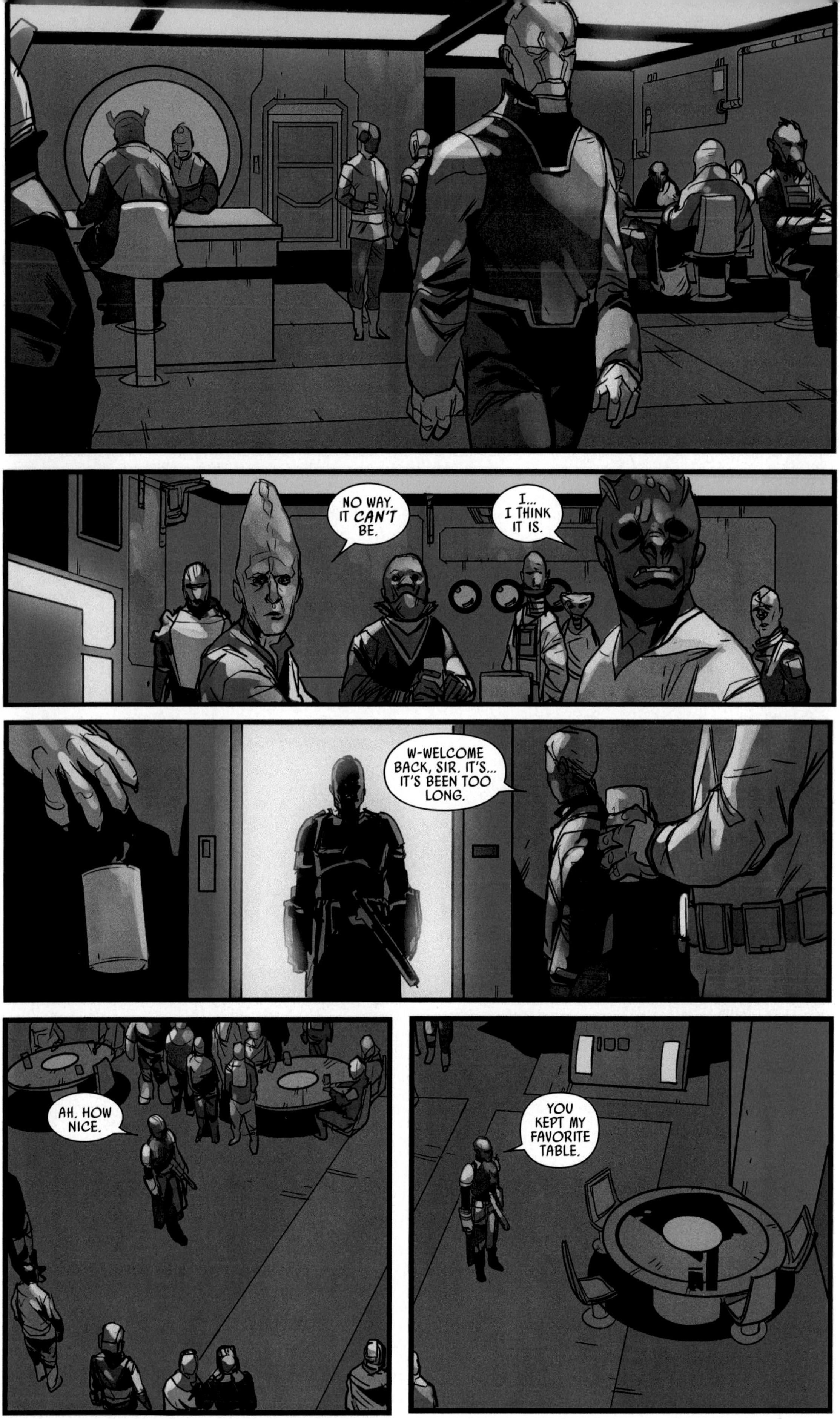
NO WAY. IT CAN'T BE.
I... I THINK IT IS.
W-WELCOME BACK, SIR. IT'S... IT'S BEEN TOO LONG.
AH. HOW NICE.
YOU KEPT MY FAVORITE TABLE.

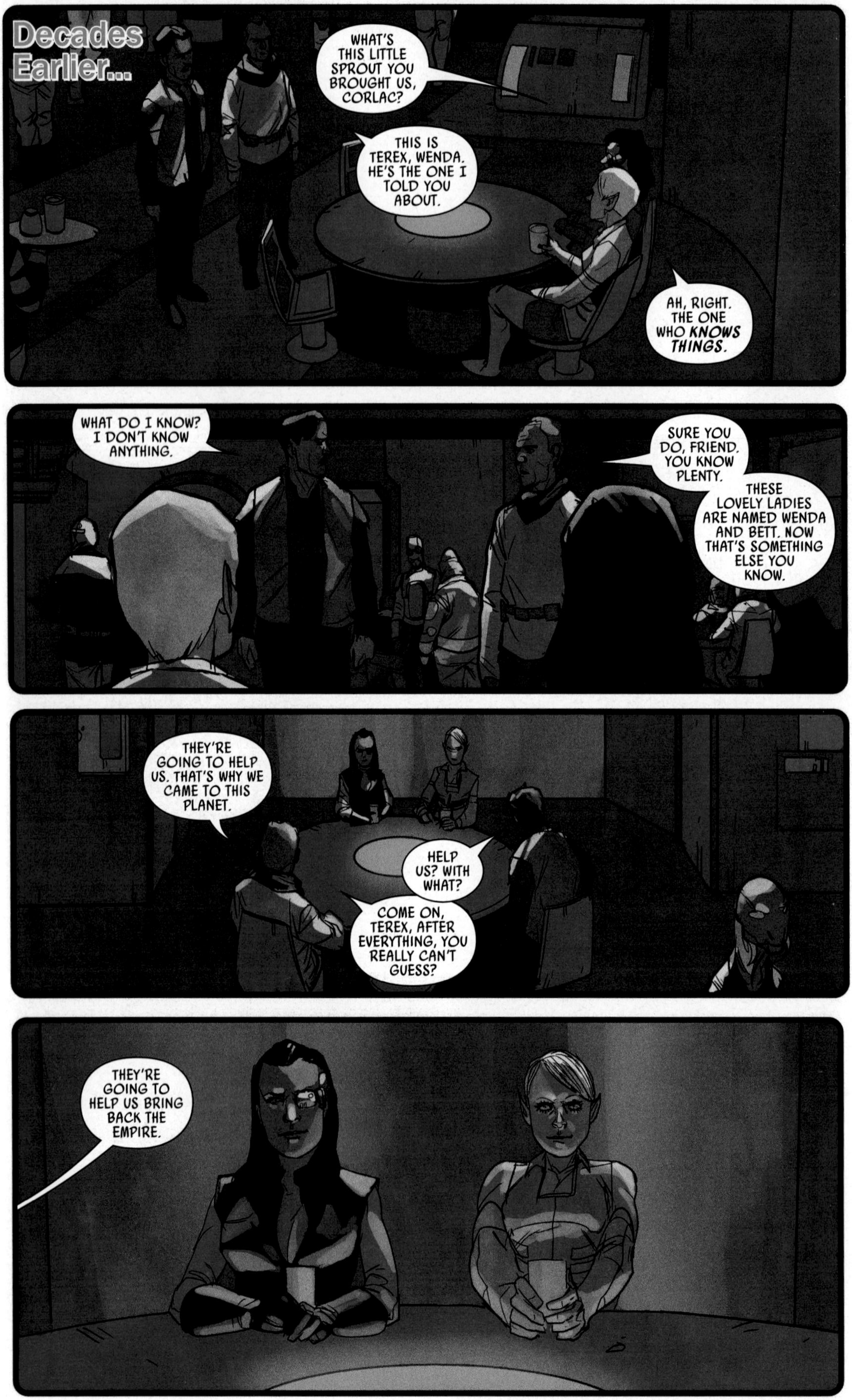
Decades Earlier...
WHAT'S THIS LITTLE SPROUT YOU BROUGHT US, CORLAC?
THIS IS TEREX, WENDA. HE'S THE ONE I TOLD YOU ABOUT.
AH, RIGHT. THE ONE WHO *KNOWS THINGS*.
WHAT DO I KNOW? I DON'T KNOW ANYTHING.
SURE YOU DO, FRIEND. YOU KNOW PLENTY.
THESE LOVELY LADIES ARE NAMED WENDA AND BETT. NOW THAT'S SOMETHING ELSE YOU KNOW.
THEY'RE GOING TO HELP US. THAT'S WHY WE CAME TO THIS PLANET.
HELP US? WITH WHAT?
COME ON, TEREX, AFTER EVERYTHING, YOU REALLY CAN'T GUESS?
THEY'RE GOING TO HELP US BRING BACK THE EMPIRE.

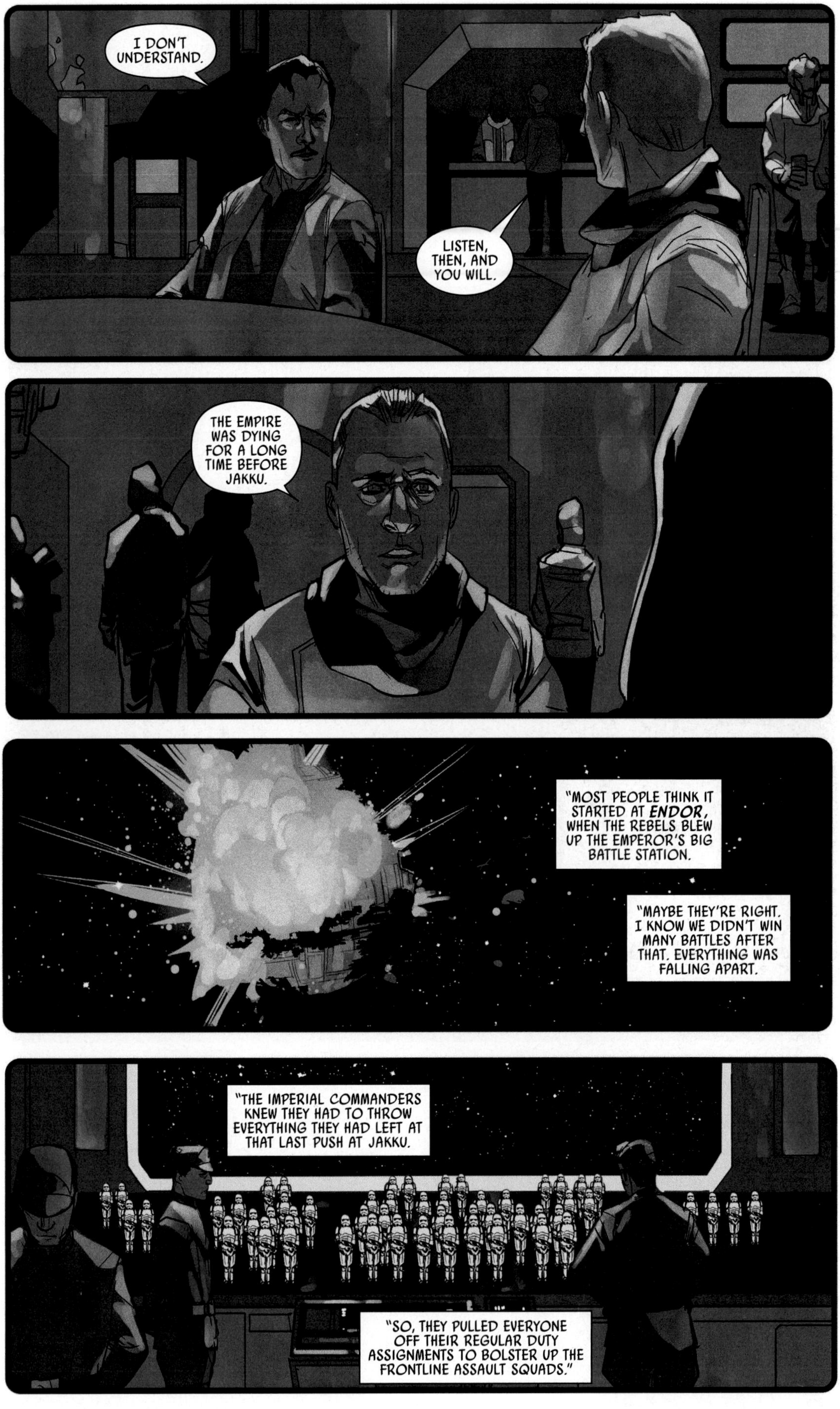
I DON'T UNDERSTAND.
LISTEN, THEN, AND YOU WILL.
THE EMPIRE WAS DYING FOR A LONG TIME BEFORE JAKKU.
"MOST PEOPLE THINK IT STARTED AT ENDOR, WHEN THE REBELS BLEW UP THE EMPEROR'S BIG BATTLE STATION.
"MAYBE THEY'RE RIGHT. I KNOW WE DIDN'T WIN MANY BATTLES AFTER THAT. EVERYTHING WAS FALLING APART.
"THE IMPERIAL COMMANDERS KNEW THEY HAD TO THROW EVERYTHING THEY HAD LEFT AT THAT LAST PUSH AT JAKKU.
"SO, THEY PULLED EVERYONE OFF THEIR REGULAR DUTY ASSIGNMENTS TO BOLSTER UP THE FRONTLINE ASSAULT SQUADS."

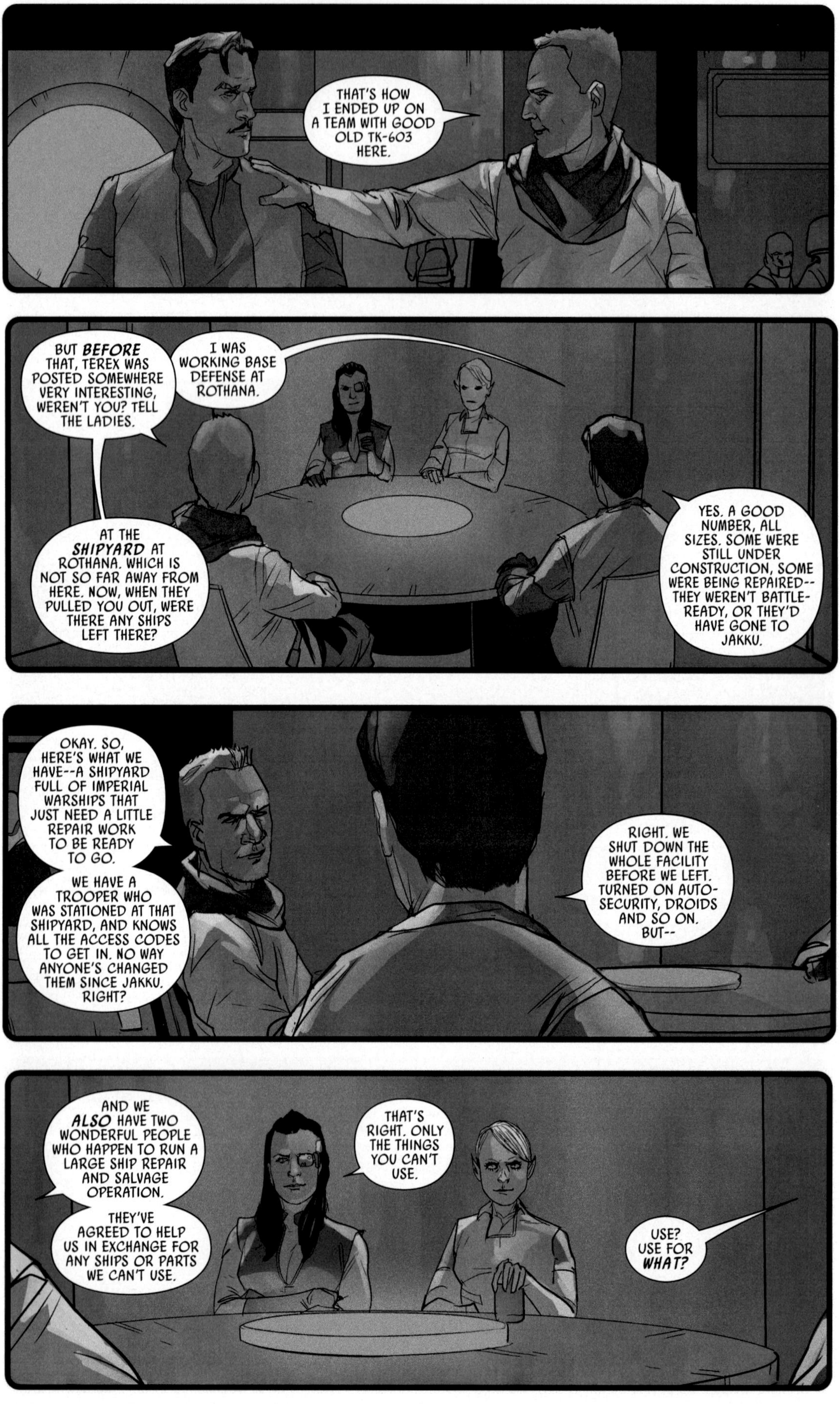
THAT'S HOW I ENDED UP ON A TEAM WITH GOOD OLD TK-603 HERE.
BUT BEFORE THAT, TEREX WAS POSTED SOMEWHERE VERY INTERESTING, WEREN'T YOU? TELL THE LADIES.
I WAS WORKING BASE DEFENSE AT ROTHANA.
AT THE SHIPYARD AT ROTHANA. WHICH IS NOT SO FAR AWAY FROM HERE. NOW, WHEN THEY PULLED YOU OUT, WERE THERE ANY SHIPS LEFT THERE?
YES. A GOOD NUMBER, ALL SIZES. SOME WERE STILL UNDER CONSTRUCTION, SOME WERE BEING REPAIRED--THEY WEREN'T BATTLE-READY, OR THEY'D HAVE GONE TO JAKKU.
OKAY. SO, HERE'S WHAT WE HAVE--A SHIPYARD FULL OF IMPERIAL WARSHIPS THAT JUST NEED A LITTLE REPAIR WORK TO BE READY TO GO.
WE HAVE A TROOPER WHO WAS STATIONED AT THAT SHIPYARD, AND KNOWS ALL THE ACCESS CODES TO GET IN. NO WAY ANYONE'S CHANGED THEM SINCE JAKKU. RIGHT?
RIGHT. WE SHUT DOWN THE WHOLE FACILITY BEFORE WE LEFT. TURNED ON AUTO-SECURITY, DROIDS AND SO ON. BUT--
AND WE ALSO HAVE TWO WONDERFUL PEOPLE WHO HAPPEN TO RUN A LARGE SHIP REPAIR AND SALVAGE OPERATION.
THEY'VE AGREED TO HELP US IN EXCHANGE FOR ANY SHIPS OR PARTS WE CAN'T USE.
THAT'S RIGHT. ONLY THE THINGS YOU CAN'T USE.
USE? USE FOR WHAT?

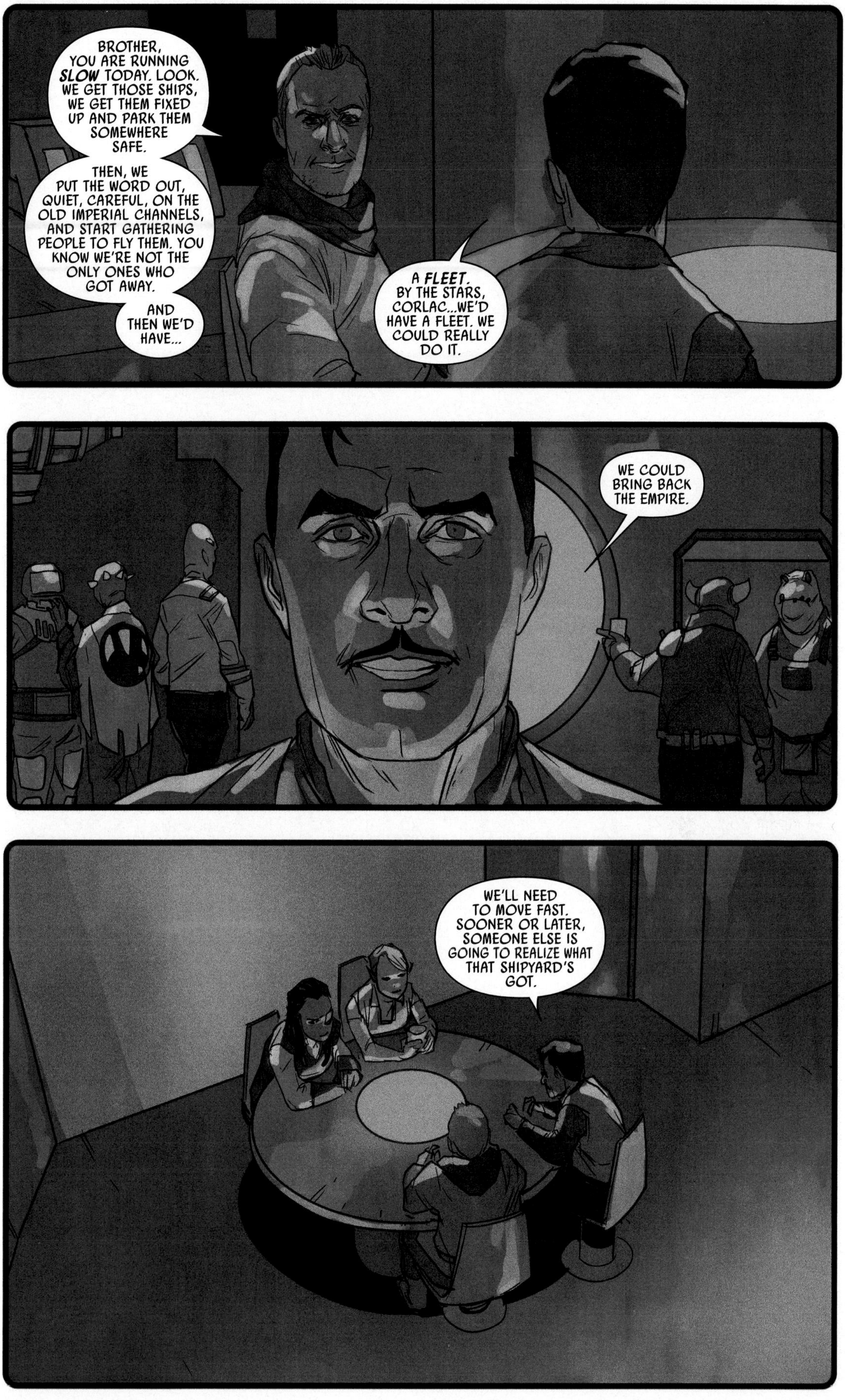
BROTHER, YOU ARE RUNNING SLOW TODAY. LOOK. WE GET THOSE SHIPS, WE GET THEM FIXED UP AND PARK THEM SOMEWHERE SAFE.
THEN, WE PUT THE WORD OUT, QUIET, CAREFUL, ON THE OLD IMPERIAL CHANNELS, AND START GATHERING PEOPLE TO FLY THEM. YOU KNOW WE'RE NOT THE ONLY ONES WHO GOT AWAY.
AND THEN WE'D HAVE...
A FLEET. BY THE STARS, CORLAC...WE'D HAVE A FLEET. WE COULD REALLY DO IT.
WE COULD BRING BACK THE EMPIRE.
WE'LL NEED TO MOVE FAST. SOONER OR LATER, SOMEONE ELSE IS GOING TO REALIZE WHAT THAT SHIPYARD'S GOT.

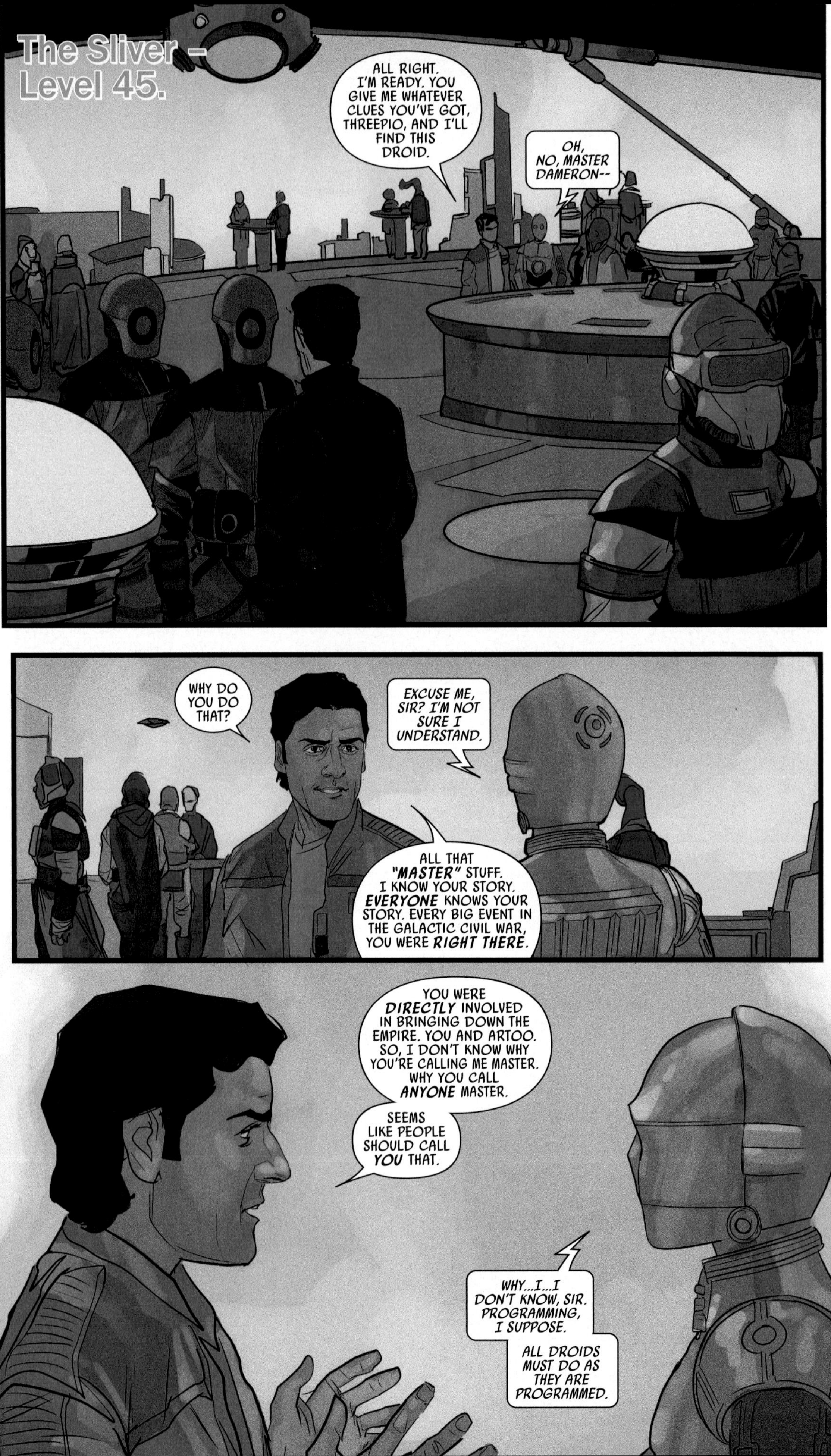
The Sliver – Level 45.
ALL RIGHT. I'M READY. YOU GIVE ME WHATEVER CLUES YOU'VE GOT, THREEPIO, AND I'LL FIND THIS DROID.
OH, NO, MASTER DAMERON--
WHY DO YOU DO THAT?
EXCUSE ME, SIR? I'M NOT SURE I UNDERSTAND.
ALL THAT "MASTER" STUFF. I KNOW YOUR STORY. EVERYONE KNOWS YOUR STORY. EVERY BIG EVENT IN THE GALACTIC CIVIL WAR, YOU WERE RIGHT THERE.
YOU WERE DIRECTLY INVOLVED IN BRINGING DOWN THE EMPIRE. YOU AND ARTOO. SO, I DON'T KNOW WHY YOU'RE CALLING ME MASTER. WHY YOU CALL ANYONE MASTER.
SEEMS LIKE PEOPLE SHOULD CALL YOU THAT.
WHY...I...I DON'T KNOW, SIR. PROGRAMMING, I SUPPOSE.
ALL DROIDS MUST DO AS THEY ARE PROGRAMMED.

BUT AS I WAS SAYING, BEFORE YOUR OVERGENEROUS ASSESSMENT OF MY ROLE IN GALACTIC EVENTS, IT IS NOT **YOUR** JOB TO FIND THE MISSING OPERATIVE.

I WILL DO THAT. YOUR JOB IS MERELY TO KEEP ME SAFE.

AND UNFORTUNATELY, I FEAR THAT I MAY HAVE THE EASIER TASK.

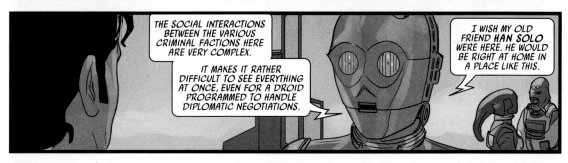

THE SOCIAL INTERACTIONS BETWEEN THE VARIOUS CRIMINAL FACTIONS HERE ARE VERY COMPLEX.

IT MAKES IT RATHER DIFFICULT TO SEE EVERYTHING AT ONCE, EVEN FOR A DROID PROGRAMMED TO HANDLE DIPLOMATIC NEGOTIATIONS.

I WISH MY OLD FRIEND **HAN SOLO** WERE HERE. HE WOULD BE RIGHT AT HOME IN A PLACE LIKE THIS.

UNFORTUNATELY, HE IS NOT AVAILABLE TO HELP US THESE DAYS, AFTER HIS ESTRANGEMENT FROM GENERAL ORGANA.

ACCORDING TO MY OPERATIVES, HE HAS RETURNED TO HIS PREVIOUS OCCUPATION AS A **SMUGGLER**.

NOT THAT IT'S MY BUSINESS, OF COURSE, BUT I UNDERSTAND HE BORROWED A SIGNIFICANT SUM FROM THE GUAVIAN DEATH GANG TO FUND HIS OPERATIONS.

SEEMS LIKE QUITE A RISKY PROPOSITION, BUT THAT'S HAN SOLO FOR YOU.

HE NEVER MUCH CARED FOR THE **ODDS**.

<WAIT-- **WHAT** DID THAT DROID JUST SAY?>

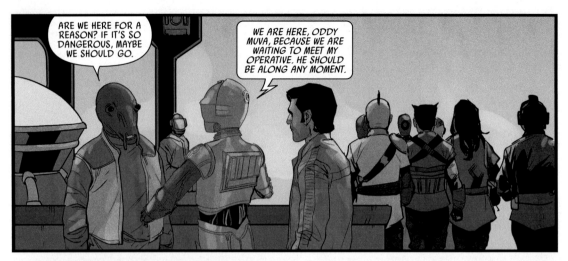

ARE WE HERE FOR A REASON? IF IT'S SO DANGEROUS, MAYBE WE SHOULD GO.

WE ARE HERE, ODDY MUVA, BECAUSE WE ARE WAITING TO MEET MY OPERATIVE. HE SHOULD BE ALONG ANY MOMENT.

AH. IN FACT...

...HERE HE IS NOW.

NICE. NICE! WHO'S GONNA LOOK TWICE AT ONE OF *THOSE* LITTLE GUYS!

YES. THE UNOBTRUSIVENESS OF THE MSE SERIES MAKES THEM *EXTREMELY* USEFUL SP-- ER, OPERATIVES.

NOW, IF YOU TWO WOULD JUST STAND IN FRONT HERE TO DIVERT ANY PRYING EYES, OUR LITTLE FRIEND CAN DOWNLOAD HIS DATABANKS INTO OUR *OTHER* LITTLE FRIEND.

I'VE HAD HIM ROLLING AROUND THE CITY'S TAVERNS ALL DAY. IF SOMEONE'S MENTIONED OUR MISSING DROID, HE'LL HAVE HEARD ABOUT IT.

THAT'S GENIUS, BUDDY.

NOT AT ALL, SIR. NOT AT ALL.

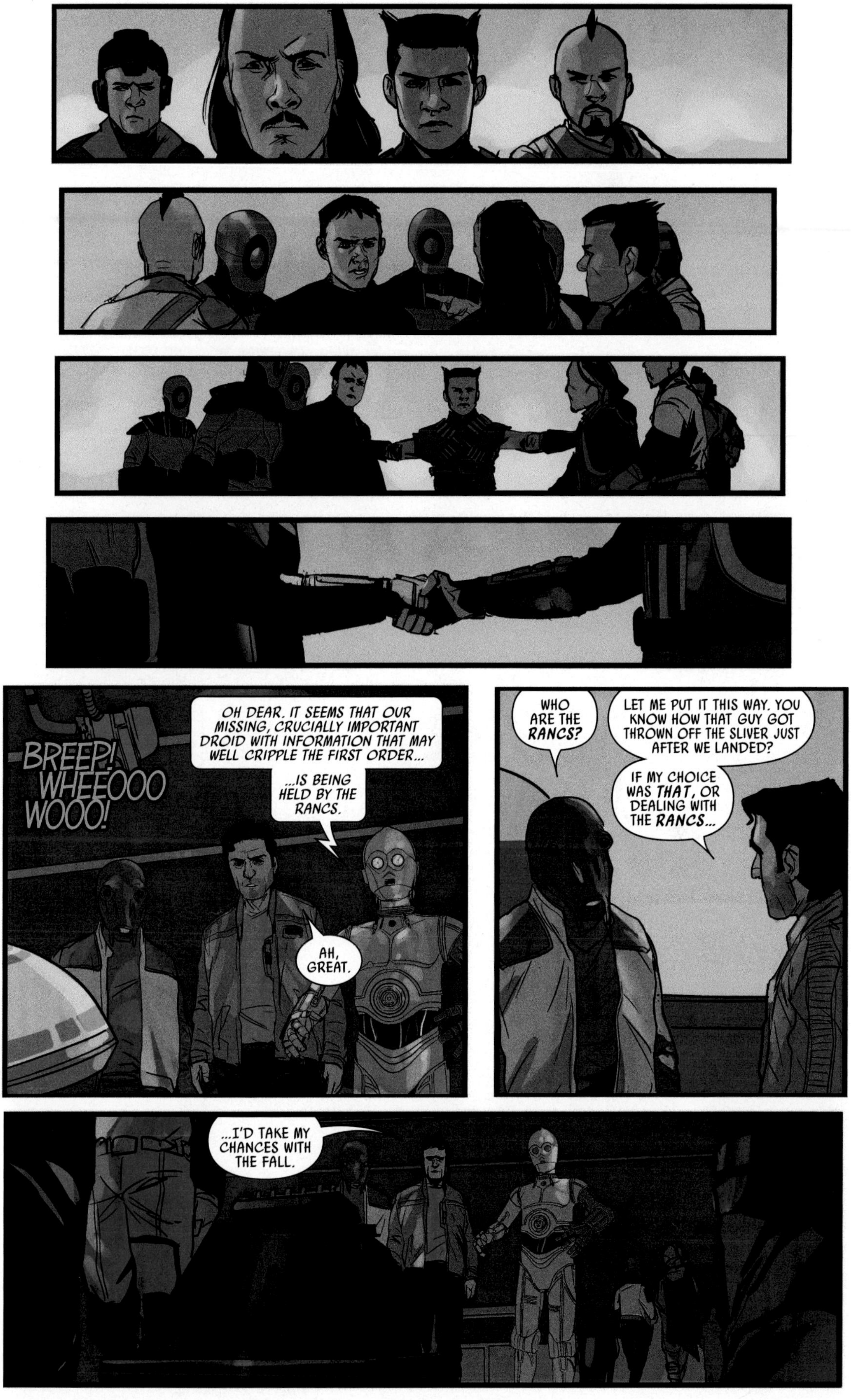
OH DEAR. IT SEEMS THAT OUR MISSING, CRUCIALLY IMPORTANT DROID WITH INFORMATION THAT MAY WELL CRIPPLE THE FIRST ORDER...
...IS BEING HELD BY THE RANCS.
BREEP! WHEEOOO WOOO!
AH, GREAT.
WHO ARE THE RANCS?
LET ME PUT IT THIS WAY. YOU KNOW HOW THAT GUY GOT THROWN OFF THE SLIVER JUST AFTER WE LANDED?
IF MY CHOICE WAS THAT, OR DEALING WITH THE RANCS...
...I'D TAKE MY CHANCES WITH THE FALL.

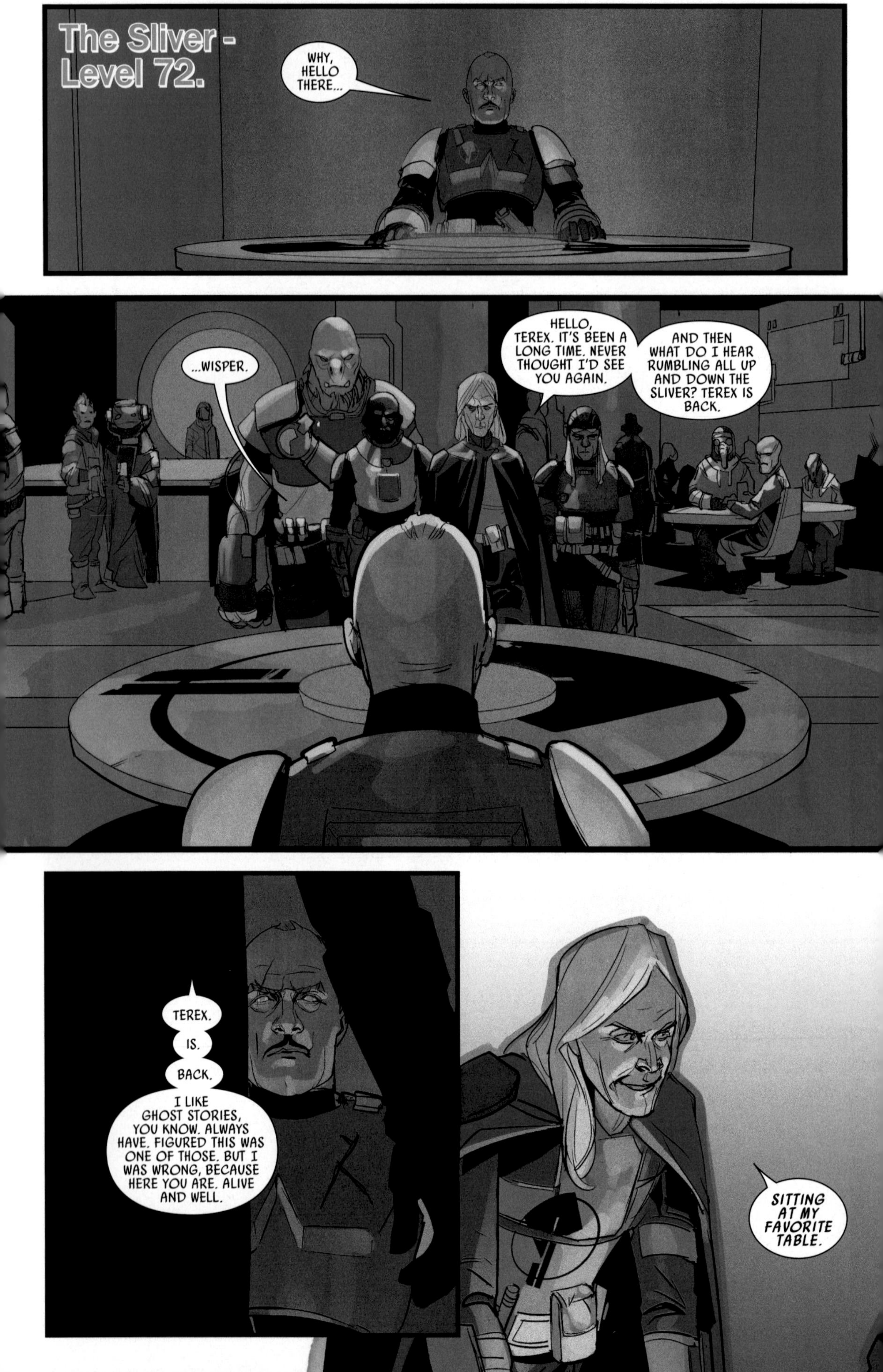
The Sliver - Level 72.
WHY, HELLO THERE...
...WISPER.
HELLO, TEREX. IT'S BEEN A LONG TIME. NEVER THOUGHT I'D SEE YOU AGAIN.
AND THEN WHAT DO I HEAR RUMBLING ALL UP AND DOWN THE SLIVER? TEREX IS BACK.
TEREX.
IS.
BACK.
I LIKE GHOST STORIES, YOU KNOW. ALWAYS HAVE. FIGURED THIS WAS ONE OF THOSE. BUT I WAS WRONG, BECAUSE HERE YOU ARE. ALIVE AND WELL.
SITTING AT MY FAVORITE TABLE.

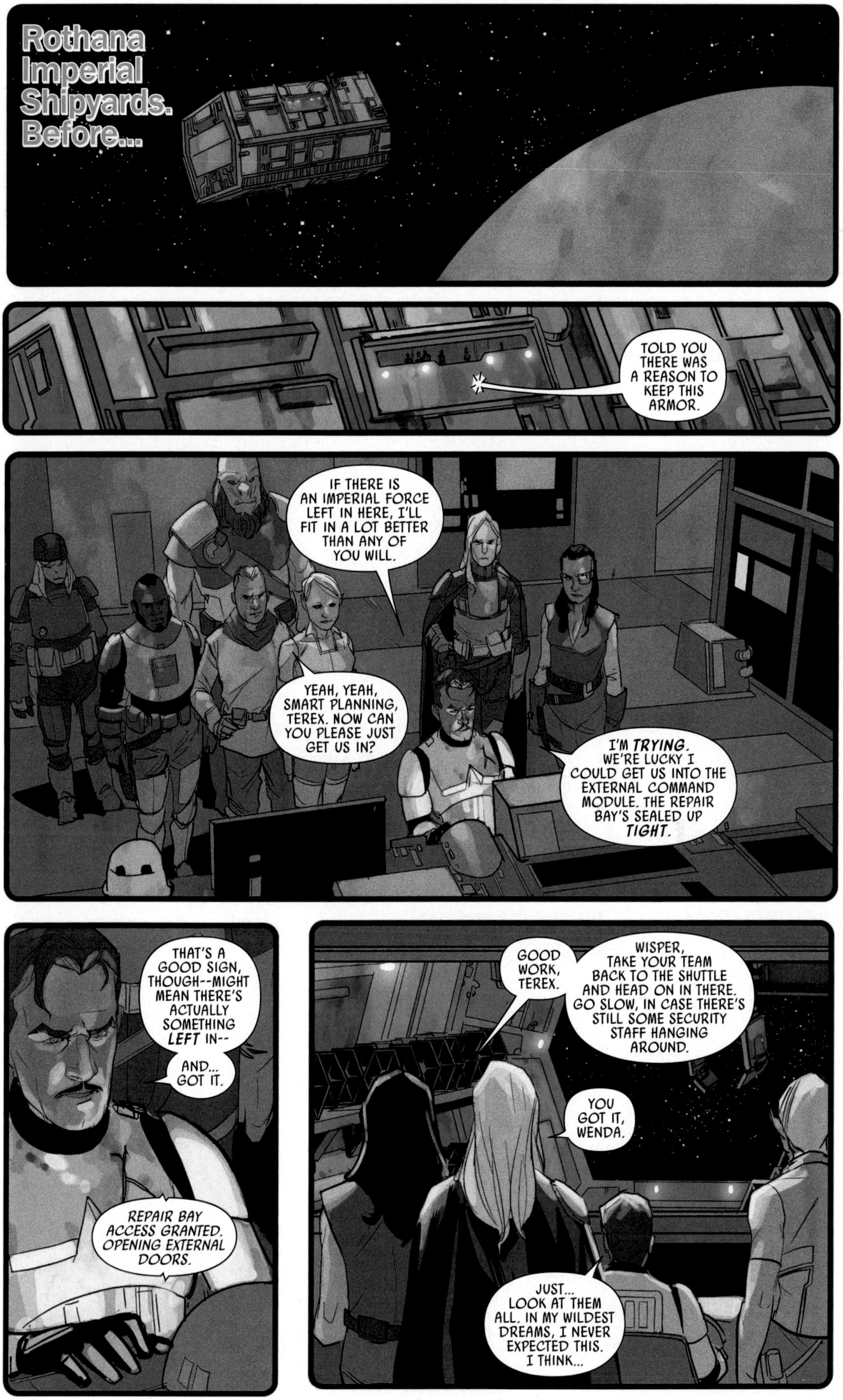
Rothana Imperial Shipyards. Before...
TOLD YOU THERE WAS A REASON TO KEEP THIS ARMOR.
IF THERE IS AN IMPERIAL FORCE LEFT IN HERE, I'LL FIT IN A LOT BETTER THAN ANY OF YOU WILL.
YEAH, YEAH, SMART PLANNING, TEREX. NOW CAN YOU PLEASE JUST GET US IN?
I'M TRYING. WE'RE LUCKY I COULD GET US INTO THE EXTERNAL COMMAND MODULE. THE REPAIR BAY'S SEALED UP TIGHT.
THAT'S A GOOD SIGN, THOUGH--MIGHT MEAN THERE'S ACTUALLY SOMETHING LEFT IN--
AND... GOT IT.
REPAIR BAY ACCESS GRANTED. OPENING EXTERNAL DOORS.
GOOD WORK, TEREX.
WISPER, TAKE YOUR TEAM BACK TO THE SHUTTLE AND HEAD ON IN THERE. GO SLOW, IN CASE THERE'S STILL SOME SECURITY STAFF HANGING AROUND.
YOU GOT IT, WENDA.
JUST... LOOK AT THEM ALL. IN MY WILDEST DREAMS, I NEVER EXPECTED THIS. I THINK...

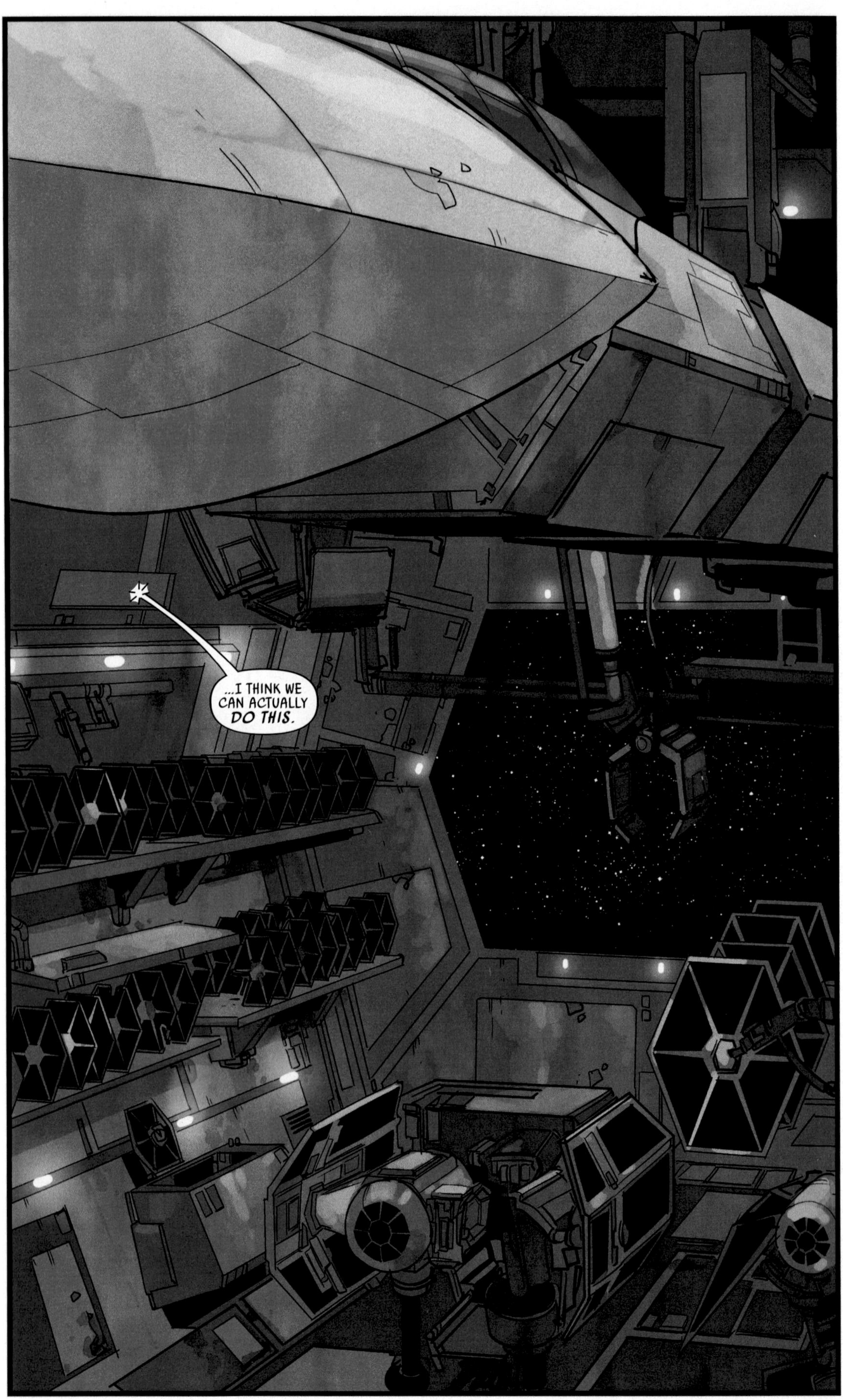
...I THINK WE CAN ACTUALLY DO THIS.

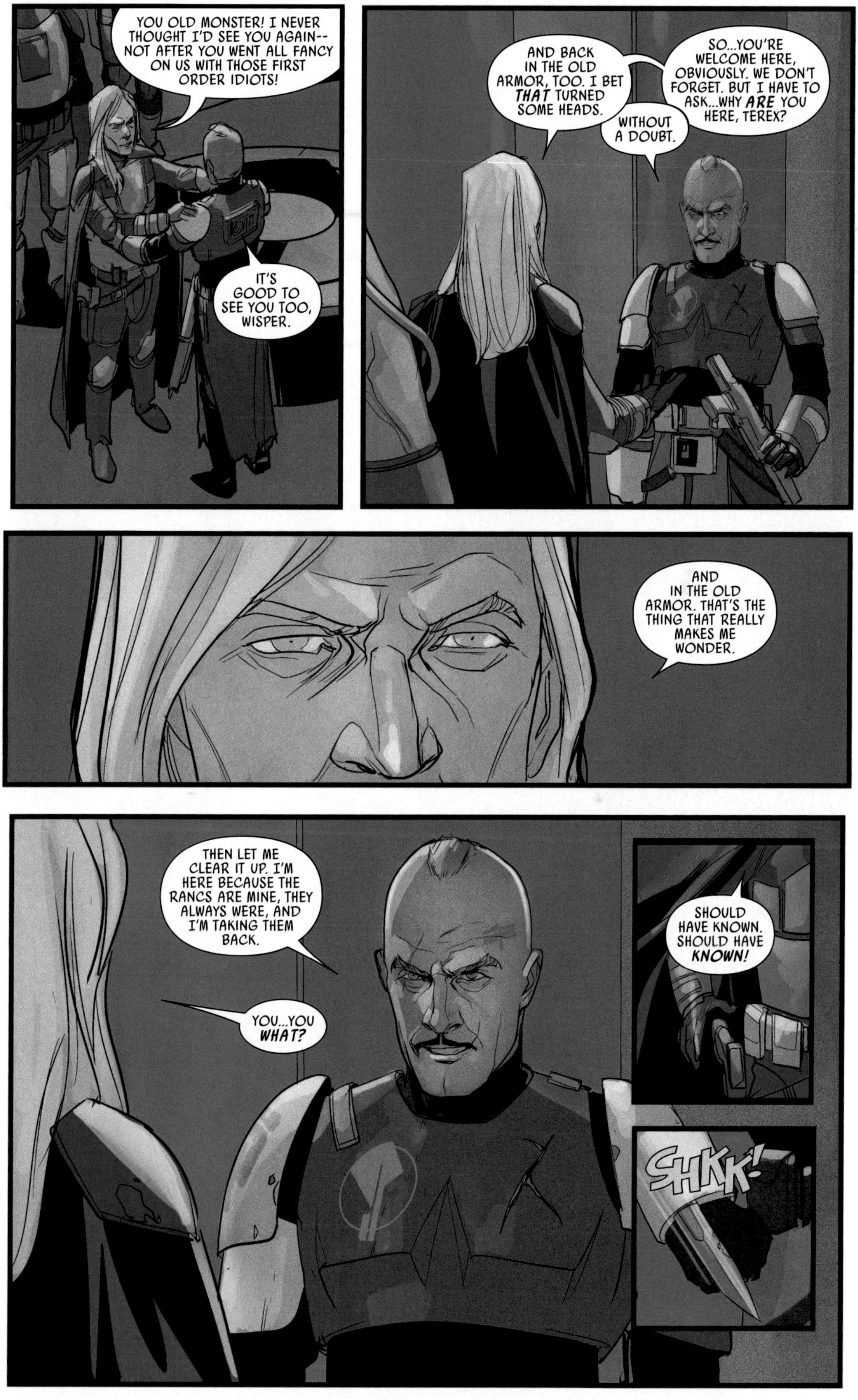

YOU OLD MONSTER! I NEVER THOUGHT I'D SEE YOU AGAIN-- NOT AFTER YOU WENT ALL FANCY ON US WITH THOSE FIRST ORDER IDIOTS!
IT'S GOOD TO SEE YOU TOO, WISPER.
AND BACK IN THE OLD ARMOR, TOO. I BET *THAT* TURNED SOME HEADS.
WITHOUT A DOUBT.
SO...YOU'RE WELCOME HERE, OBVIOUSLY. WE DON'T FORGET. BUT I HAVE TO ASK...WHY *ARE* YOU HERE, TEREX?
AND IN THE OLD ARMOR. THAT'S THE THING THAT REALLY MAKES ME WONDER.
THEN LET ME CLEAR IT UP. I'M HERE BECAUSE THE RANCS ARE MINE, THEY ALWAYS WERE, AND I'M TAKING THEM BACK.
YOU...YOU *WHAT?*
SHOULD HAVE KNOWN. SHOULD HAVE *KNOWN!*
SHKK!

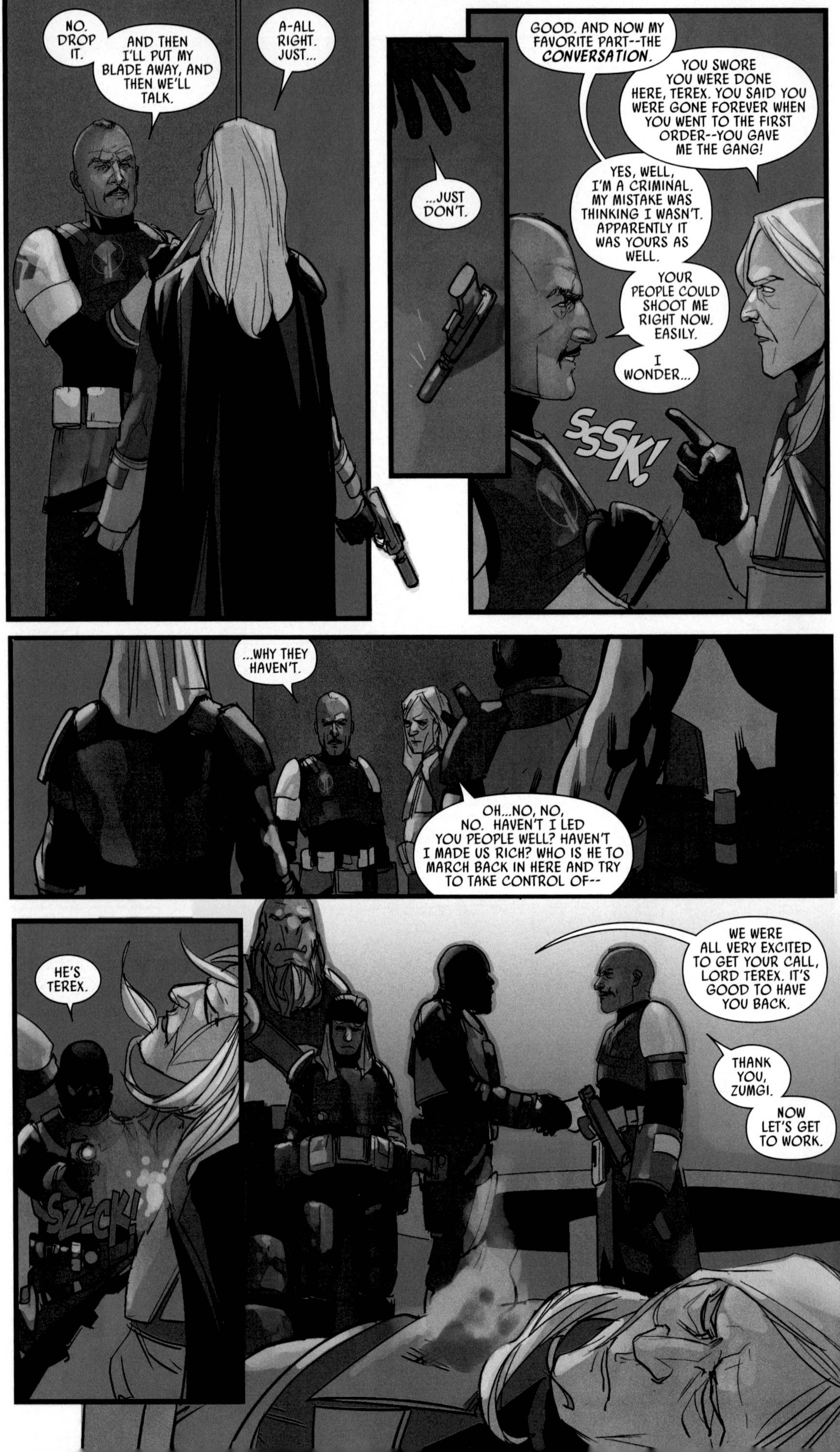
NO. DROP IT.
AND THEN I'LL PUT MY BLADE AWAY, AND THEN WE'LL TALK.
A-ALL RIGHT. JUST...
...JUST DON'T.
GOOD. AND NOW MY FAVORITE PART--THE CONVERSATION.
YOU SWORE YOU WERE DONE HERE, TEREX. YOU SAID YOU WERE GONE FOREVER WHEN YOU WENT TO THE FIRST ORDER--YOU GAVE ME THE GANG!
YES, WELL, I'M A CRIMINAL. MY MISTAKE WAS THINKING I WASN'T. APPARENTLY IT WAS YOURS AS WELL.
YOUR PEOPLE COULD SHOOT ME RIGHT NOW. EASILY.
I WONDER...
SSSK!
...WHY THEY HAVEN'T.
OH...NO, NO, NO. HAVEN'T I LED YOU PEOPLE WELL? HAVEN'T I MADE US RICH? WHO IS HE TO MARCH BACK IN HERE AND TRY TO TAKE CONTROL OF--
HE'S TEREX.
SZZCK!
WE WERE ALL VERY EXCITED TO GET YOUR CALL, LORD TEREX. IT'S GOOD TO HAVE YOU BACK.
THANK YOU, ZUMGI.
NOW LET'S GET TO WORK.

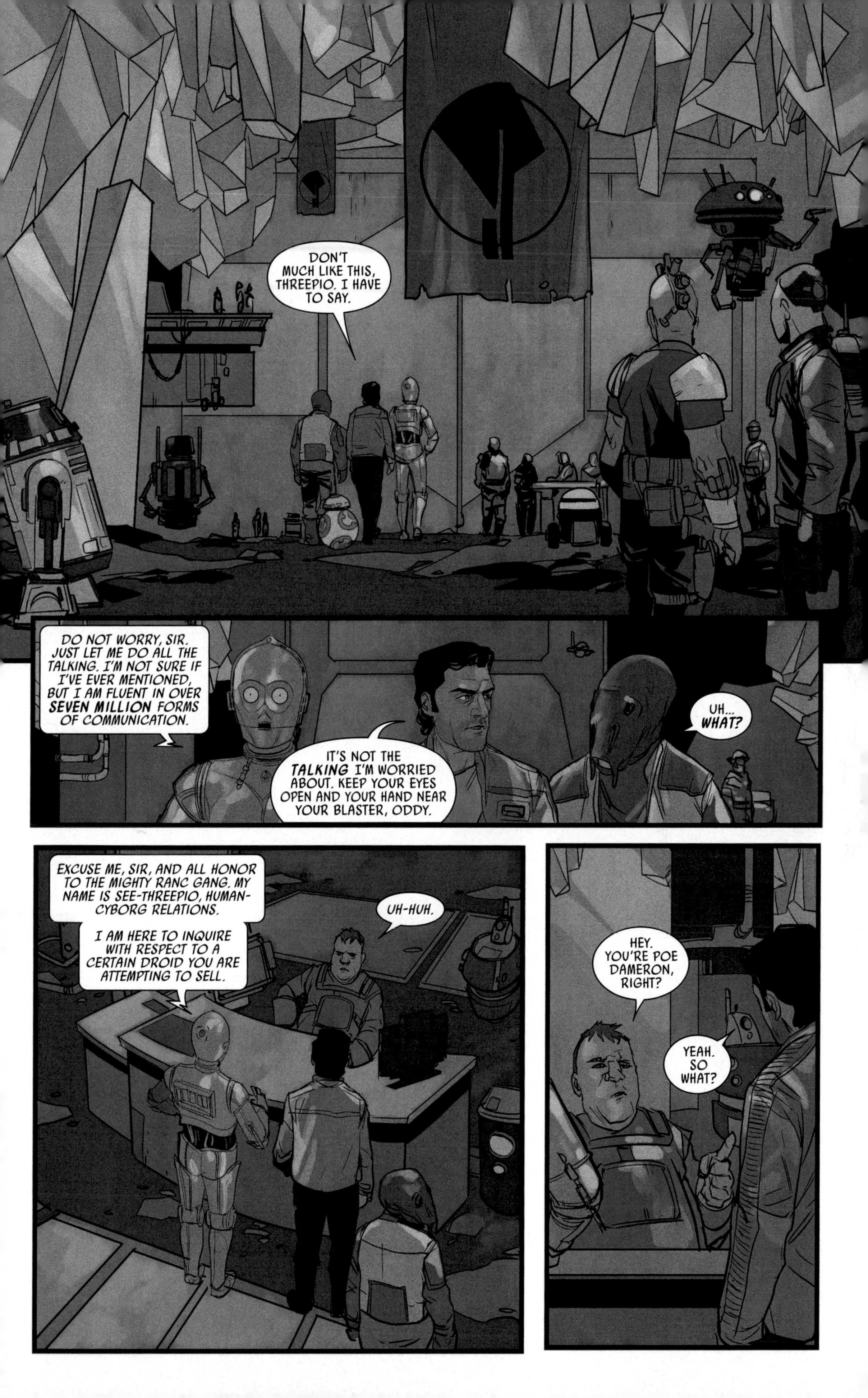
DON'T MUCH LIKE THIS, THREEPIO. I HAVE TO SAY.
DO NOT WORRY, SIR. JUST LET ME DO ALL THE TALKING. I'M NOT SURE IF I'VE EVER MENTIONED, BUT I AM FLUENT IN OVER SEVEN MILLION FORMS OF COMMUNICATION.
IT'S NOT THE TALKING I'M WORRIED ABOUT. KEEP YOUR EYES OPEN AND YOUR HAND NEAR YOUR BLASTER, ODDY.
UH... WHAT?
EXCUSE ME, SIR, AND ALL HONOR TO THE MIGHTY RANC GANG. MY NAME IS SEE-THREEPIO, HUMAN-CYBORG RELATIONS.
I AM HERE TO INQUIRE WITH RESPECT TO A CERTAIN DROID YOU ARE ATTEMPTING TO SELL.
UH-HUH.
HEY. YOU'RE POE DAMERON, RIGHT?
YEAH. SO WHAT?

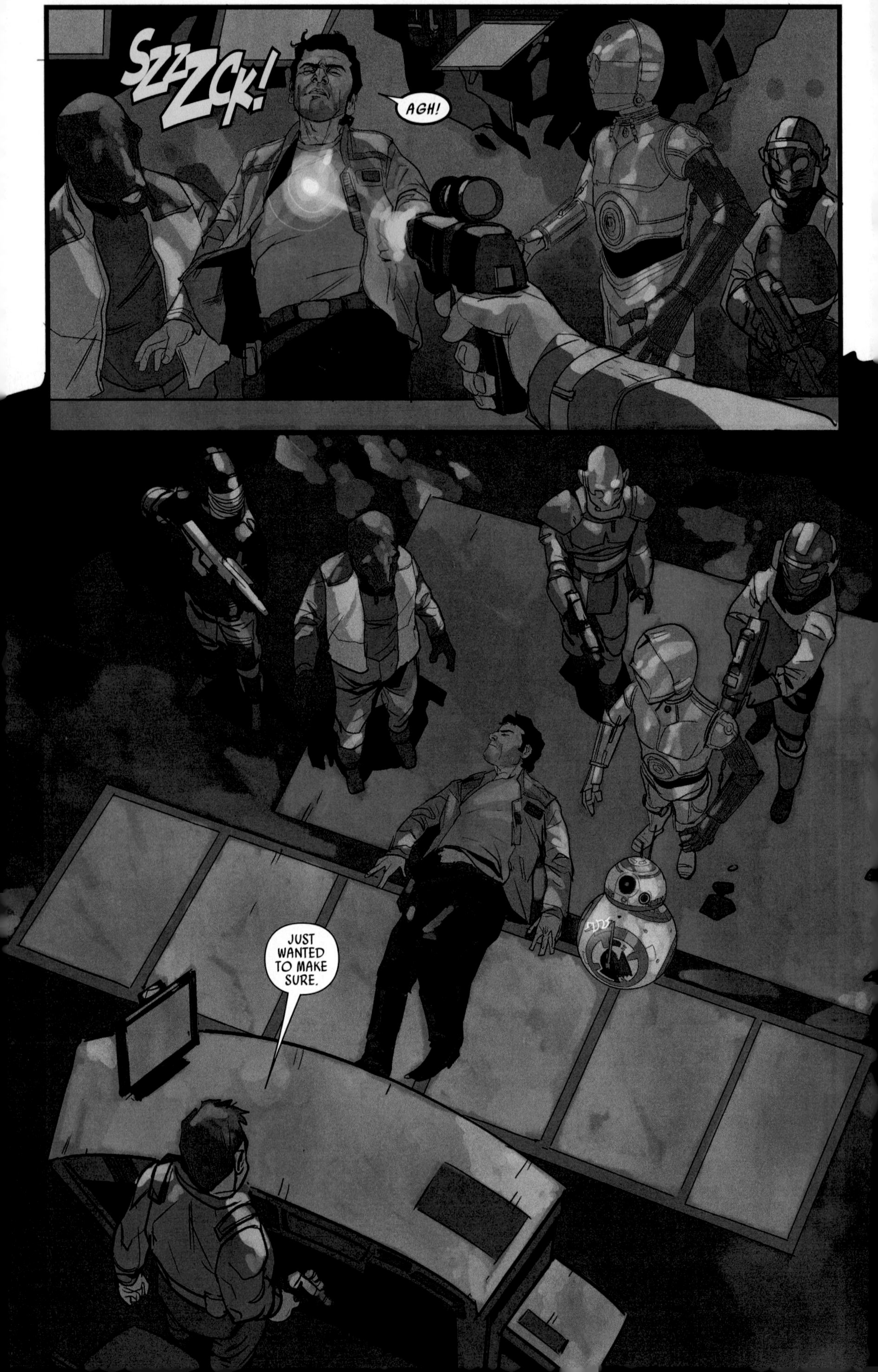
SZZZCK!
AGH!
JUST WANTED TO MAKE SURE.

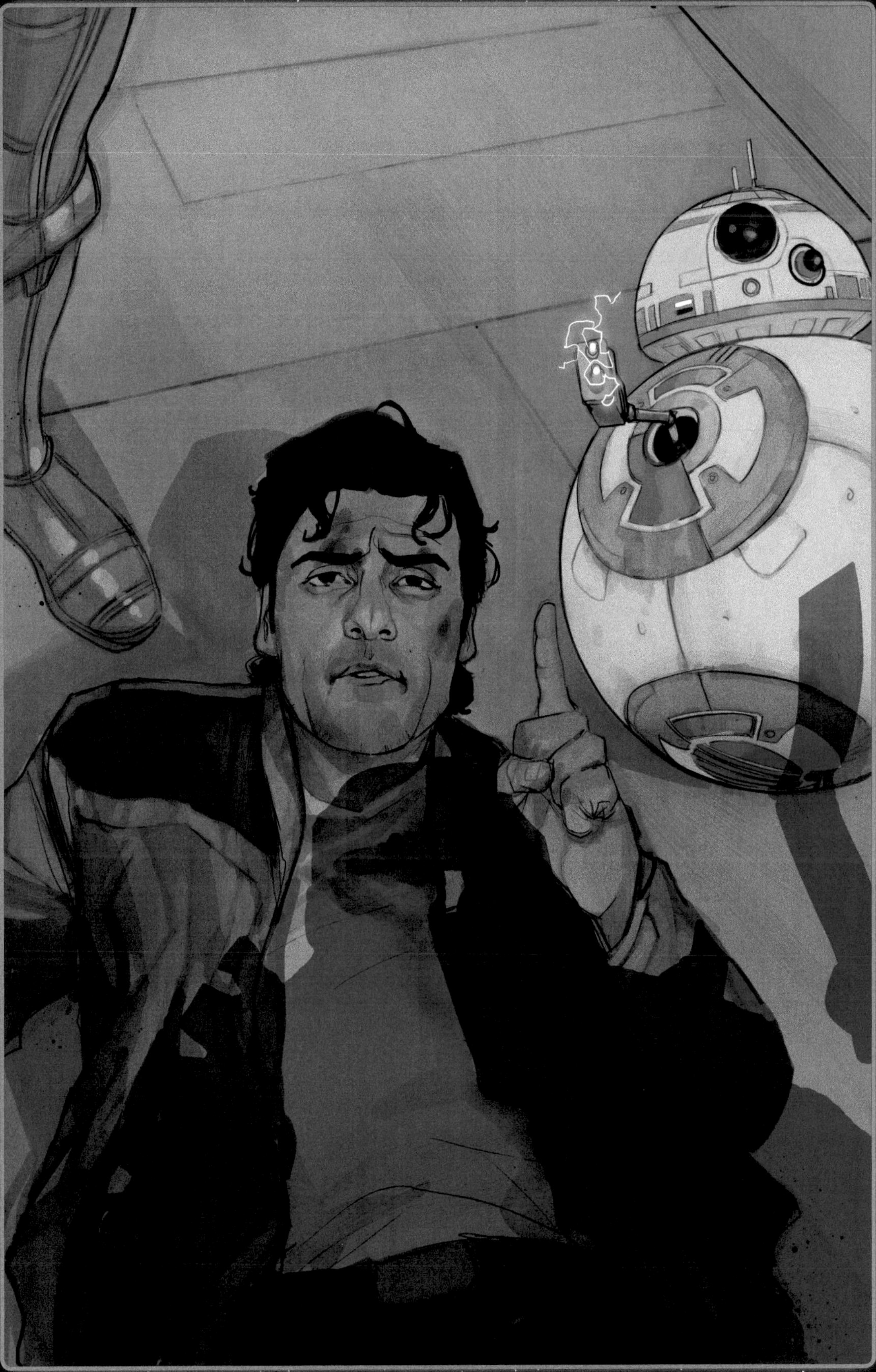

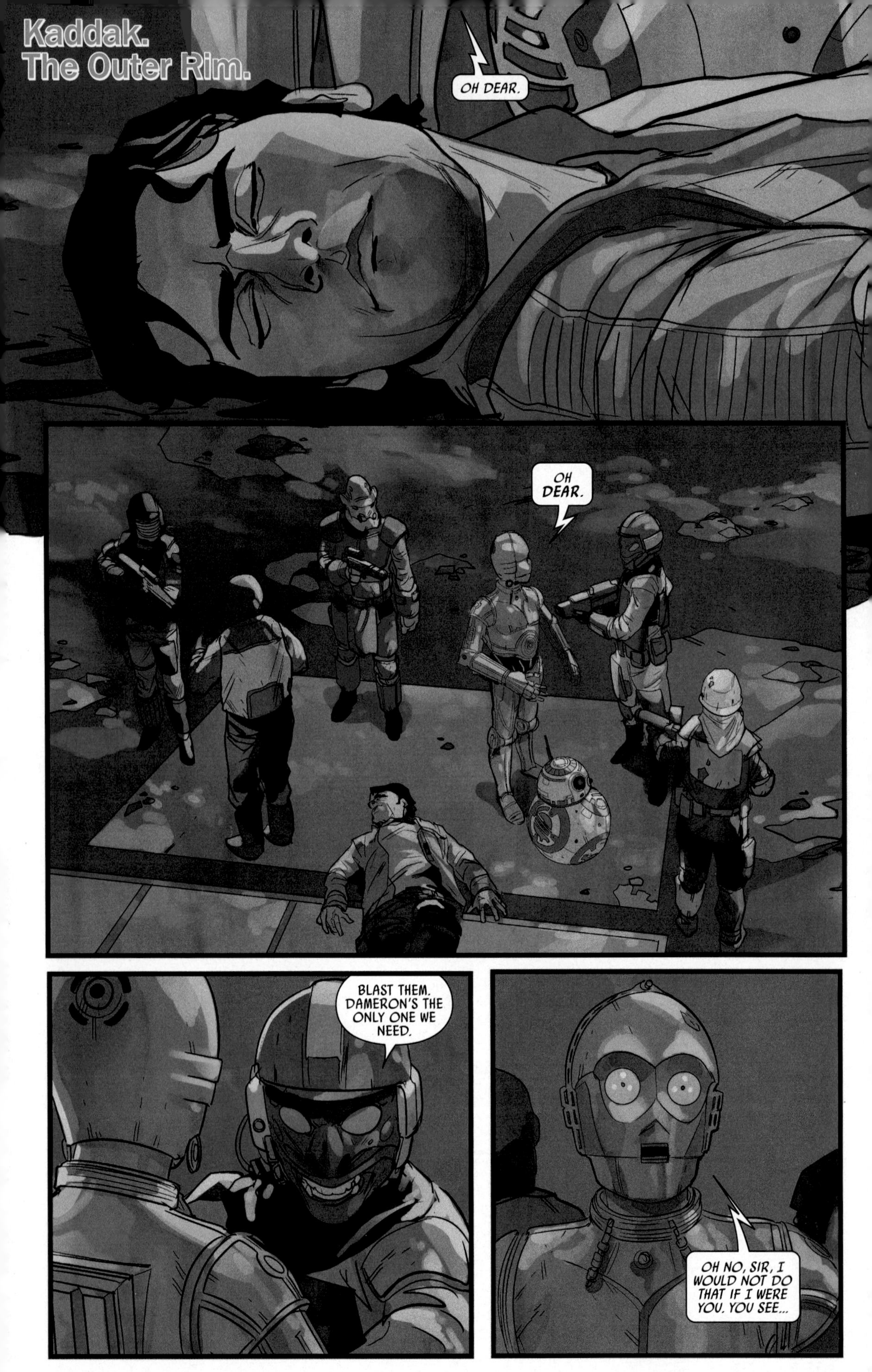
Kaddak.
The Outer Rim.
OH DEAR.
OH DEAR.
BLAST THEM. DAMERON'S THE ONLY ONE WE NEED.
OH NO, SIR, I WOULD NOT DO THAT IF I WERE YOU. YOU SEE...

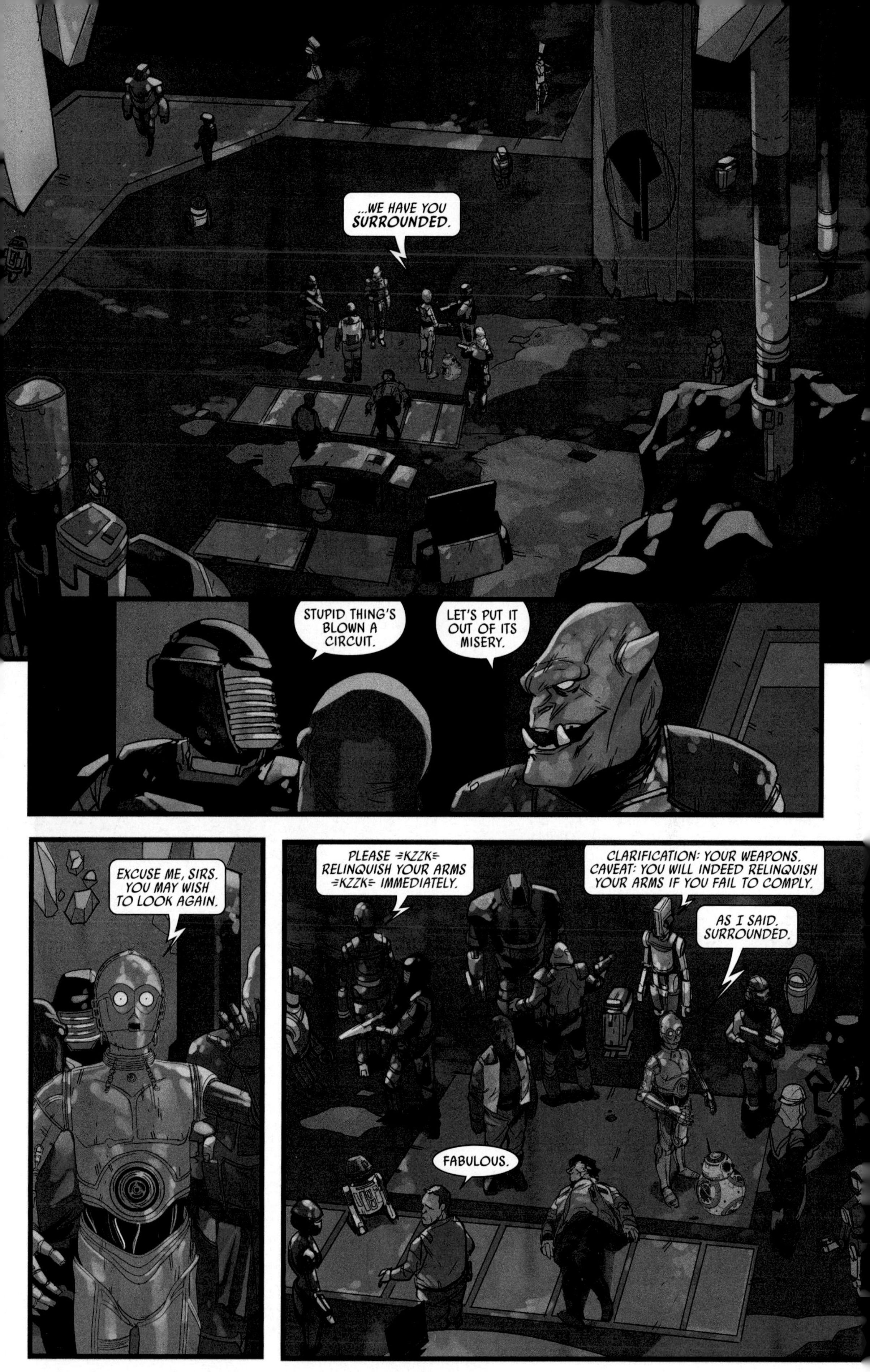
...WE HAVE YOU SURROUNDED.
STUPID THING'S BLOWN A CIRCUIT.
LET'S PUT IT OUT OF ITS MISERY.
EXCUSE ME, SIRS. YOU MAY WISH TO LOOK AGAIN.
PLEASE =KZZK= RELINQUISH YOUR ARMS =KZZK= IMMEDIATELY.
CLARIFICATION: YOUR WEAPONS. CAVEAT: YOU WILL INDEED RELINQUISH YOUR ARMS IF YOU FAIL TO COMPLY.
AS I SAID. SURROUNDED.
FABULOUS.

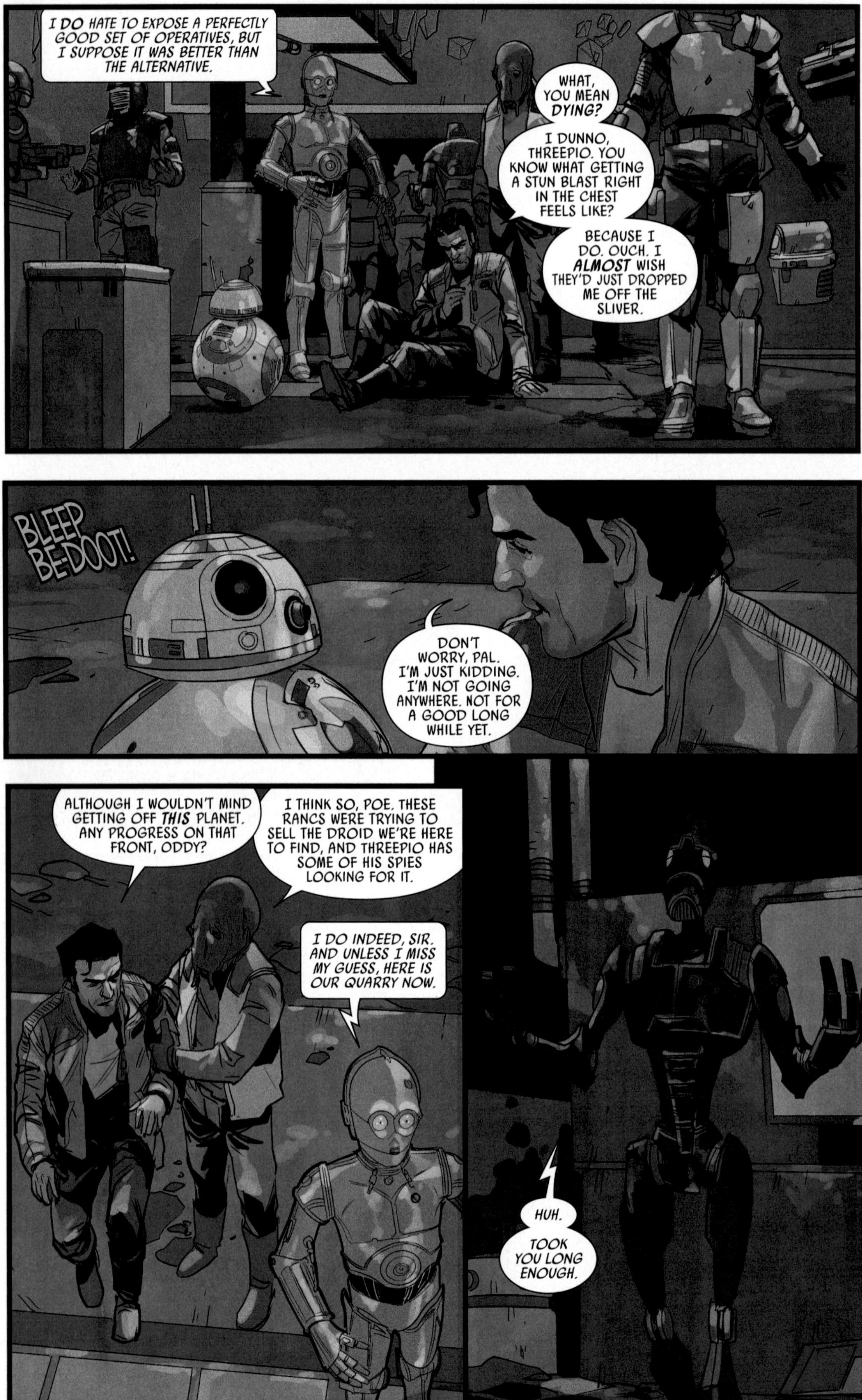
I DO HATE TO EXPOSE A PERFECTLY GOOD SET OF OPERATIVES, BUT I SUPPOSE IT WAS BETTER THAN THE ALTERNATIVE.
WHAT, YOU MEAN DYING?
I DUNNO, THREEPIO. YOU KNOW WHAT GETTING A STUN BLAST RIGHT IN THE CHEST FEELS LIKE?
BECAUSE I DO. OUCH. I ALMOST WISH THEY'D JUST DROPPED ME OFF THE SLIVER.
BLEEP BE-DOOT!
DON'T WORRY, PAL. I'M JUST KIDDING. I'M NOT GOING ANYWHERE. NOT FOR A GOOD LONG WHILE YET.
ALTHOUGH I WOULDN'T MIND GETTING OFF THIS PLANET. ANY PROGRESS ON THAT FRONT, ODDY?
I THINK SO, POE. THESE RANCS WERE TRYING TO SELL THE DROID WE'RE HERE TO FIND, AND THREEPIO HAS SOME OF HIS SPIES LOOKING FOR IT.
I DO INDEED, SIR. AND UNLESS I MISS MY GUESS, HERE IS OUR QUARRY NOW.
HUH.
TOOK YOU LONG ENOUGH.

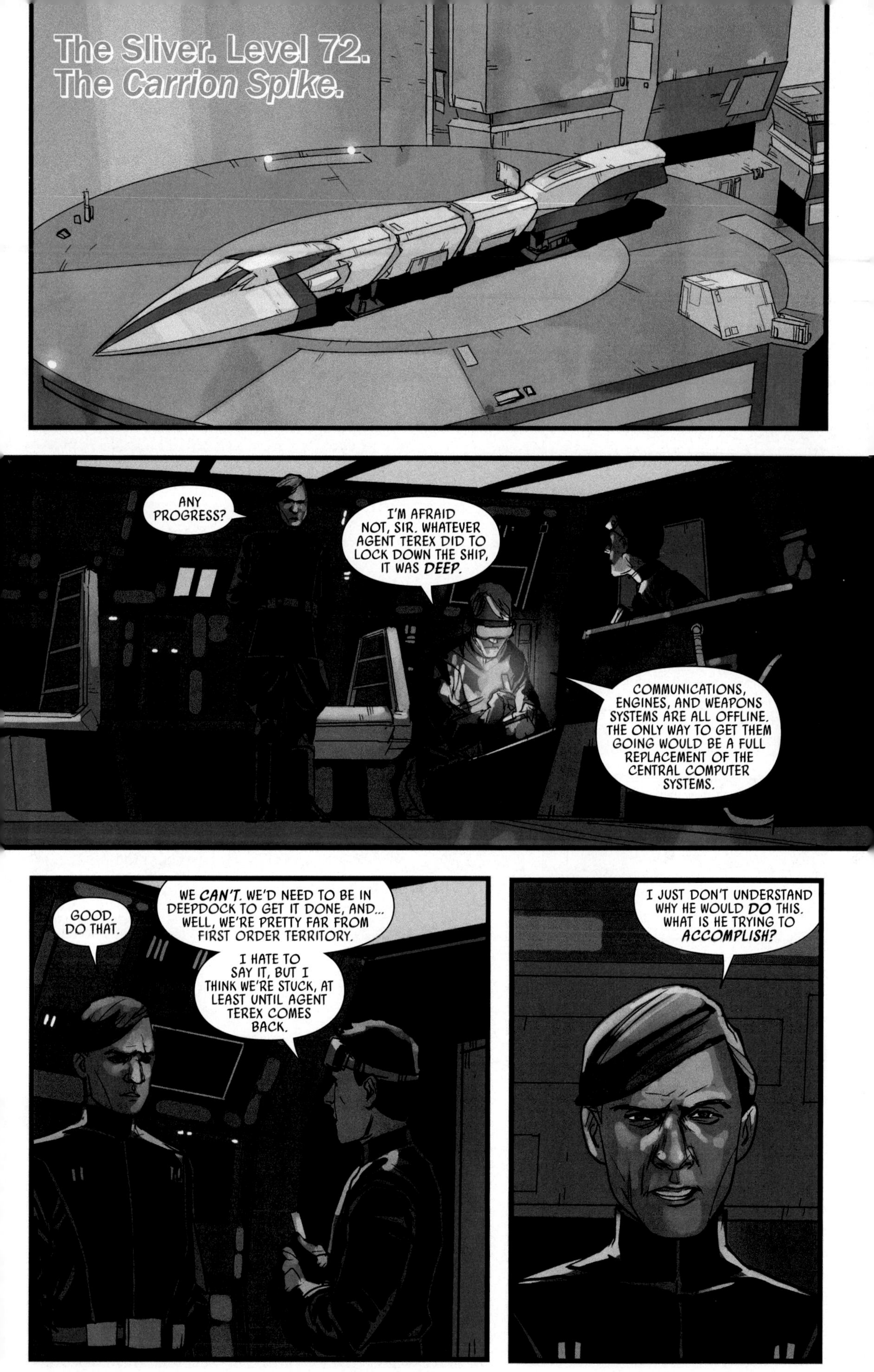
The Sliver. Level 72.
The *Carrion Spike.*
ANY PROGRESS?
I'M AFRAID NOT, SIR. WHATEVER AGENT TEREX DID TO LOCK DOWN THE SHIP, IT WAS **DEEP**.
COMMUNICATIONS, ENGINES, AND WEAPONS SYSTEMS ARE ALL OFFLINE. THE ONLY WAY TO GET THEM GOING WOULD BE A FULL REPLACEMENT OF THE CENTRAL COMPUTER SYSTEMS.
GOOD. DO THAT.
WE **CAN'T**. WE'D NEED TO BE IN DEEPDOCK TO GET IT DONE, AND... WELL, WE'RE PRETTY FAR FROM FIRST ORDER TERRITORY.
I HATE TO SAY IT, BUT I THINK WE'RE STUCK, AT LEAST UNTIL AGENT TEREX COMES BACK.
I JUST DON'T UNDERSTAND WHY HE WOULD **DO** THIS. WHAT IS HE TRYING TO **ACCOMPLISH?**

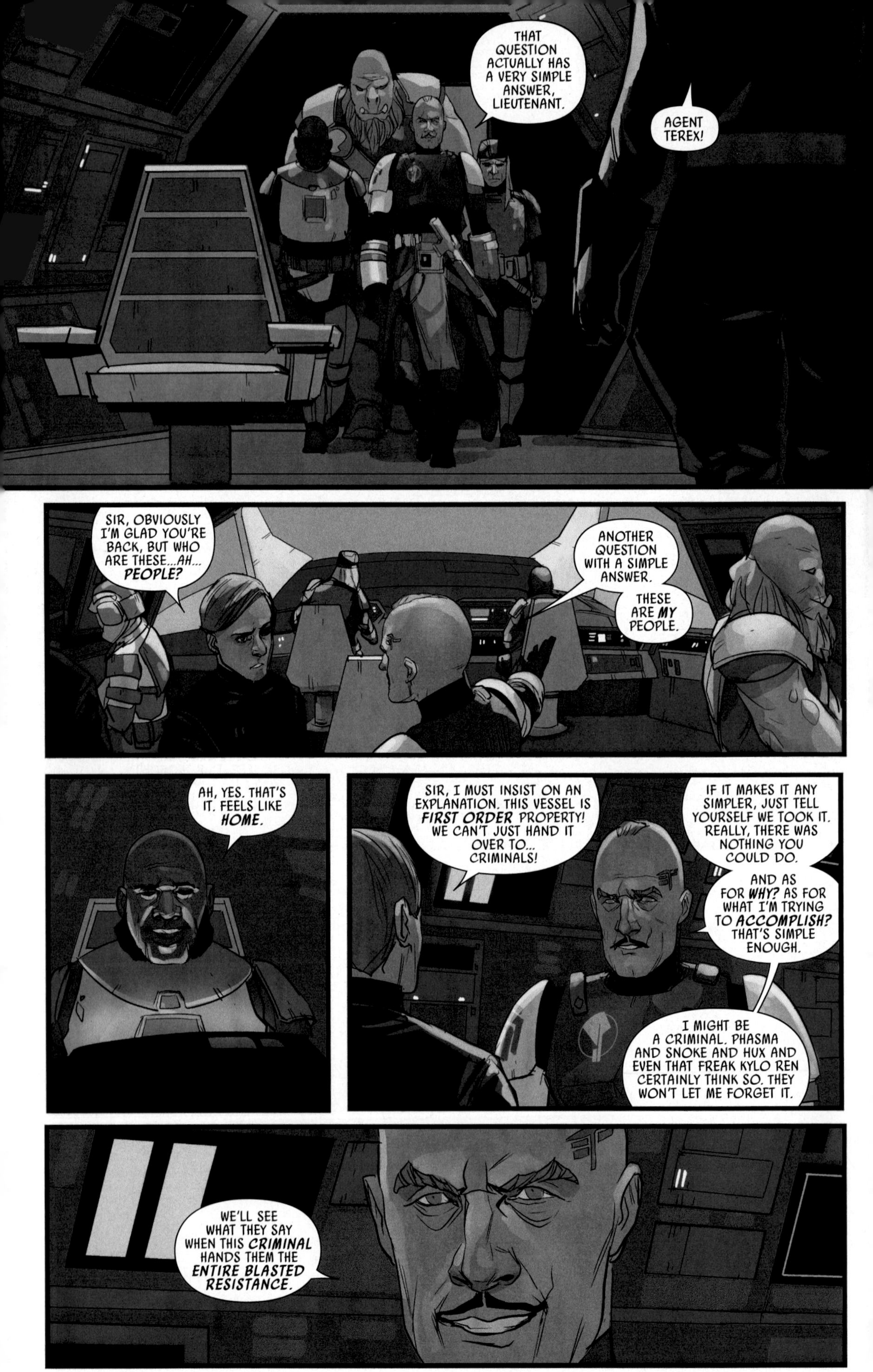
THAT QUESTION ACTUALLY HAS A VERY SIMPLE ANSWER, LIEUTENANT.
AGENT TEREX!
SIR, OBVIOUSLY I'M GLAD YOU'RE BACK, BUT WHO ARE THESE...AH... PEOPLE?
ANOTHER QUESTION WITH A SIMPLE ANSWER.
THESE ARE MY PEOPLE.
AH, YES. THAT'S IT. FEELS LIKE HOME.
SIR, I MUST INSIST ON AN EXPLANATION. THIS VESSEL IS FIRST ORDER PROPERTY! WE CAN'T JUST HAND IT OVER TO... CRIMINALS!
IF IT MAKES IT ANY SIMPLER, JUST TELL YOURSELF WE TOOK IT. REALLY, THERE WAS NOTHING YOU COULD DO.
AND AS FOR WHY? AS FOR WHAT I'M TRYING TO ACCOMPLISH? THAT'S SIMPLE ENOUGH.
I MIGHT BE A CRIMINAL. PHASMA AND SNOKE AND HUX AND EVEN THAT FREAK KYLO REN CERTAINLY THINK SO. THEY WON'T LET ME FORGET IT.
WE'LL SEE WHAT THEY SAY WHEN THIS CRIMINAL HANDS THEM THE ENTIRE BLASTED RESISTANCE.

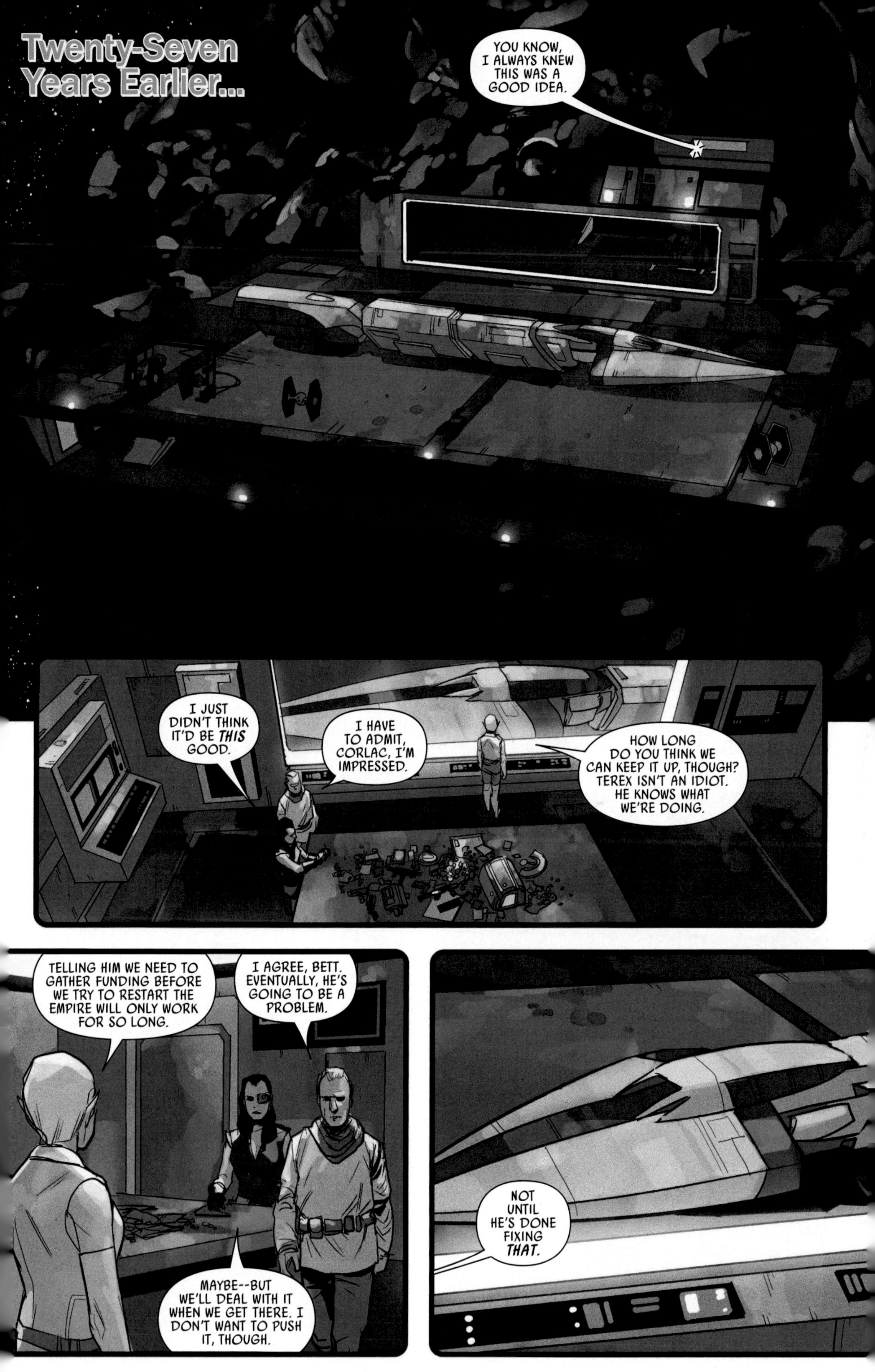
Twenty-Seven Years Earlier...
YOU KNOW, I ALWAYS KNEW THIS WAS A GOOD IDEA.
I JUST DIDN'T THINK IT'D BE THIS GOOD.
I HAVE TO ADMIT, CORLAC, I'M IMPRESSED.
HOW LONG DO YOU THINK WE CAN KEEP IT UP, THOUGH? TEREX ISN'T AN IDIOT. HE KNOWS WHAT WE'RE DOING.
TELLING HIM WE NEED TO GATHER FUNDING BEFORE WE TRY TO RESTART THE EMPIRE WILL ONLY WORK FOR SO LONG.
I AGREE, BETT. EVENTUALLY, HE'S GOING TO BE A PROBLEM.
MAYBE--BUT WE'LL DEAL WITH IT WHEN WE GET THERE. I DON'T WANT TO PUSH IT, THOUGH.
NOT UNTIL HE'S DONE FIXING THAT.

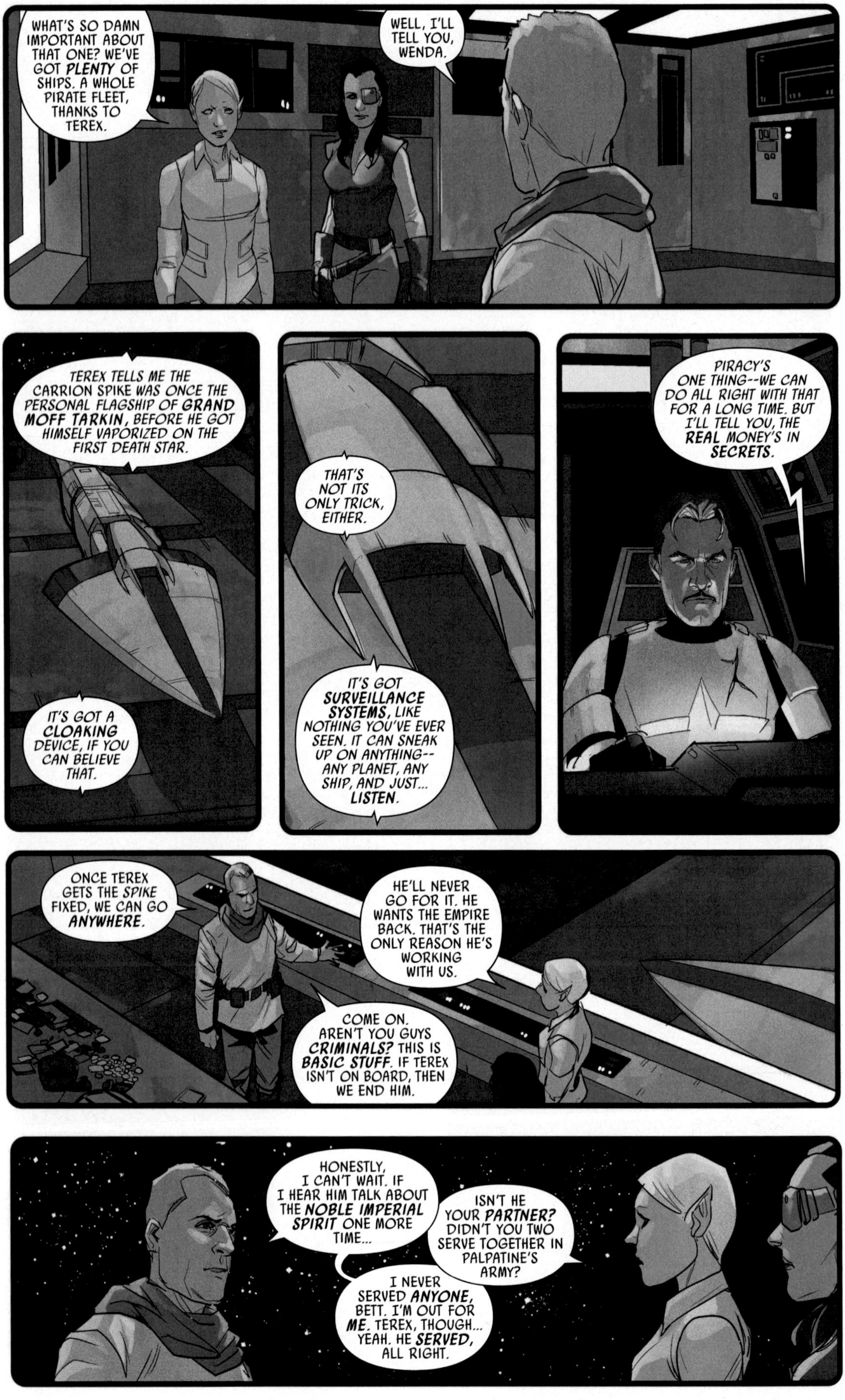
WHAT'S SO DAMN IMPORTANT ABOUT THAT ONE? WE'VE GOT PLENTY OF SHIPS. A WHOLE PIRATE FLEET, THANKS TO TEREX.
WELL, I'LL TELL YOU, WENDA.
TEREX TELLS ME THE CARRION SPIKE WAS ONCE THE PERSONAL FLAGSHIP OF GRAND MOFF TARKIN, BEFORE HE GOT HIMSELF VAPORIZED ON THE FIRST DEATH STAR.
IT'S GOT A CLOAKING DEVICE, IF YOU CAN BELIEVE THAT.
THAT'S NOT ITS ONLY TRICK, EITHER.
IT'S GOT SURVEILLANCE SYSTEMS, LIKE NOTHING YOU'VE EVER SEEN. IT CAN SNEAK UP ON ANYTHING--ANY PLANET, ANY SHIP, AND JUST... LISTEN.
PIRACY'S ONE THING--WE CAN DO ALL RIGHT WITH THAT FOR A LONG TIME. BUT I'LL TELL YOU, THE REAL MONEY'S IN SECRETS.
ONCE TEREX GETS THE SPIKE FIXED, WE CAN GO ANYWHERE.
HE'LL NEVER GO FOR IT. HE WANTS THE EMPIRE BACK. THAT'S THE ONLY REASON HE'S WORKING WITH US.
COME ON. AREN'T YOU GUYS CRIMINALS? THIS IS BASIC STUFF. IF TEREX ISN'T ON BOARD, THEN WE END HIM.
HONESTLY, I CAN'T WAIT. IF I HEAR HIM TALK ABOUT THE NOBLE IMPERIAL SPIRIT ONE MORE TIME...
ISN'T HE YOUR PARTNER? DIDN'T YOU TWO SERVE TOGETHER IN PALPATINE'S ARMY?
I NEVER SERVED ANYONE, BETT. I'M OUT FOR ME. TEREX, THOUGH... YEAH. HE SERVED, ALL RIGHT.

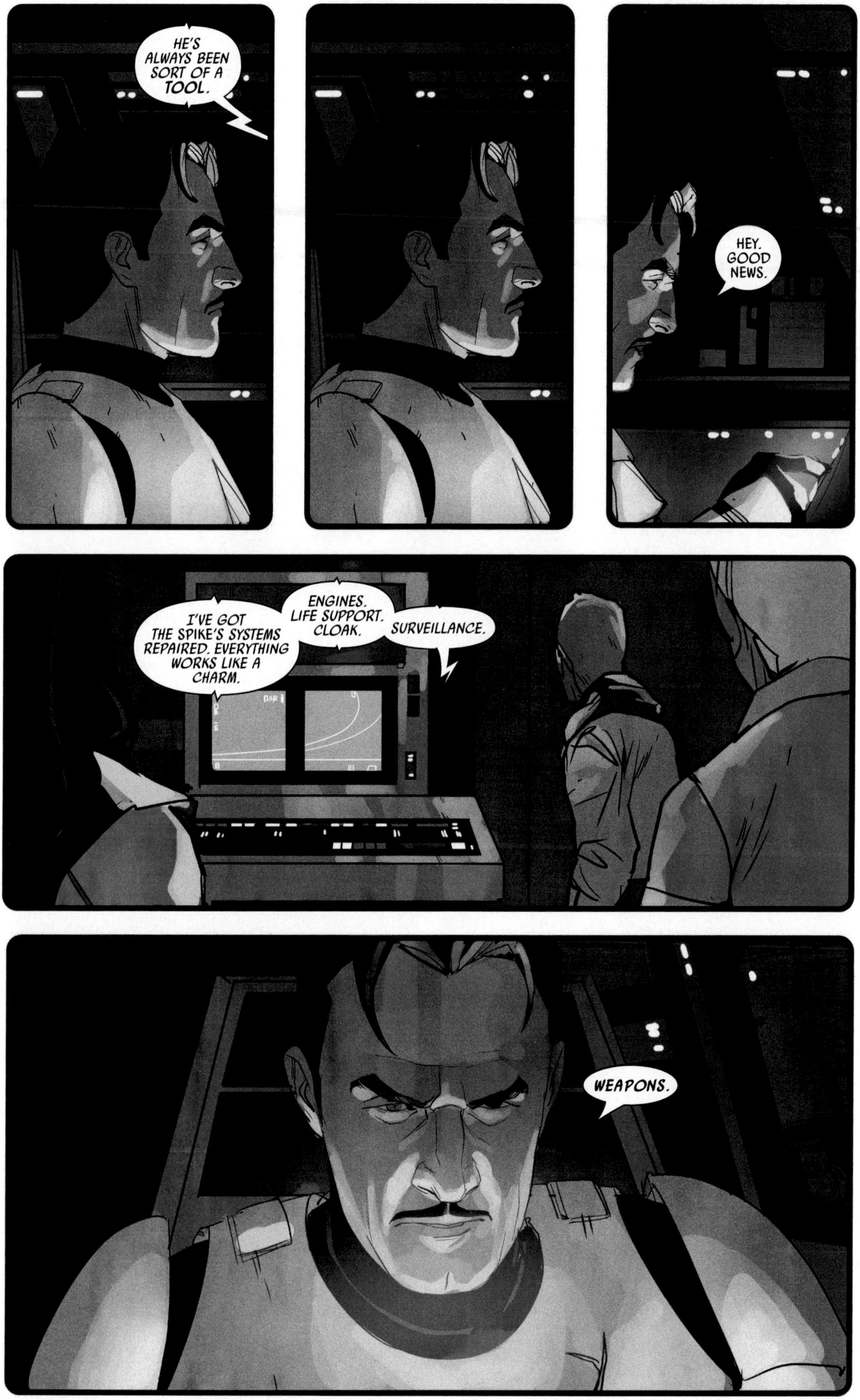
HE'S ALWAYS BEEN SORT OF A TOOL.
HEY. GOOD NEWS.
I'VE GOT THE SPIKE'S SYSTEMS REPAIRED. EVERYTHING WORKS LIKE A CHARM.
ENGINES. LIFE SUPPORT. CLOAK.
SURVEILLANCE.
WEAPONS.

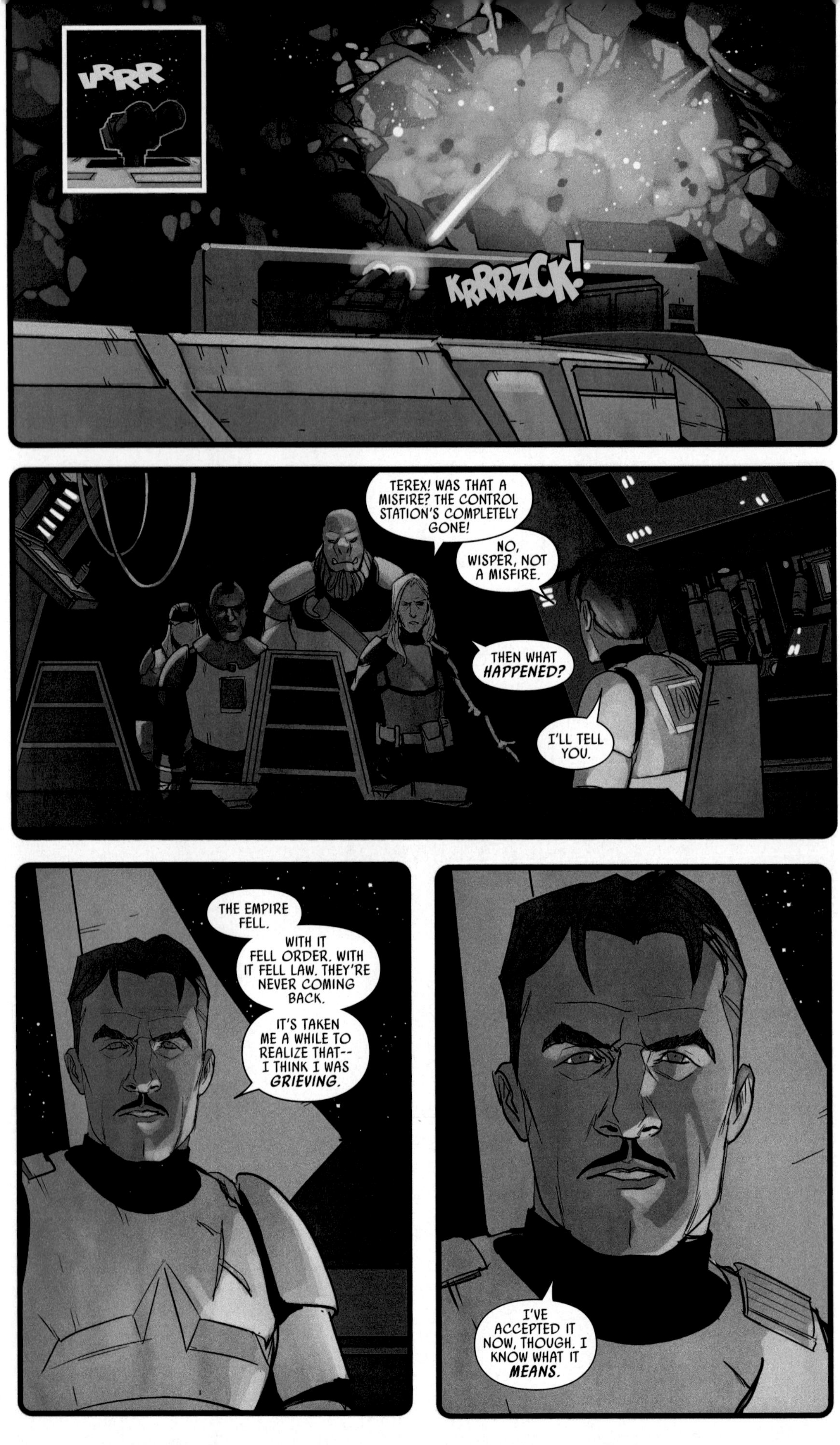
VRRR
KRRRZCK!
TEREX! WAS THAT A MISFIRE? THE CONTROL STATION'S COMPLETELY GONE!
NO, WISPER, NOT A MISFIRE.
THEN WHAT HAPPENED?
I'LL TELL YOU.
THE EMPIRE FELL.
WITH IT FELL ORDER. WITH IT FELL LAW. THEY'RE NEVER COMING BACK.
IT'S TAKEN ME A WHILE TO REALIZE THAT-- I THINK I WAS GRIEVING.
I'VE ACCEPTED IT NOW, THOUGH. I KNOW WHAT IT MEANS.

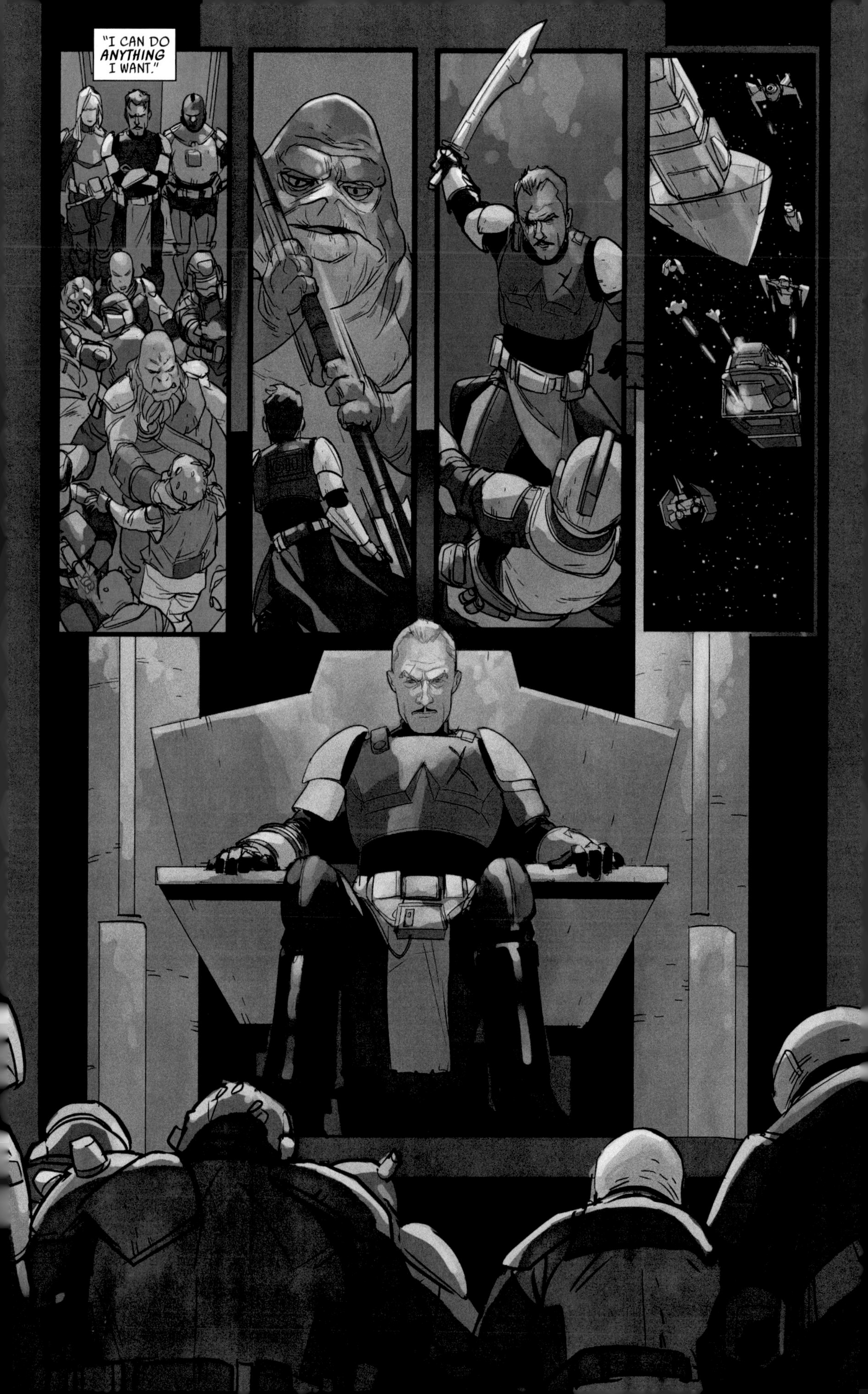
"I CAN DO ANYTHING I WANT."

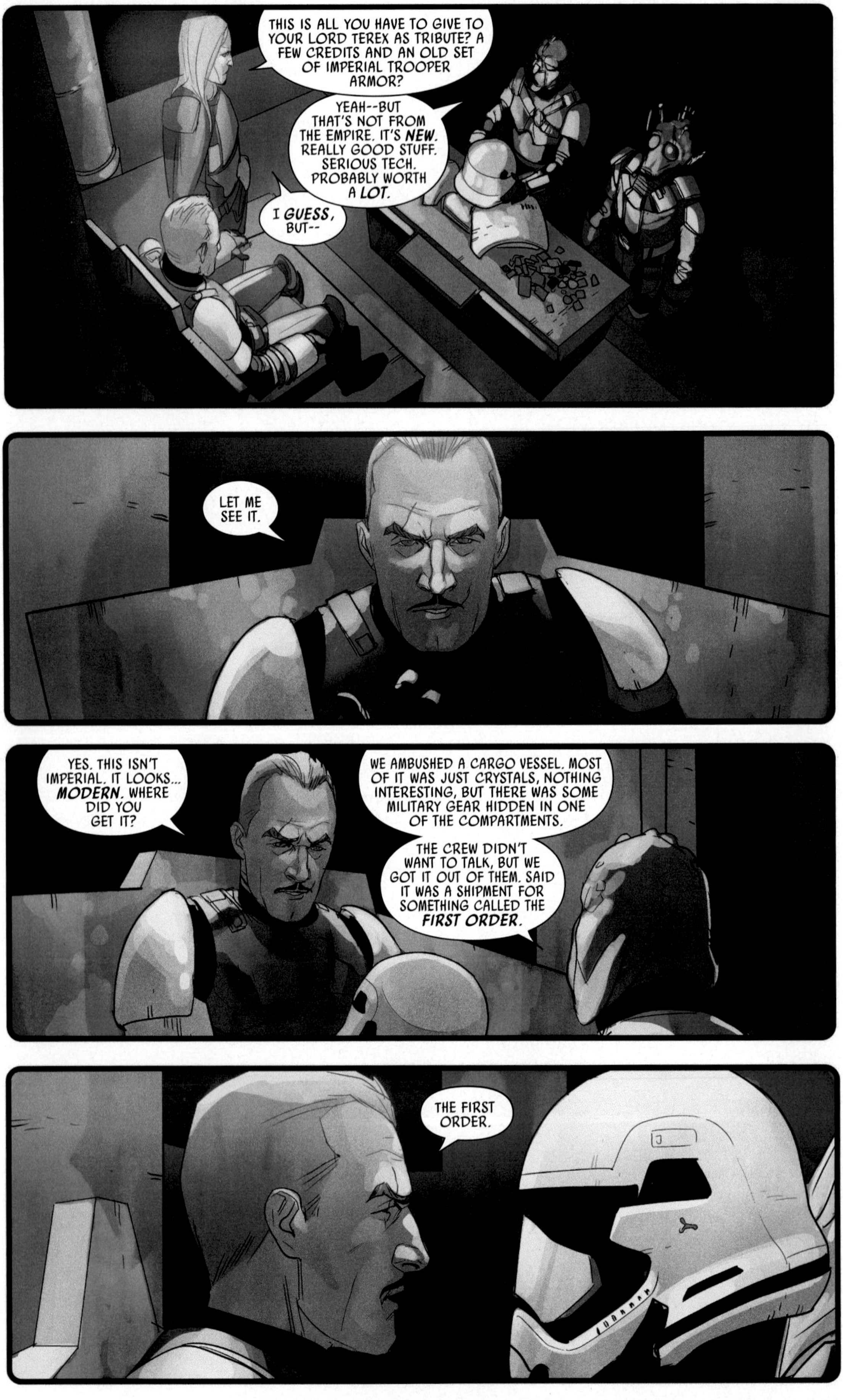
THIS IS ALL YOU HAVE TO GIVE TO YOUR LORD TEREX AS TRIBUTE? A FEW CREDITS AND AN OLD SET OF IMPERIAL TROOPER ARMOR?
YEAH--BUT THAT'S NOT FROM THE EMPIRE. IT'S NEW. REALLY GOOD STUFF. SERIOUS TECH. PROBABLY WORTH A LOT.
I GUESS, BUT--
LET ME SEE IT.
YES. THIS ISN'T IMPERIAL. IT LOOKS... MODERN. WHERE DID YOU GET IT?
WE AMBUSHED A CARGO VESSEL. MOST OF IT WAS JUST CRYSTALS, NOTHING INTERESTING, BUT THERE WAS SOME MILITARY GEAR HIDDEN IN ONE OF THE COMPARTMENTS.
THE CREW DIDN'T WANT TO TALK, BUT WE GOT IT OUT OF THEM. SAID IT WAS A SHIPMENT FOR SOMETHING CALLED THE FIRST ORDER.
THE FIRST ORDER.

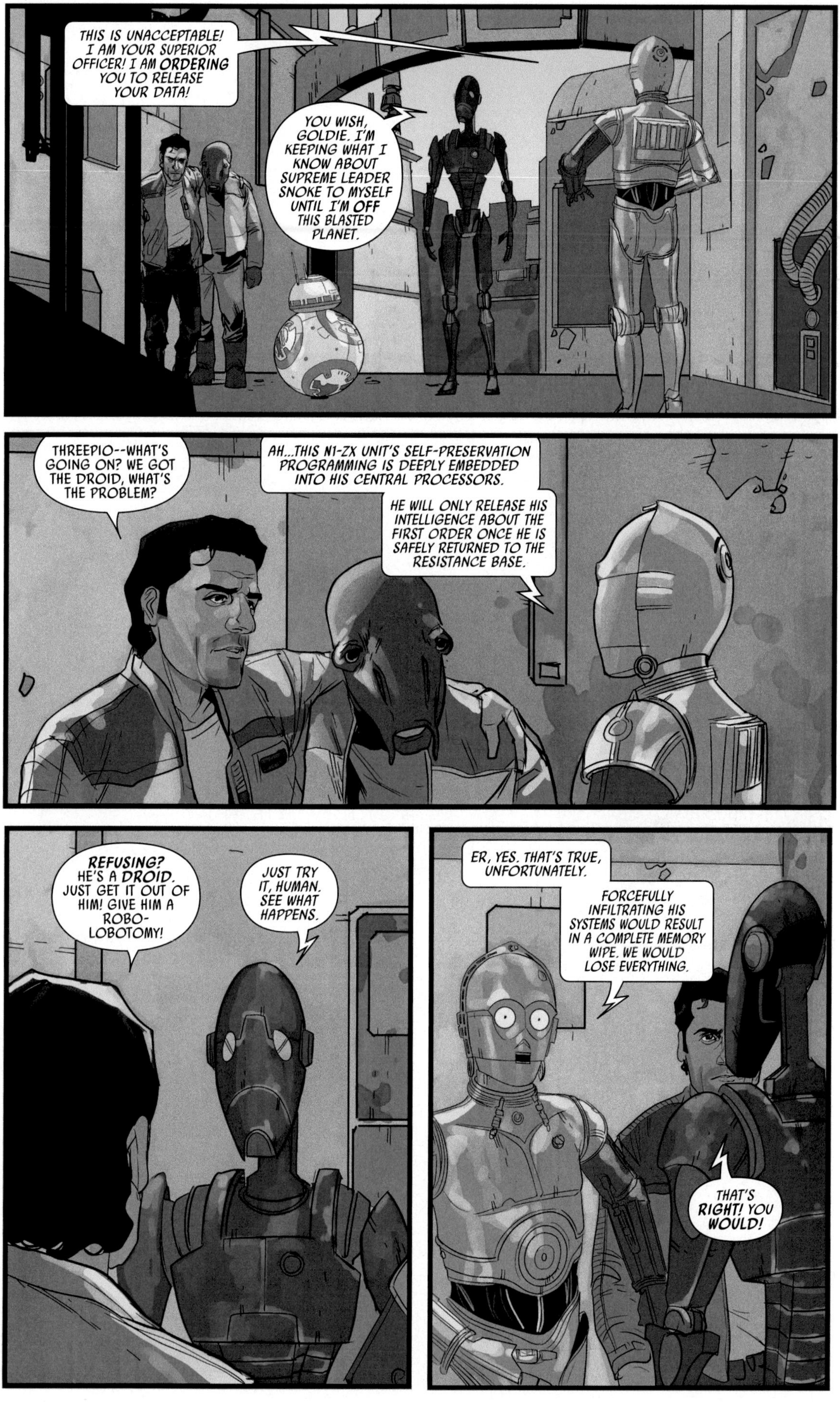
THIS IS UNACCEPTABLE! I AM YOUR SUPERIOR OFFICER! I AM ORDERING YOU TO RELEASE YOUR DATA!
YOU WISH, GOLDIE. I'M KEEPING WHAT I KNOW ABOUT SUPREME LEADER SNOKE TO MYSELF UNTIL I'M OFF THIS BLASTED PLANET.
THREEPIO--WHAT'S GOING ON? WE GOT THE DROID, WHAT'S THE PROBLEM?
AH...THIS N1-ZX UNIT'S SELF-PRESERVATION PROGRAMMING IS DEEPLY EMBEDDED INTO HIS CENTRAL PROCESSORS.
HE WILL ONLY RELEASE HIS INTELLIGENCE ABOUT THE FIRST ORDER ONCE HE IS SAFELY RETURNED TO THE RESISTANCE BASE.
REFUSING? HE'S A DROID. JUST GET IT OUT OF HIM! GIVE HIM A ROBO-LOBOTOMY!
JUST TRY IT, HUMAN. SEE WHAT HAPPENS.
ER, YES. THAT'S TRUE, UNFORTUNATELY.
FORCEFULLY INFILTRATING HIS SYSTEMS WOULD RESULT IN A COMPLETE MEMORY WIPE. WE WOULD LOSE EVERYTHING.
THAT'S RIGHT! YOU WOULD!

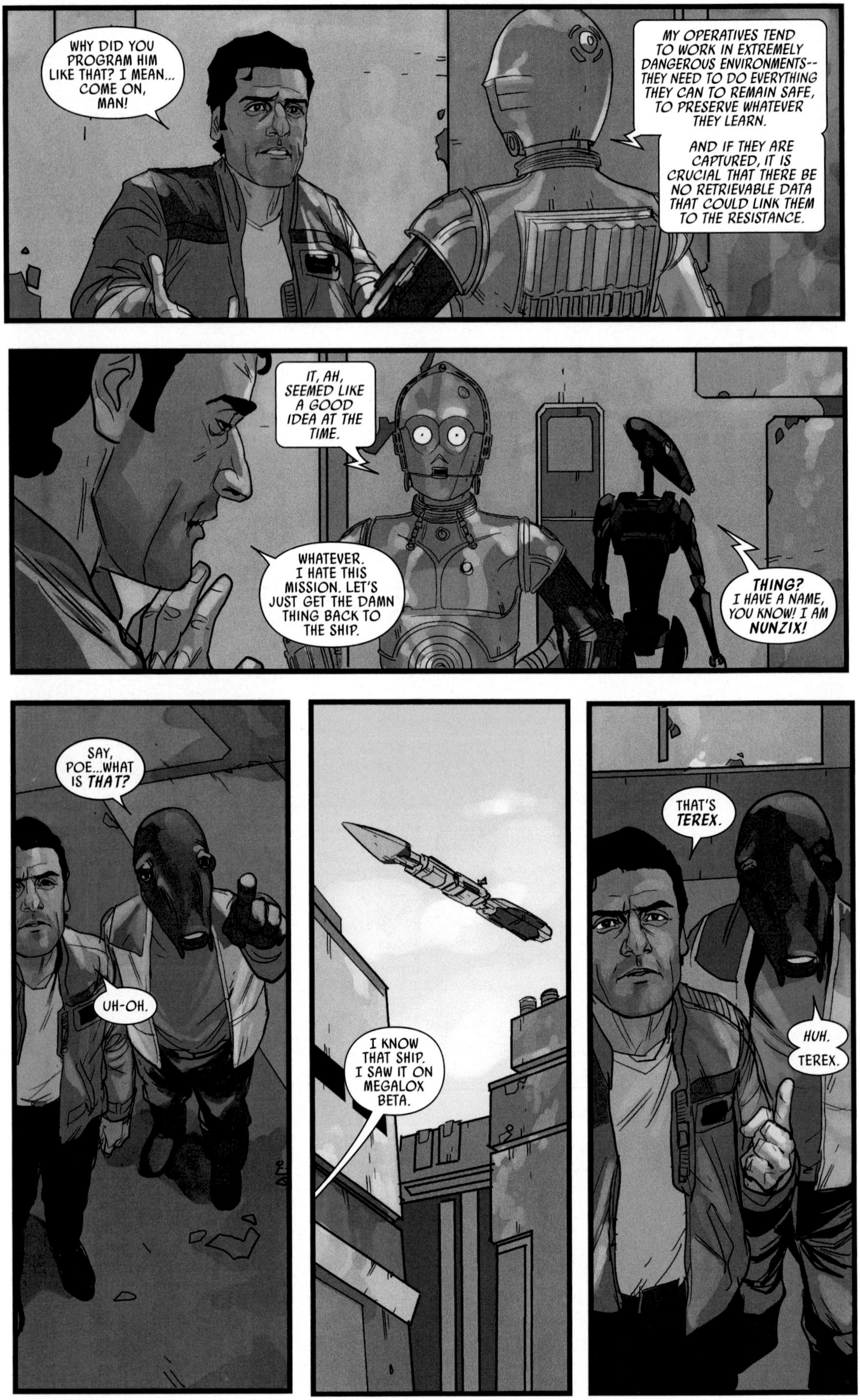
WHY DID YOU PROGRAM HIM LIKE THAT? I MEAN... COME ON, MAN!
MY OPERATIVES TEND TO WORK IN EXTREMELY DANGEROUS ENVIRONMENTS-- THEY NEED TO DO EVERYTHING THEY CAN TO REMAIN SAFE, TO PRESERVE WHATEVER THEY LEARN.
AND IF THEY ARE CAPTURED, IT IS CRUCIAL THAT THERE BE NO RETRIEVABLE DATA THAT COULD LINK THEM TO THE RESISTANCE.
IT, AH, SEEMED LIKE A GOOD IDEA AT THE TIME.
WHATEVER. I HATE THIS MISSION. LET'S JUST GET THE DAMN THING BACK TO THE SHIP.
THING? I HAVE A NAME, YOU KNOW! I AM NUNZIX!
SAY, POE...WHAT IS THAT?
UH-OH.
I KNOW THAT SHIP. I SAW IT ON MEGALOX BETA.
THAT'S TEREX.
HUH.
TEREX.

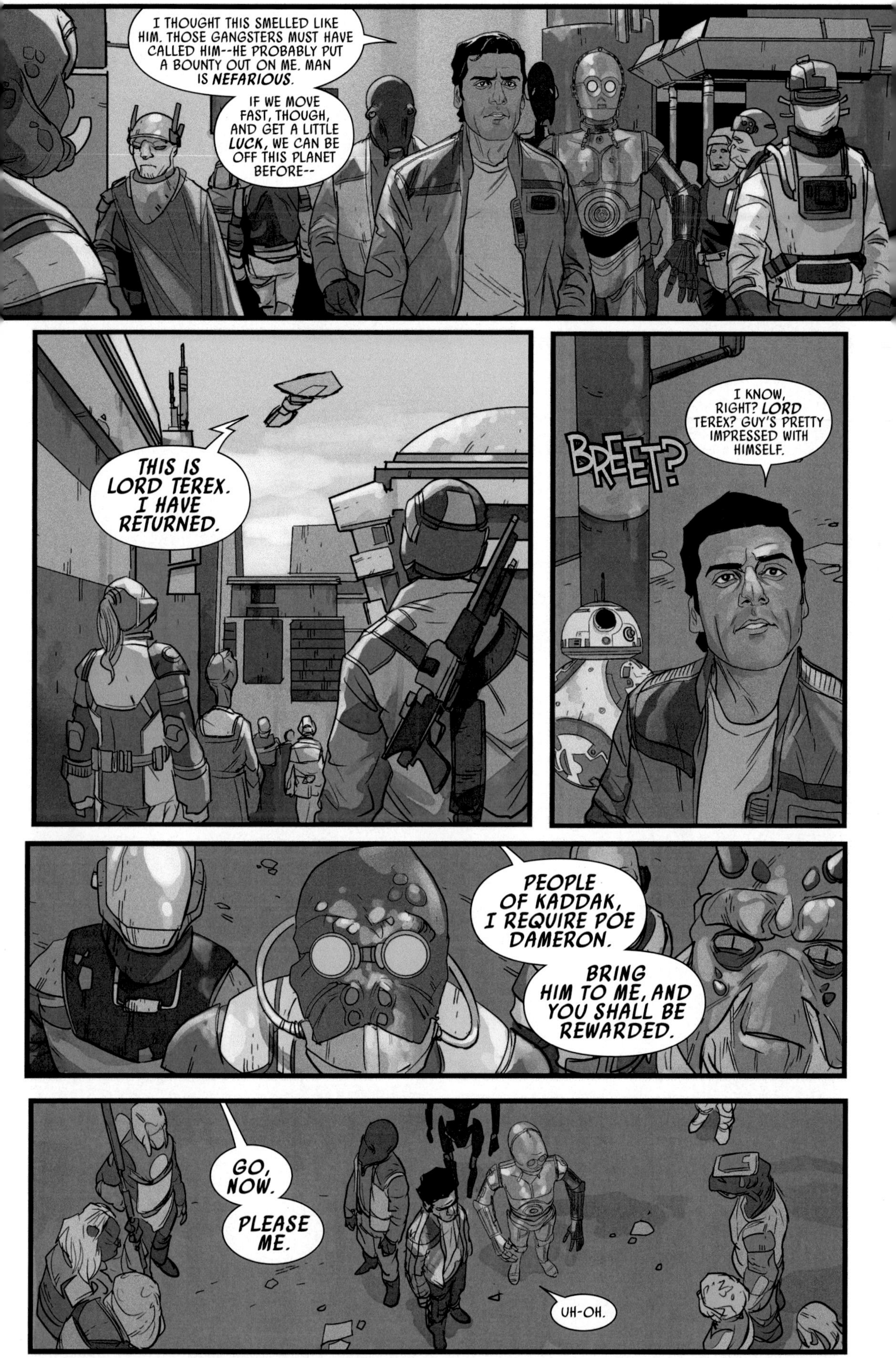
I THOUGHT THIS SMELLED LIKE HIM. THOSE GANGSTERS MUST HAVE CALLED HIM--HE PROBABLY PUT A BOUNTY OUT ON ME. MAN IS NEFARIOUS.
IF WE MOVE FAST, THOUGH, AND GET A LITTLE LUCK, WE CAN BE OFF THIS PLANET BEFORE--
THIS IS LORD TEREX. I HAVE RETURNED.
BREET?
I KNOW, RIGHT? LORD TEREX? GUY'S PRETTY IMPRESSED WITH HIMSELF.
PEOPLE OF KADDAK, I REQUIRE POE DAMERON.
BRING HIM TO ME, AND YOU SHALL BE REWARDED.
GO, NOW.
PLEASE ME.
UH-OH.

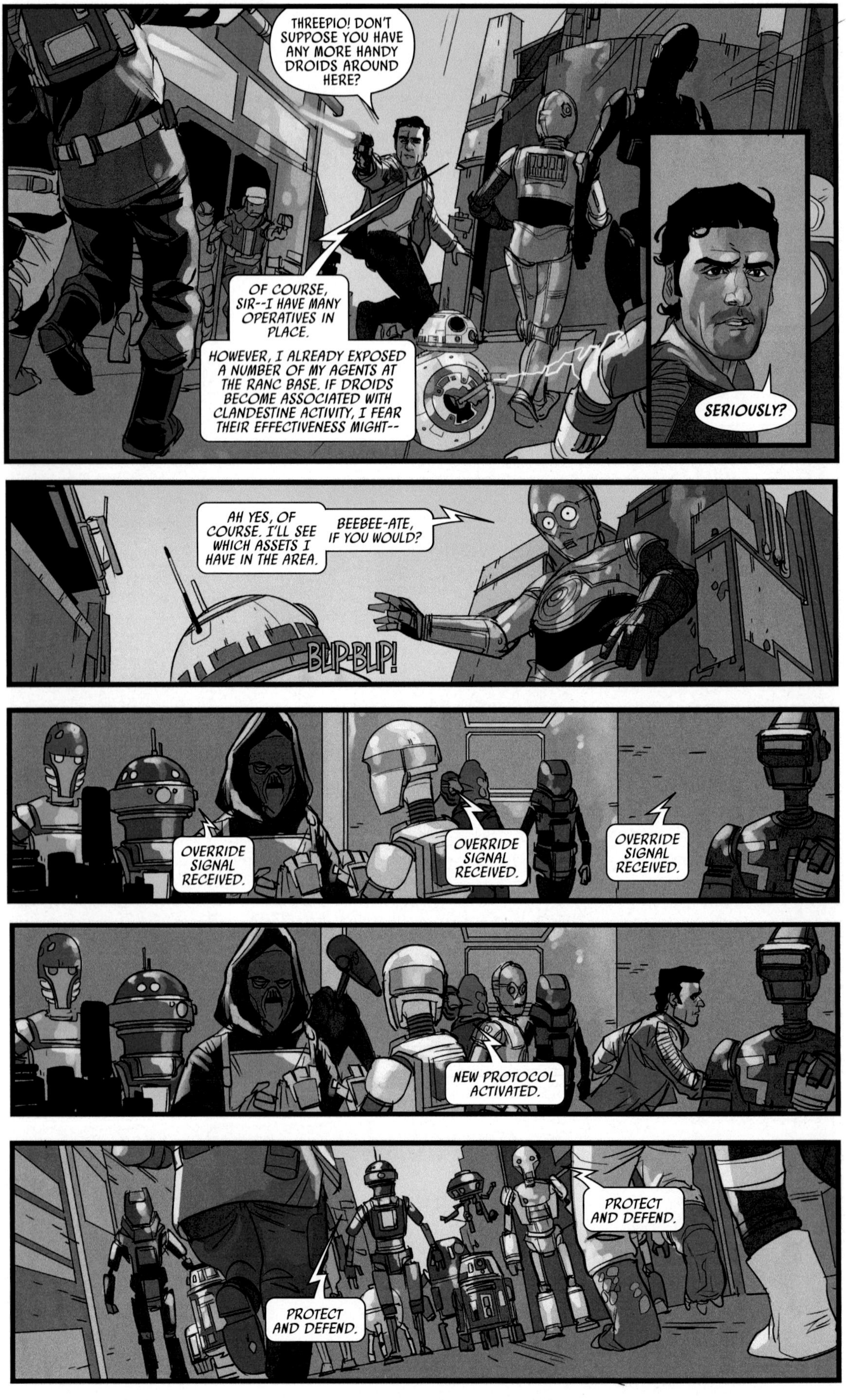
THREEPIO! DON'T SUPPOSE YOU HAVE ANY MORE HANDY DROIDS AROUND HERE?
OF COURSE, SIR--I HAVE MANY OPERATIVES IN PLACE.
HOWEVER, I ALREADY EXPOSED A NUMBER OF MY AGENTS AT THE RANC BASE. IF DROIDS BECOME ASSOCIATED WITH CLANDESTINE ACTIVITY, I FEAR THEIR EFFECTIVENESS MIGHT--
SERIOUSLY?
AH YES, OF COURSE. I'LL SEE WHICH ASSETS I HAVE IN THE AREA.
BEEBEE-ATE, IF YOU WOULD?
BLIP-BLIP!
OVERRIDE SIGNAL RECEIVED.
OVERRIDE SIGNAL RECEIVED.
OVERRIDE SIGNAL RECEIVED.
NEW PROTOCOL ACTIVATED.
PROTECT AND DEFEND.
PROTECT AND DEFEND.

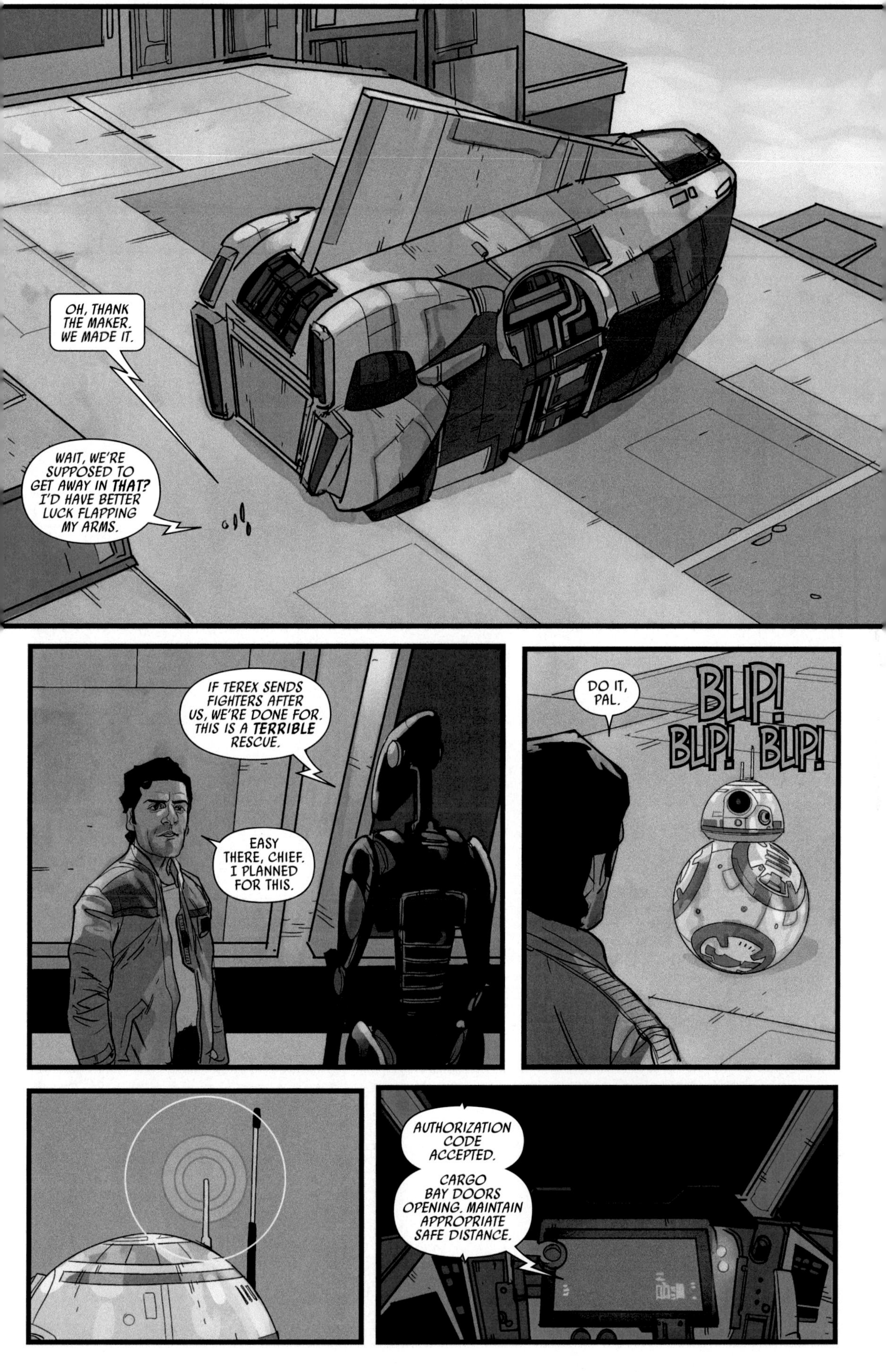
OH, THANK THE MAKER. WE MADE IT.
WAIT, WE'RE SUPPOSED TO GET AWAY IN THAT? I'D HAVE BETTER LUCK FLAPPING MY ARMS.
IF TEREX SENDS FIGHTERS AFTER US, WE'RE DONE FOR. THIS IS A TERRIBLE RESCUE.
EASY THERE, CHIEF. I PLANNED FOR THIS.
DO IT, PAL.
BLIP! BLIP! BLIP!
AUTHORIZATION CODE ACCEPTED.
CARGO BAY DOORS OPENING. MAINTAIN APPROPRIATE SAFE DISTANCE.

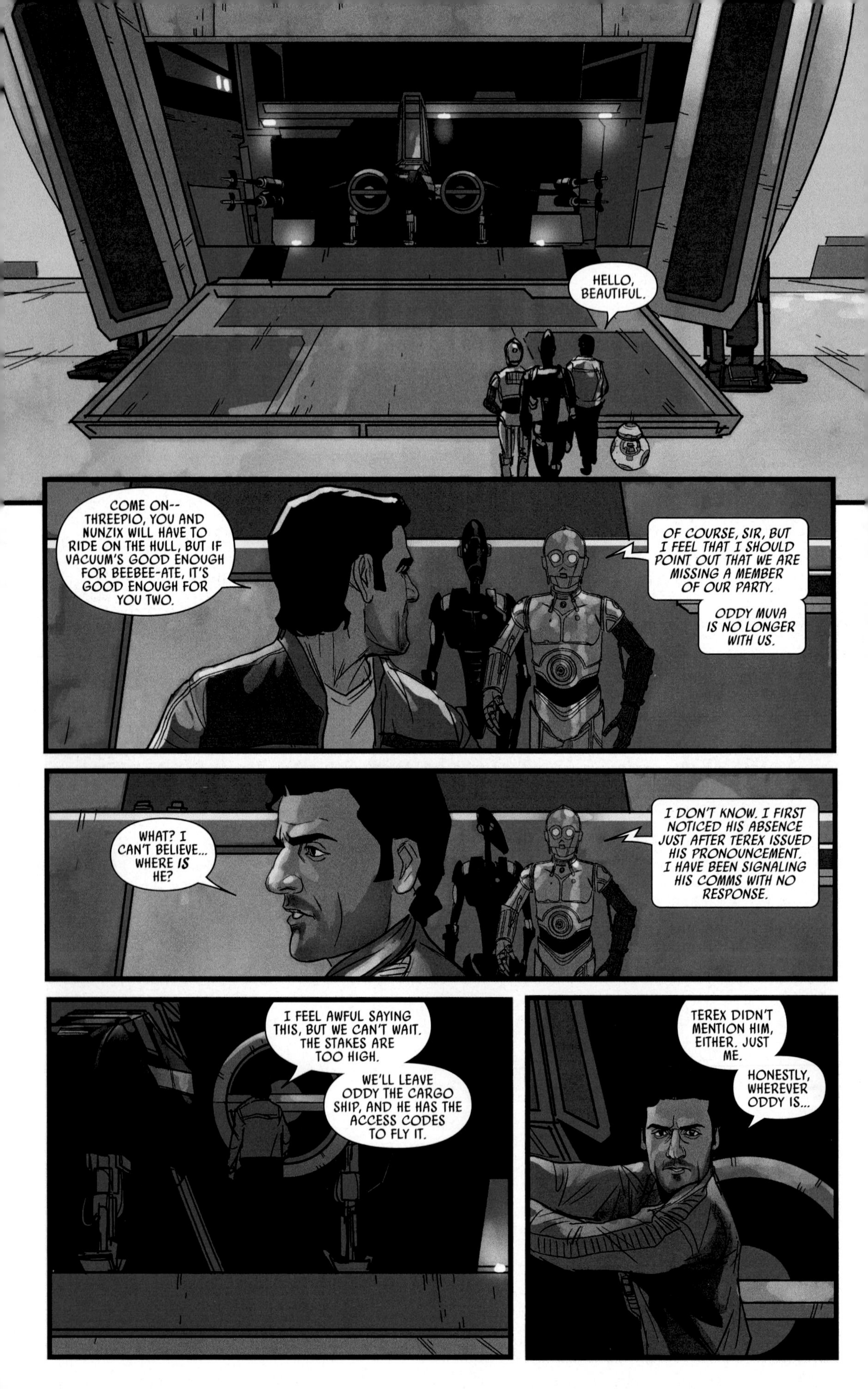

HELLO, BEAUTIFUL.
COME ON-- THREEPIO, YOU AND NUNZIX WILL HAVE TO RIDE ON THE HULL, BUT IF VACUUM'S GOOD ENOUGH FOR BEEBEE-ATE, IT'S GOOD ENOUGH FOR YOU TWO.
OF COURSE, SIR, BUT I FEEL THAT I SHOULD POINT OUT THAT WE ARE MISSING A MEMBER OF OUR PARTY.
ODDY MUVA IS NO LONGER WITH US.
WHAT? I CAN'T BELIEVE... WHERE *IS* HE?
I DON'T KNOW. I FIRST NOTICED HIS ABSENCE JUST AFTER TEREX ISSUED HIS PRONOUNCEMENT. I HAVE BEEN SIGNALING HIS COMMS WITH NO RESPONSE.
I FEEL AWFUL SAYING THIS, BUT WE CAN'T WAIT. THE STAKES ARE TOO HIGH.
WE'LL LEAVE ODDY THE CARGO SHIP, AND HE HAS THE ACCESS CODES TO FLY IT.
TEREX DIDN'T MENTION HIM, EITHER. JUST ME.
HONESTLY, WHEREVER ODDY IS...

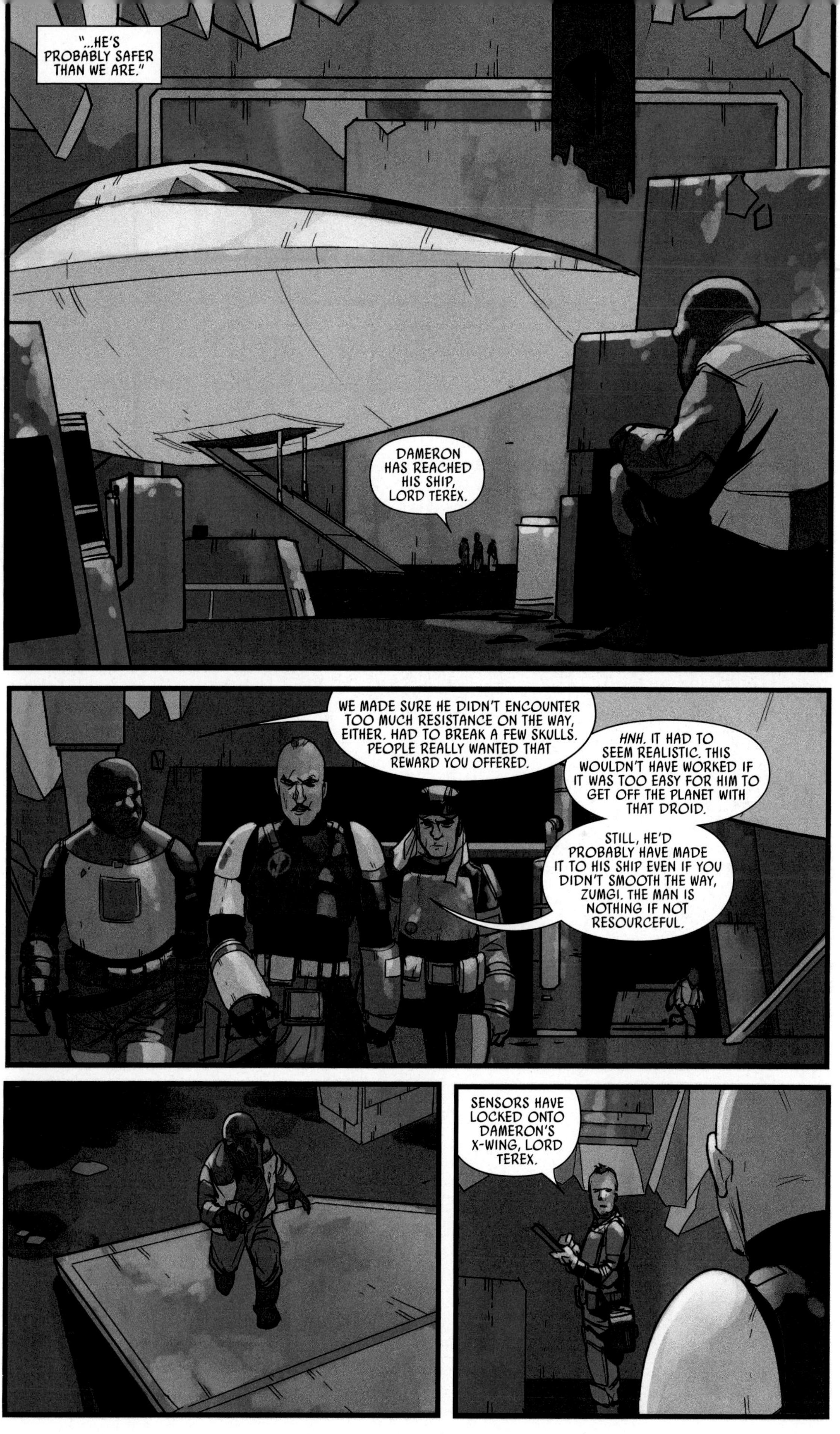
"...HE'S PROBABLY SAFER THAN WE ARE."
DAMERON HAS REACHED HIS SHIP, LORD TEREX.
WE MADE SURE HE DIDN'T ENCOUNTER TOO MUCH RESISTANCE ON THE WAY, EITHER. HAD TO BREAK A FEW SKULLS. PEOPLE REALLY WANTED THAT REWARD YOU OFFERED.
HNH. IT HAD TO SEEM REALISTIC. THIS WOULDN'T HAVE WORKED IF IT WAS TOO EASY FOR HIM TO GET OFF THE PLANET WITH THAT DROID.
STILL, HE'D PROBABLY HAVE MADE IT TO HIS SHIP EVEN IF YOU DIDN'T SMOOTH THE WAY, ZUMGI. THE MAN IS NOTHING IF NOT RESOURCEFUL.
SENSORS HAVE LOCKED ONTO DAMERON'S X-WING, LORD TEREX.

"HE'S OFF-PLANET."

GOOD-BYE, KADDAK, AND BY THE FORCE ITSELF, I HOPE I NEVER SET FOOT ON YOU AGAIN.

AH, VERY GOOD.

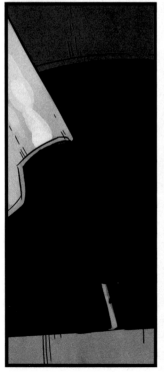

KRRRRRRK

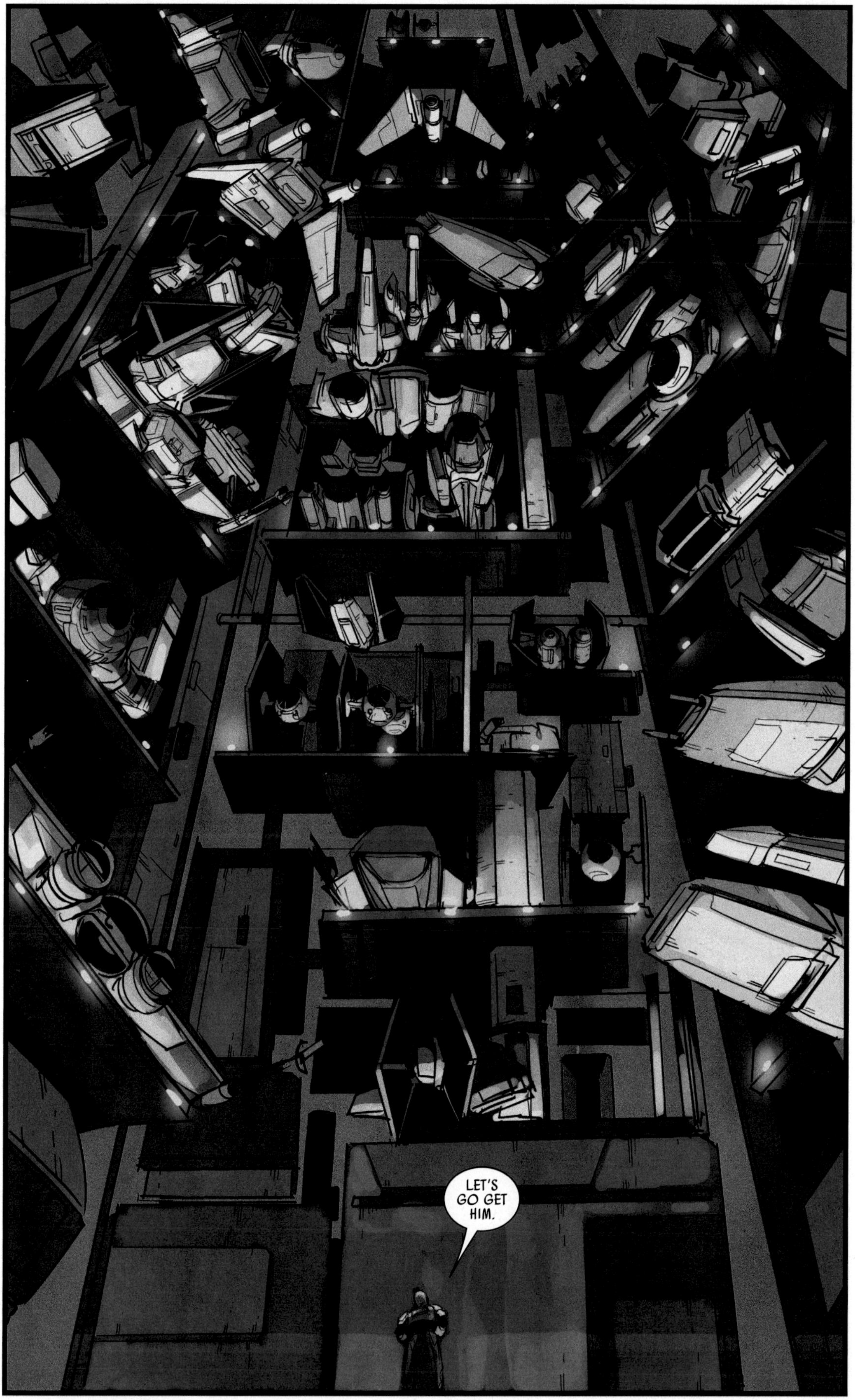
LET'S GO GET HIM.

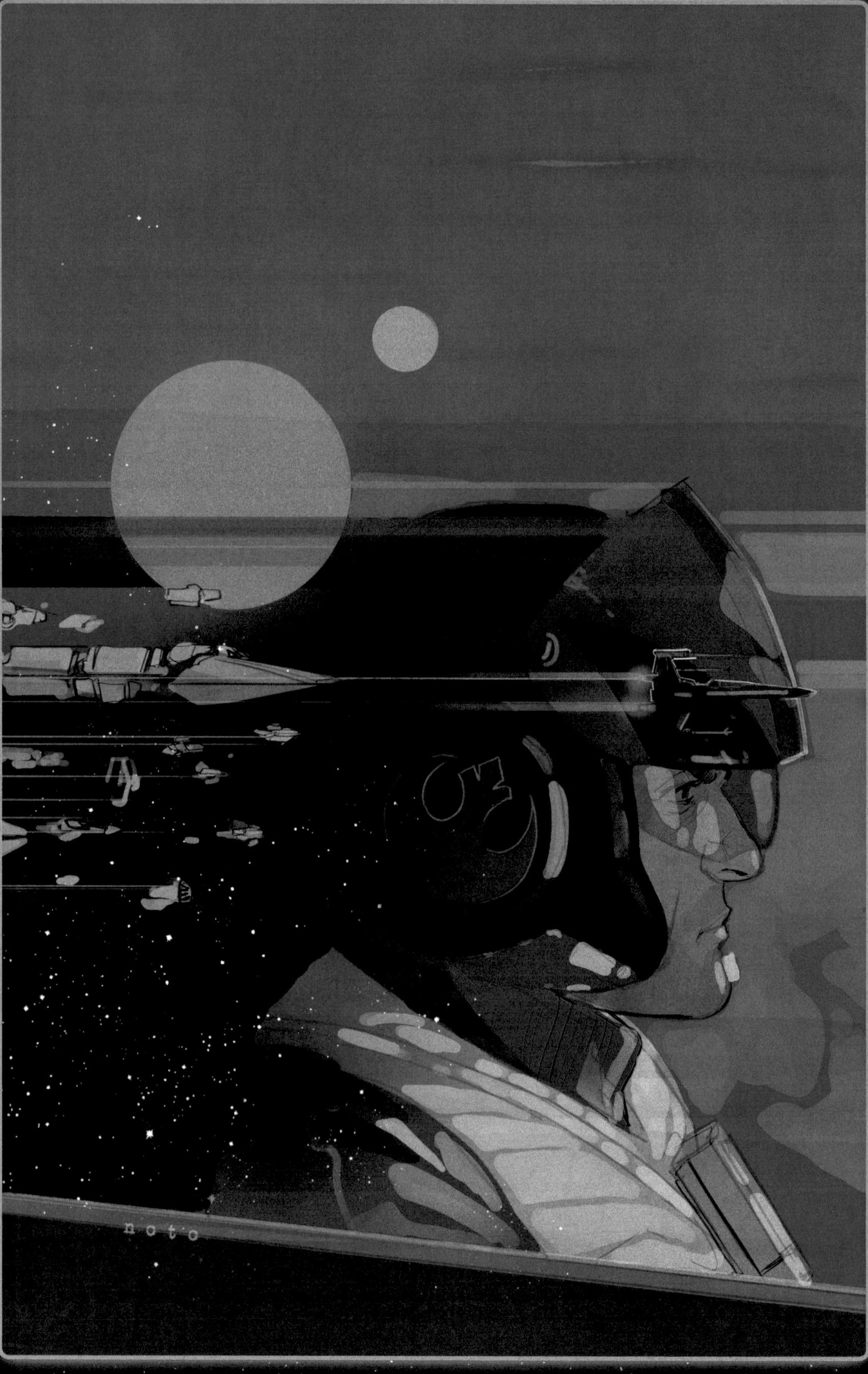
noto

11

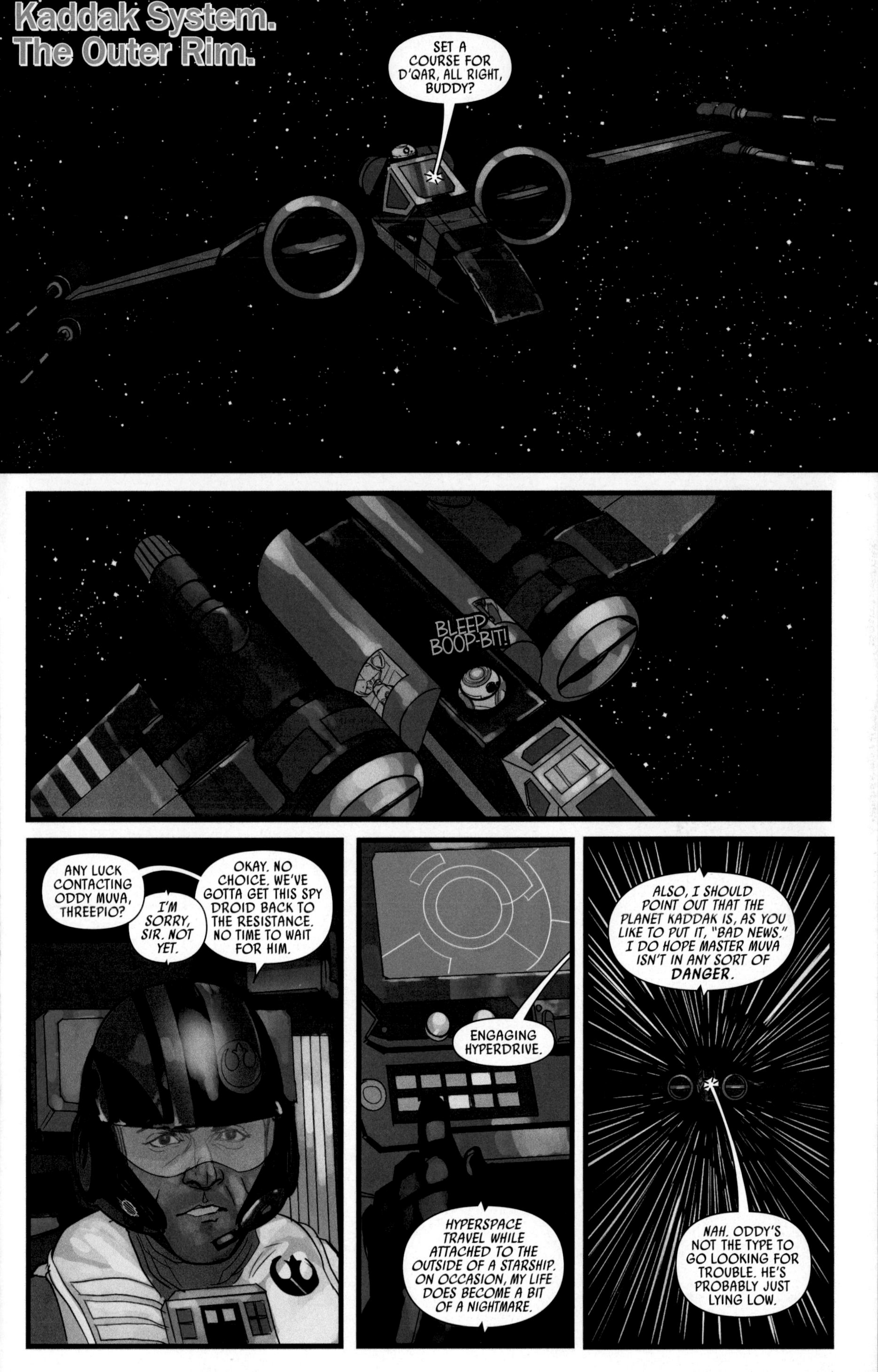
Kaddak System.
The Outer Rim.
SET A COURSE FOR D'QAR, ALL RIGHT, BUDDY?
BLEEP BOOP-BIT!
ANY LUCK CONTACTING ODDY MUVA, THREEPIO?
I'M SORRY, SIR. NOT YET.
OKAY. NO CHOICE. WE'VE GOTTA GET THIS SPY DROID BACK TO THE RESISTANCE. NO TIME TO WAIT FOR HIM.
ENGAGING HYPERDRIVE.
HYPERSPACE TRAVEL WHILE ATTACHED TO THE OUTSIDE OF A STARSHIP. ON OCCASION, MY LIFE DOES BECOME A BIT OF A NIGHTMARE.
ALSO, I SHOULD POINT OUT THAT THE PLANET KADDAK IS, AS YOU LIKE TO PUT IT, "BAD NEWS." I DO HOPE MASTER MUVA ISN'T IN ANY SORT OF DANGER.
NAH. ODDY'S NOT THE TYPE TO GO LOOKING FOR TROUBLE. HE'S PROBABLY JUST LYING LOW.

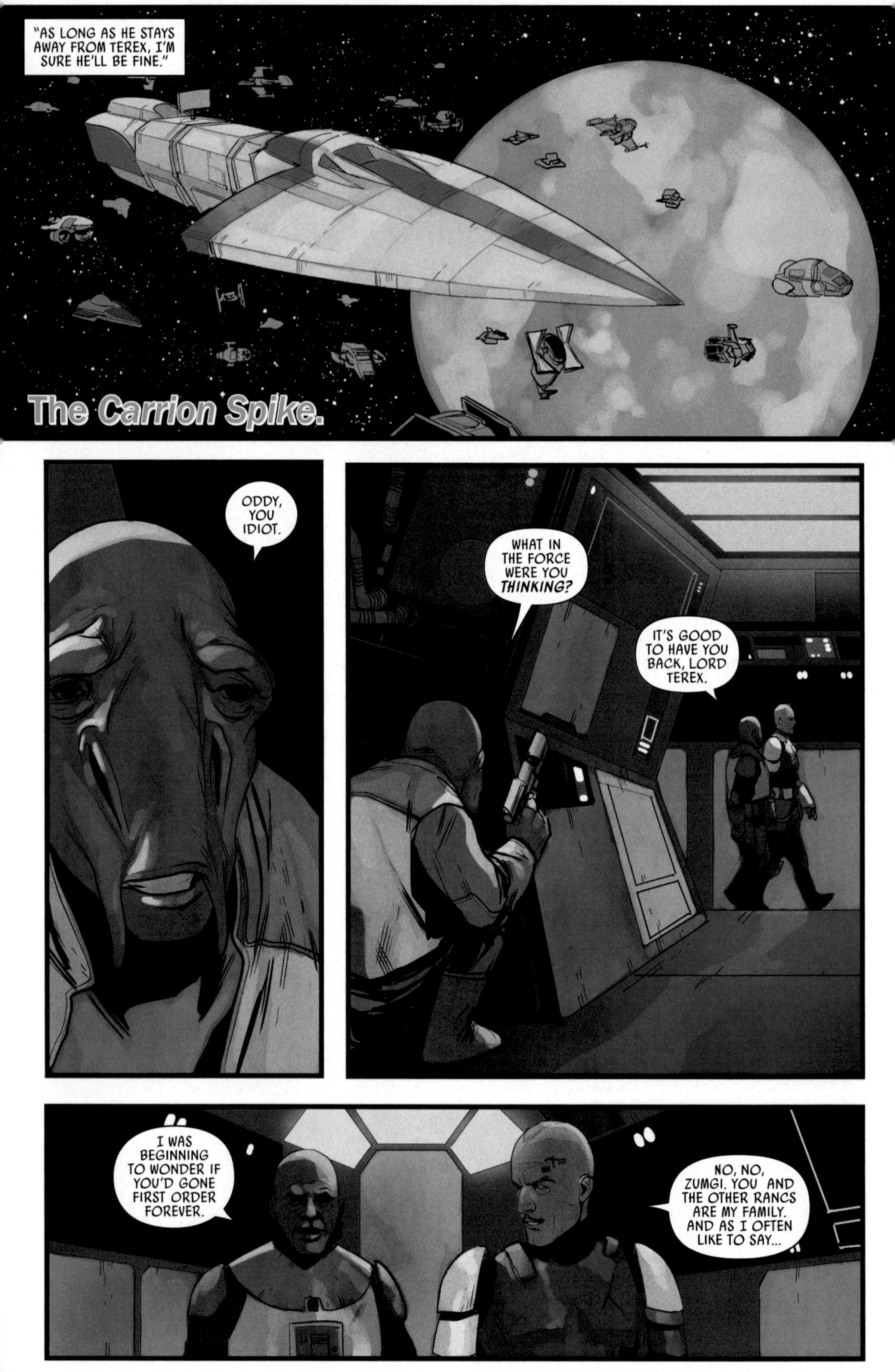
"AS LONG AS HE STAYS AWAY FROM TEREX, I'M SURE HE'LL BE FINE."
The Carrion Spike.
ODDY, YOU IDIOT.
WHAT IN THE FORCE WERE YOU THINKING?
IT'S GOOD TO HAVE YOU BACK, LORD TEREX.
I WAS BEGINNING TO WONDER IF YOU'D GONE FIRST ORDER FOREVER.
NO, NO, ZUMGI. YOU AND THE OTHER RANCS ARE MY FAMILY. AND AS I OFTEN LIKE TO SAY...

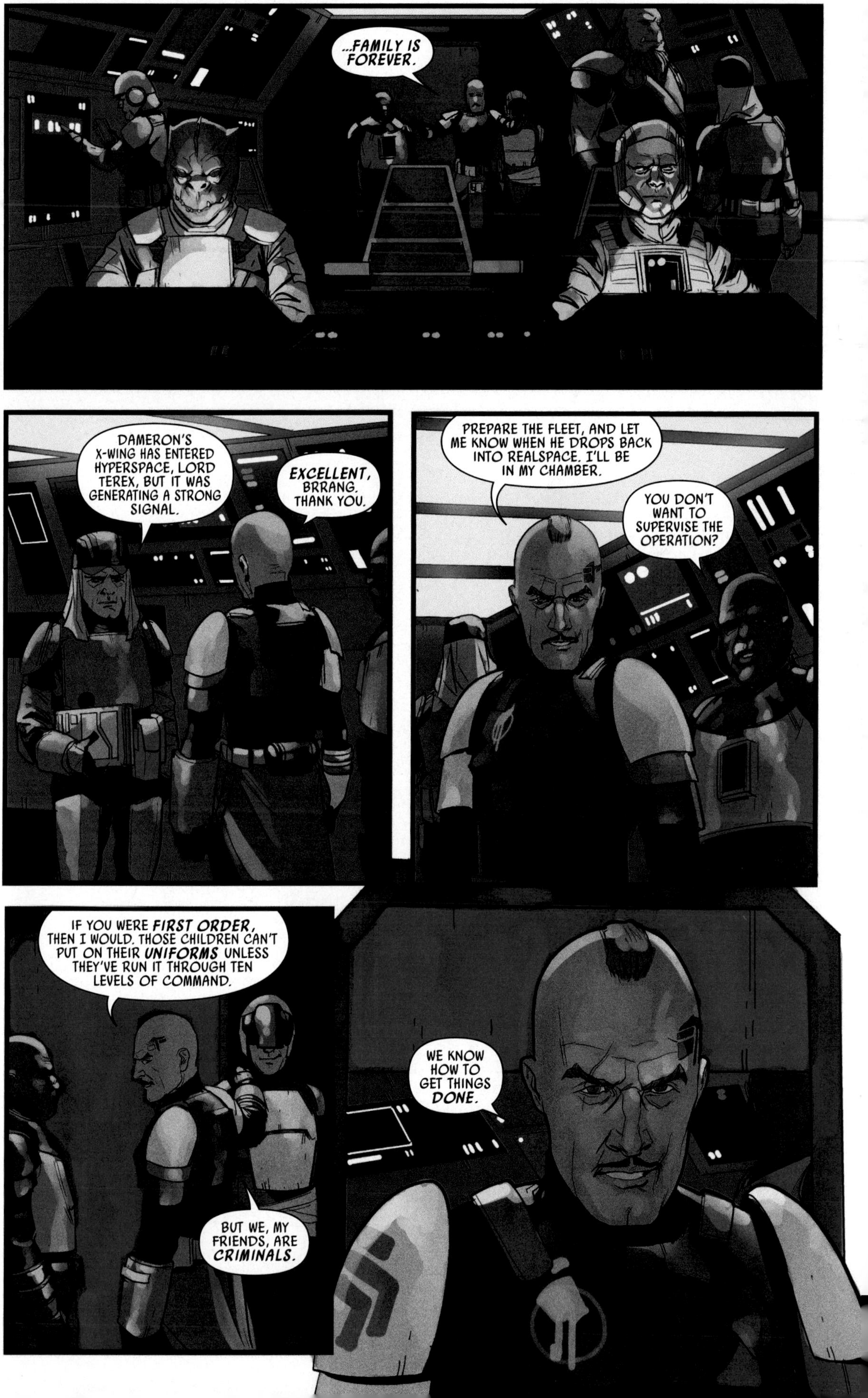
...FAMILY IS FOREVER.
DAMERON'S X-WING HAS ENTERED HYPERSPACE, LORD TEREX, BUT IT WAS GENERATING A STRONG SIGNAL.
EXCELLENT, BRRANG. THANK YOU.
PREPARE THE FLEET, AND LET ME KNOW WHEN HE DROPS BACK INTO REALSPACE. I'LL BE IN MY CHAMBER.
YOU DON'T WANT TO SUPERVISE THE OPERATION?
IF YOU WERE FIRST ORDER, THEN I WOULD. THOSE CHILDREN CAN'T PUT ON THEIR UNIFORMS UNLESS THEY'VE RUN IT THROUGH TEN LEVELS OF COMMAND.
BUT WE, MY FRIENDS, ARE CRIMINALS.
WE KNOW HOW TO GET THINGS DONE.

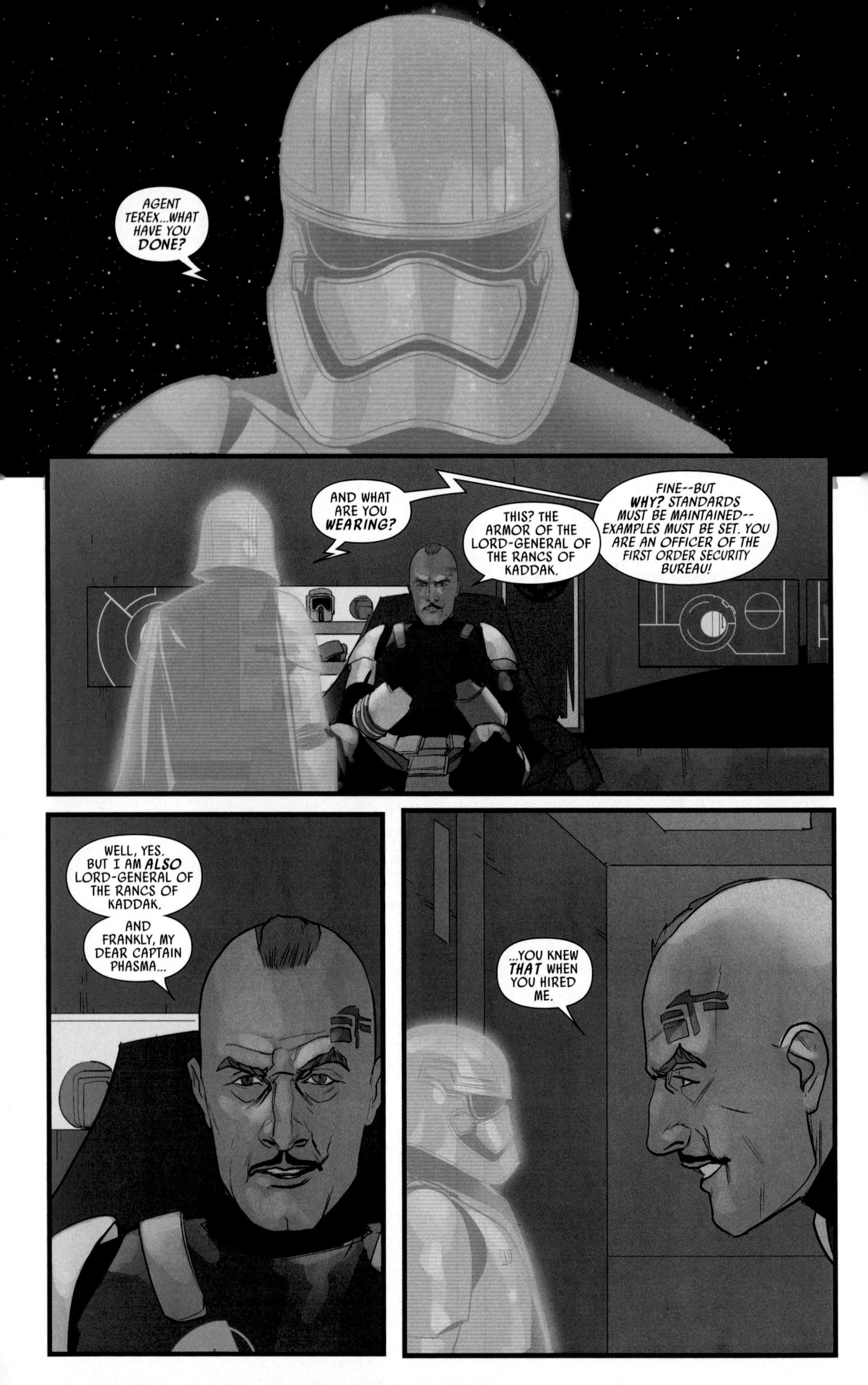
AGENT TEREX...WHAT HAVE YOU DONE?
AND WHAT ARE YOU WEARING?
THIS? THE ARMOR OF THE LORD-GENERAL OF THE RANCS OF KADDAK.
FINE--BUT WHY? STANDARDS MUST BE MAINTAINED--EXAMPLES MUST BE SET. YOU ARE AN OFFICER OF THE FIRST ORDER SECURITY BUREAU!
WELL, YES. BUT I AM ALSO LORD-GENERAL OF THE RANCS OF KADDAK.
AND FRANKLY, MY DEAR CAPTAIN PHASMA...
...YOU KNEW THAT WHEN YOU HIRED ME.

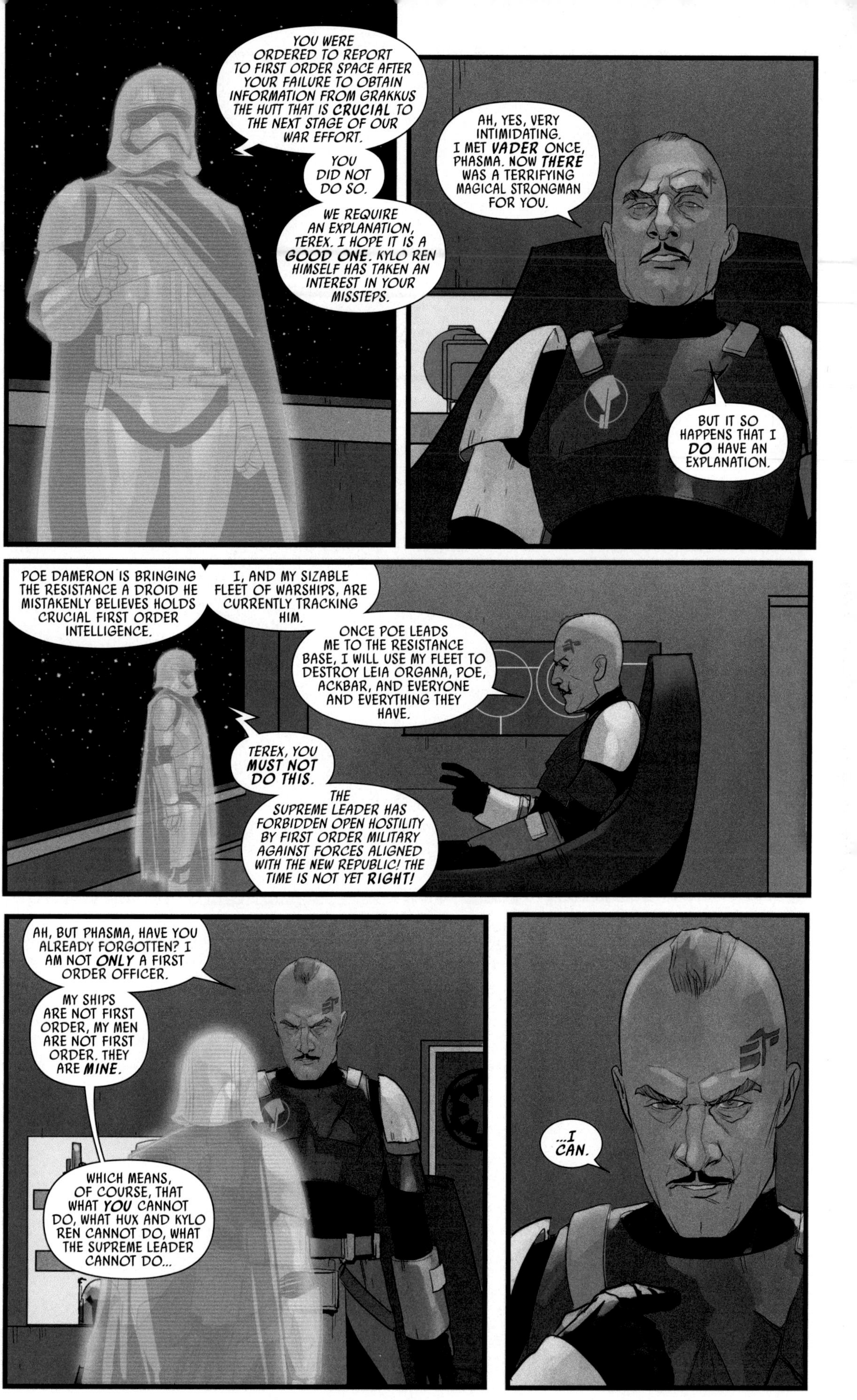
YOU WERE ORDERED TO REPORT TO FIRST ORDER SPACE AFTER YOUR FAILURE TO OBTAIN INFORMATION FROM GRAKKUS THE HUTT THAT IS CRUCIAL TO THE NEXT STAGE OF OUR WAR EFFORT.
YOU DID NOT DO SO.
WE REQUIRE AN EXPLANATION, TEREX. I HOPE IT IS A GOOD ONE. KYLO REN HIMSELF HAS TAKEN AN INTEREST IN YOUR MISSTEPS.
AH, YES, VERY INTIMIDATING. I MET VADER ONCE, PHASMA. NOW THERE WAS A TERRIFYING MAGICAL STRONGMAN FOR YOU.
BUT IT SO HAPPENS THAT I DO HAVE AN EXPLANATION.
POE DAMERON IS BRINGING THE RESISTANCE A DROID HE MISTAKENLY BELIEVES HOLDS CRUCIAL FIRST ORDER INTELLIGENCE.
I, AND MY SIZABLE FLEET OF WARSHIPS, ARE CURRENTLY TRACKING HIM.
ONCE POE LEADS ME TO THE RESISTANCE BASE, I WILL USE MY FLEET TO DESTROY LEIA ORGANA, POE, ACKBAR, AND EVERYONE AND EVERYTHING THEY HAVE.
TEREX, YOU MUST NOT DO THIS.
THE SUPREME LEADER HAS FORBIDDEN OPEN HOSTILITY BY FIRST ORDER MILITARY AGAINST FORCES ALIGNED WITH THE NEW REPUBLIC! THE TIME IS NOT YET RIGHT!
AH, BUT PHASMA, HAVE YOU ALREADY FORGOTTEN? I AM NOT ONLY A FIRST ORDER OFFICER.
MY SHIPS ARE NOT FIRST ORDER, MY MEN ARE NOT FIRST ORDER. THEY ARE MINE.
WHICH MEANS, OF COURSE, THAT WHAT YOU CANNOT DO, WHAT HUX AND KYLO REN CANNOT DO, WHAT THE SUPREME LEADER CANNOT DO...
...I CAN.

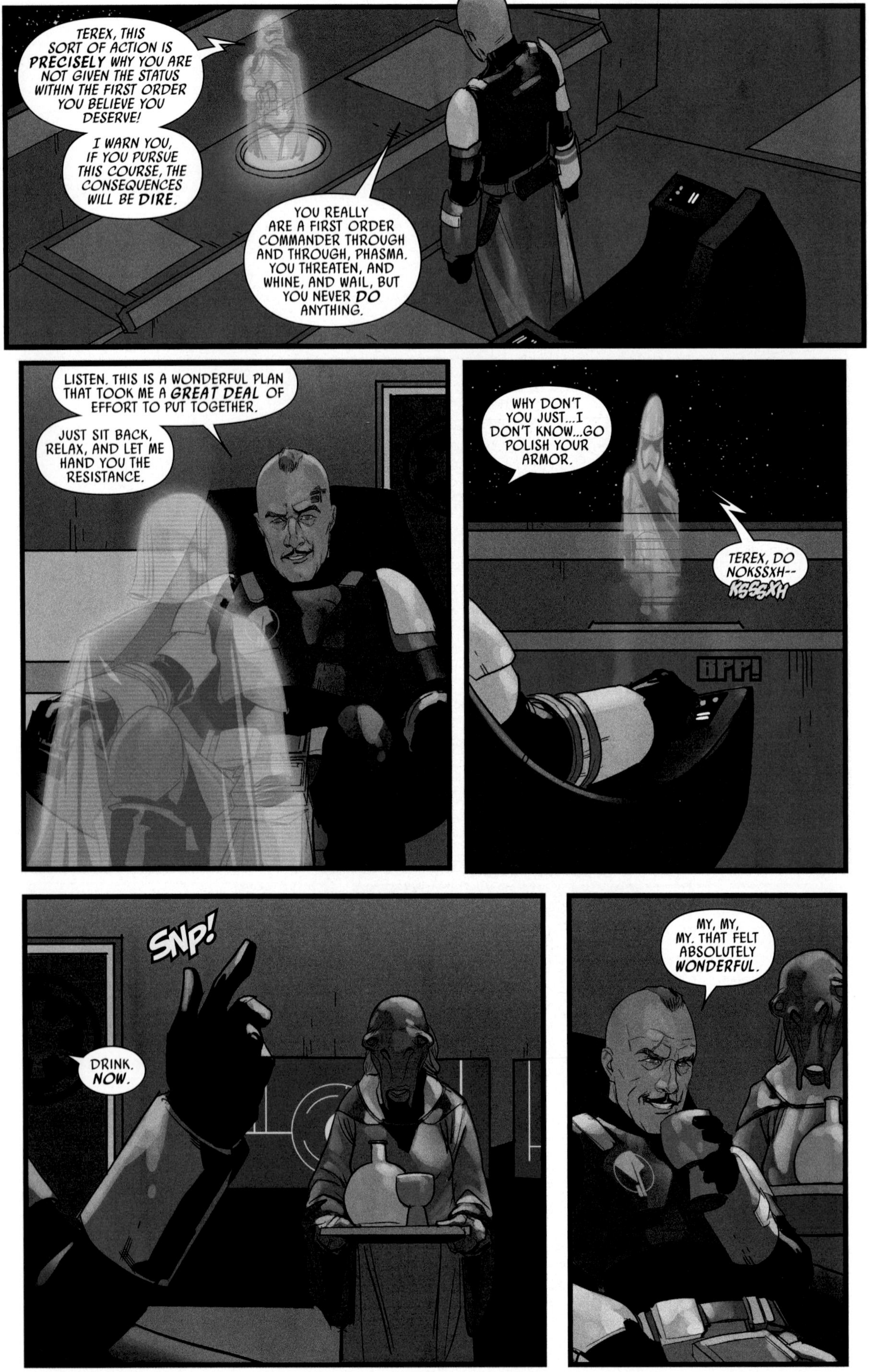
TEREX, THIS SORT OF ACTION IS PRECISELY WHY YOU ARE NOT GIVEN THE STATUS WITHIN THE FIRST ORDER YOU BELIEVE YOU DESERVE!
I WARN YOU, IF YOU PURSUE THIS COURSE, THE CONSEQUENCES WILL BE DIRE.
YOU REALLY ARE A FIRST ORDER COMMANDER THROUGH AND THROUGH, PHASMA. YOU THREATEN, AND WHINE, AND WAIL, BUT YOU NEVER DO ANYTHING.
LISTEN. THIS IS A WONDERFUL PLAN THAT TOOK ME A GREAT DEAL OF EFFORT TO PUT TOGETHER.
JUST SIT BACK, RELAX, AND LET ME HAND YOU THE RESISTANCE.
WHY DON'T YOU JUST...I DON'T KNOW...GO POLISH YOUR ARMOR.
TEREX, DO NOKSSXH-- KSSSXH
BPP!
SNP!
DRINK. NOW.
MY, MY, MY. THAT FELT ABSOLUTELY WONDERFUL.

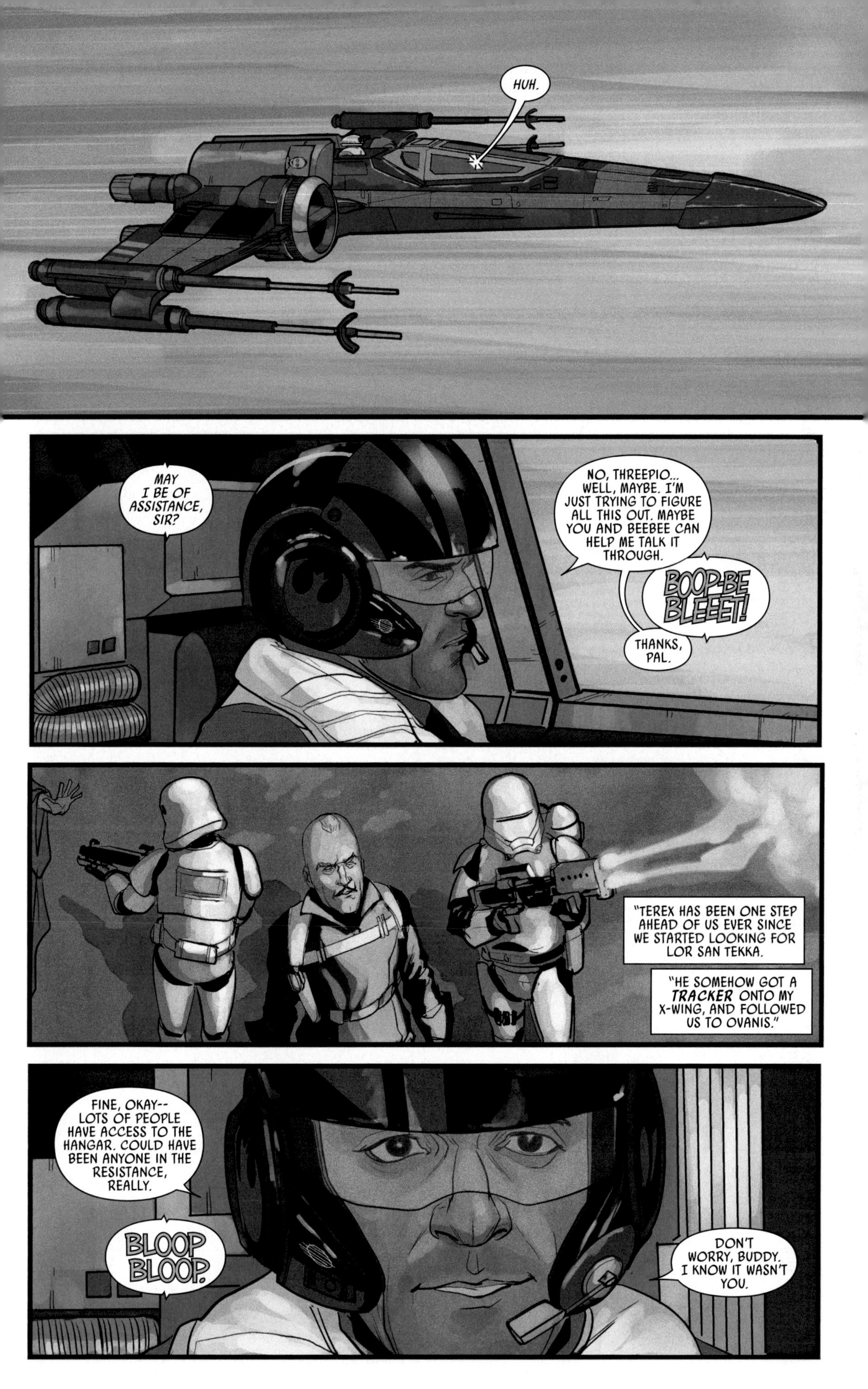
HUH.
MAY I BE OF ASSISTANCE, SIR?
NO, THREEPIO... WELL, MAYBE. I'M JUST TRYING TO FIGURE ALL THIS OUT. MAYBE YOU AND BEEBEE CAN HELP ME TALK IT THROUGH.
BOOP-BE BLEEET!
THANKS, PAL.
"TEREX HAS BEEN ONE STEP AHEAD OF US EVER SINCE WE STARTED LOOKING FOR LOR SAN TEKKA.
"HE SOMEHOW GOT A *TRACKER* ONTO MY X-WING, AND FOLLOWED US TO OVANIS."
FINE, OKAY-- LOTS OF PEOPLE HAVE ACCESS TO THE HANGAR. COULD HAVE BEEN ANYONE IN THE RESISTANCE, REALLY.
BLOOP BLOOP.
DON'T WORRY, BUDDY. I KNOW IT WASN'T YOU.

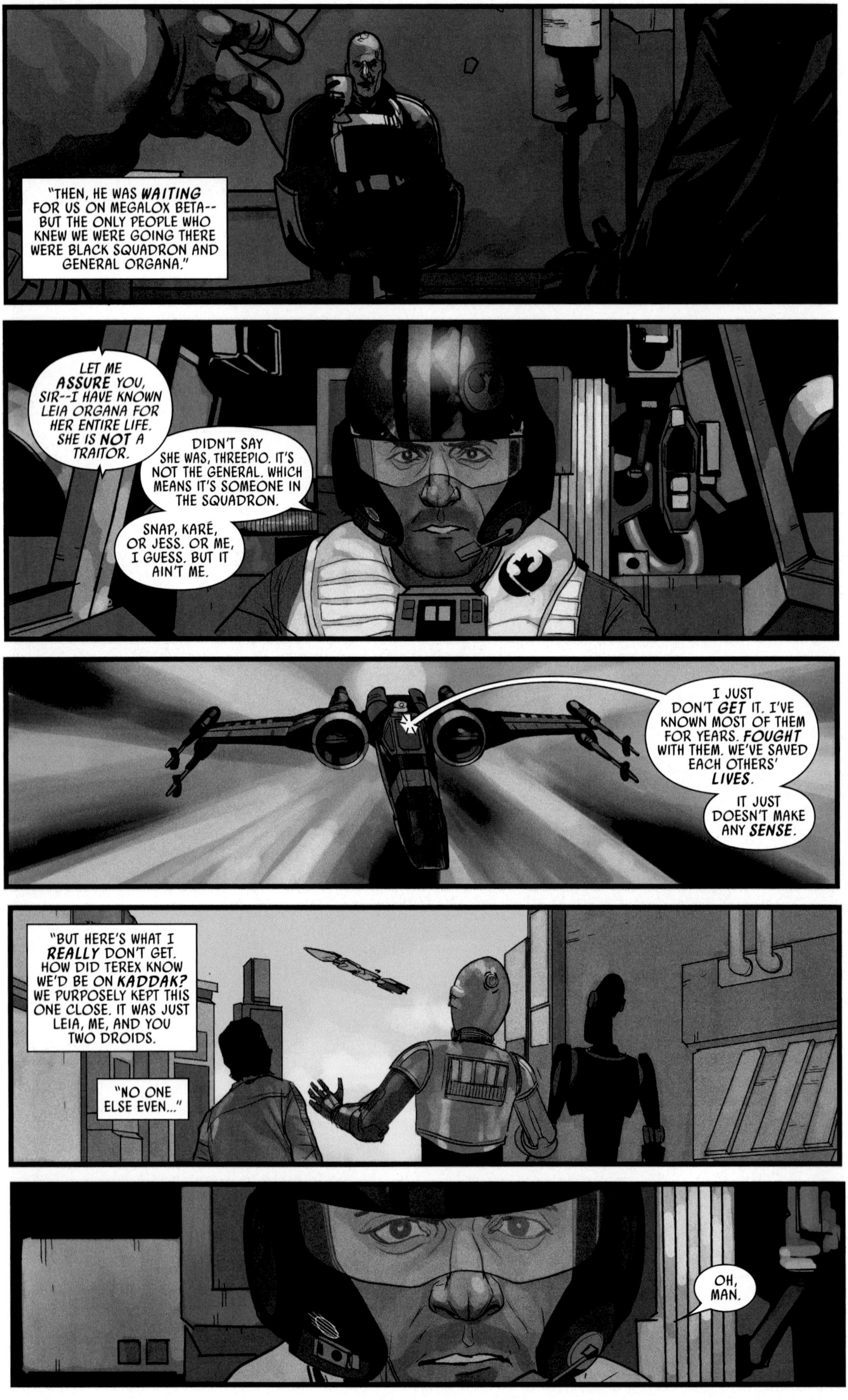
"THEN, HE WAS WAITING FOR US ON MEGALOX BETA--BUT THE ONLY PEOPLE WHO KNEW WE WERE GOING THERE WERE BLACK SQUADRON AND GENERAL ORGANA."
LET ME ASSURE YOU, SIR--I HAVE KNOWN LEIA ORGANA FOR HER ENTIRE LIFE. SHE IS NOT A TRAITOR.
DIDN'T SAY SHE WAS, THREEPIO. IT'S NOT THE GENERAL. WHICH MEANS IT'S SOMEONE IN THE SQUADRON.
SNAP, KARÉ, OR JESS. OR ME, I GUESS. BUT IT AIN'T ME.
I JUST DON'T GET IT. I'VE KNOWN MOST OF THEM FOR YEARS. FOUGHT WITH THEM. WE'VE SAVED EACH OTHERS' LIVES.
IT JUST DOESN'T MAKE ANY SENSE.
"BUT HERE'S WHAT I REALLY DON'T GET. HOW DID TEREX KNOW WE'D BE ON KADDAK? WE PURPOSELY KEPT THIS ONE CLOSE. IT WAS JUST LEIA, ME, AND YOU TWO DROIDS.
"NO ONE ELSE EVEN..."
OH, MAN.

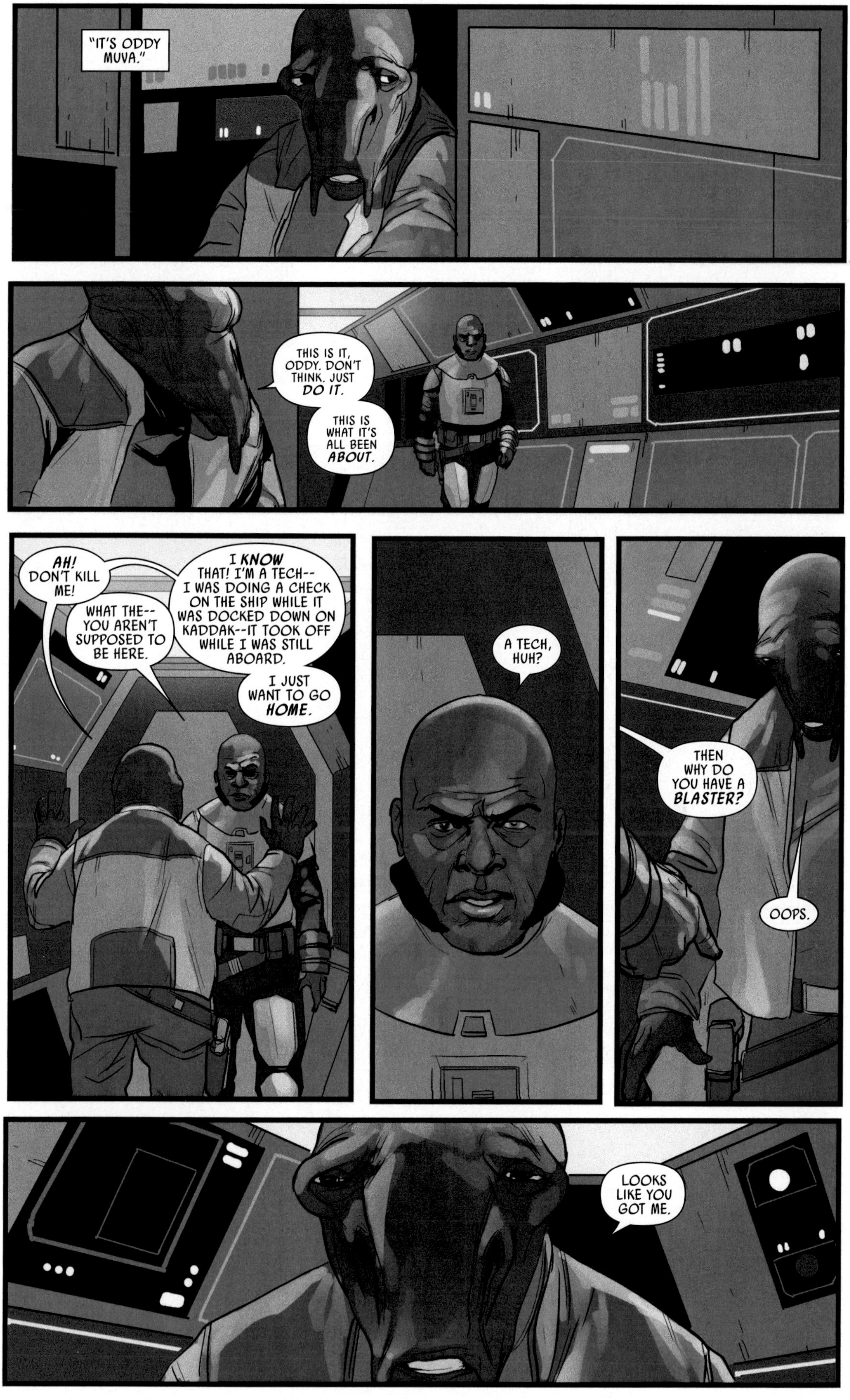
"IT'S ODDY MUVA."
THIS IS IT, ODDY. DON'T THINK. JUST DO IT.
THIS IS WHAT IT'S ALL BEEN ABOUT.
AH! DON'T KILL ME!
WHAT THE-- YOU AREN'T SUPPOSED TO BE HERE.
I KNOW THAT! I'M A TECH-- I WAS DOING A CHECK ON THE SHIP WHILE IT WAS DOCKED DOWN ON KADDAK--IT TOOK OFF WHILE I WAS STILL ABOARD.
I JUST WANT TO GO HOME.
A TECH, HUH?
THEN WHY DO YOU HAVE A BLASTER?
OOPS.
LOOKS LIKE YOU GOT ME.

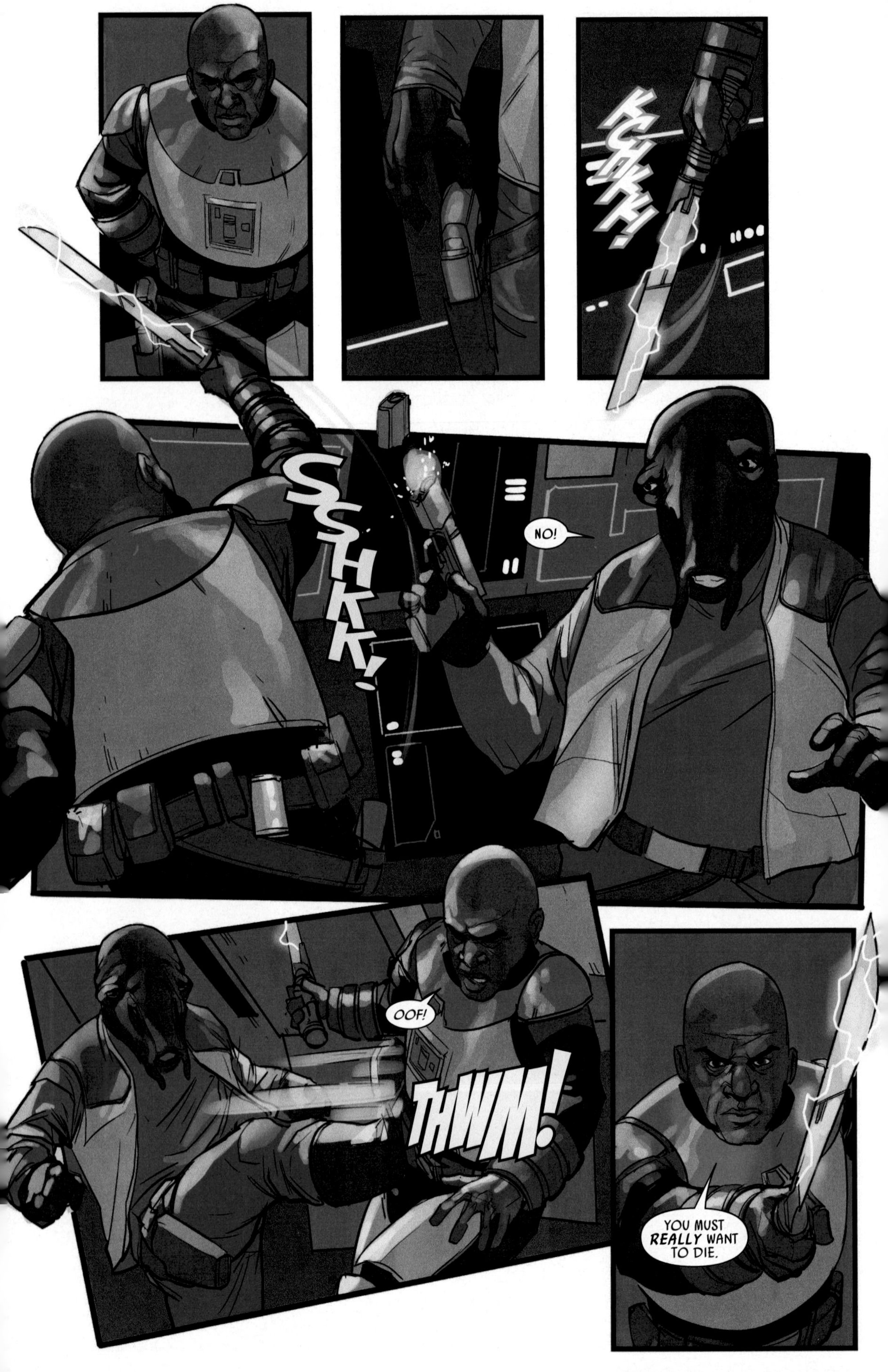
K-CHKKK!
SSHKK!
NO!
OOF!
THWM!
YOU MUST REALLY WANT TO DIE.

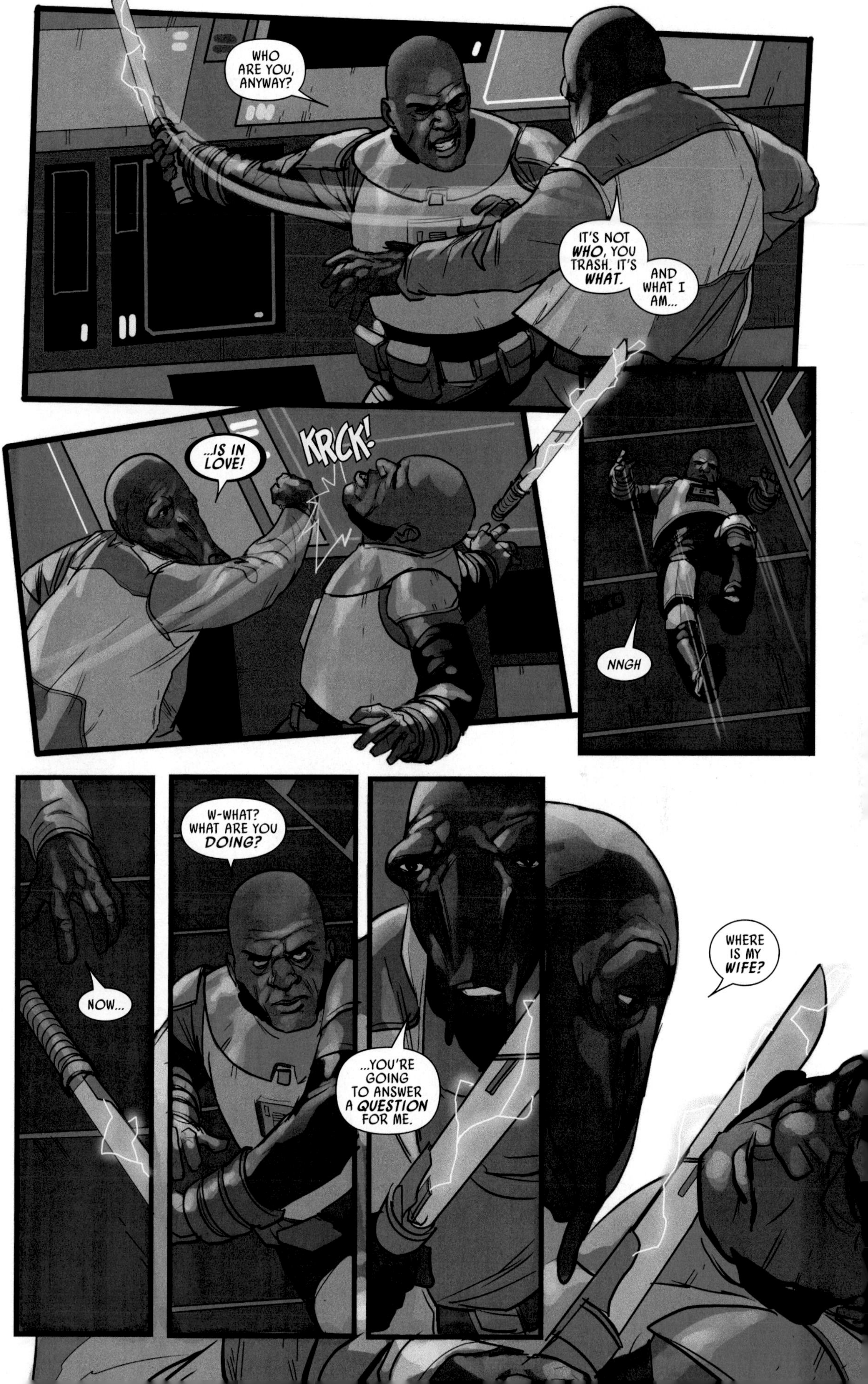
WHO ARE YOU, ANYWAY?
IT'S NOT WHO, YOU TRASH. IT'S WHAT.
AND WHAT I AM...
...IS IN LOVE!
KRCK!
NNGH
NOW...
W-WHAT? WHAT ARE YOU DOING?
...YOU'RE GOING TO ANSWER A QUESTION FOR ME.
WHERE IS MY WIFE?

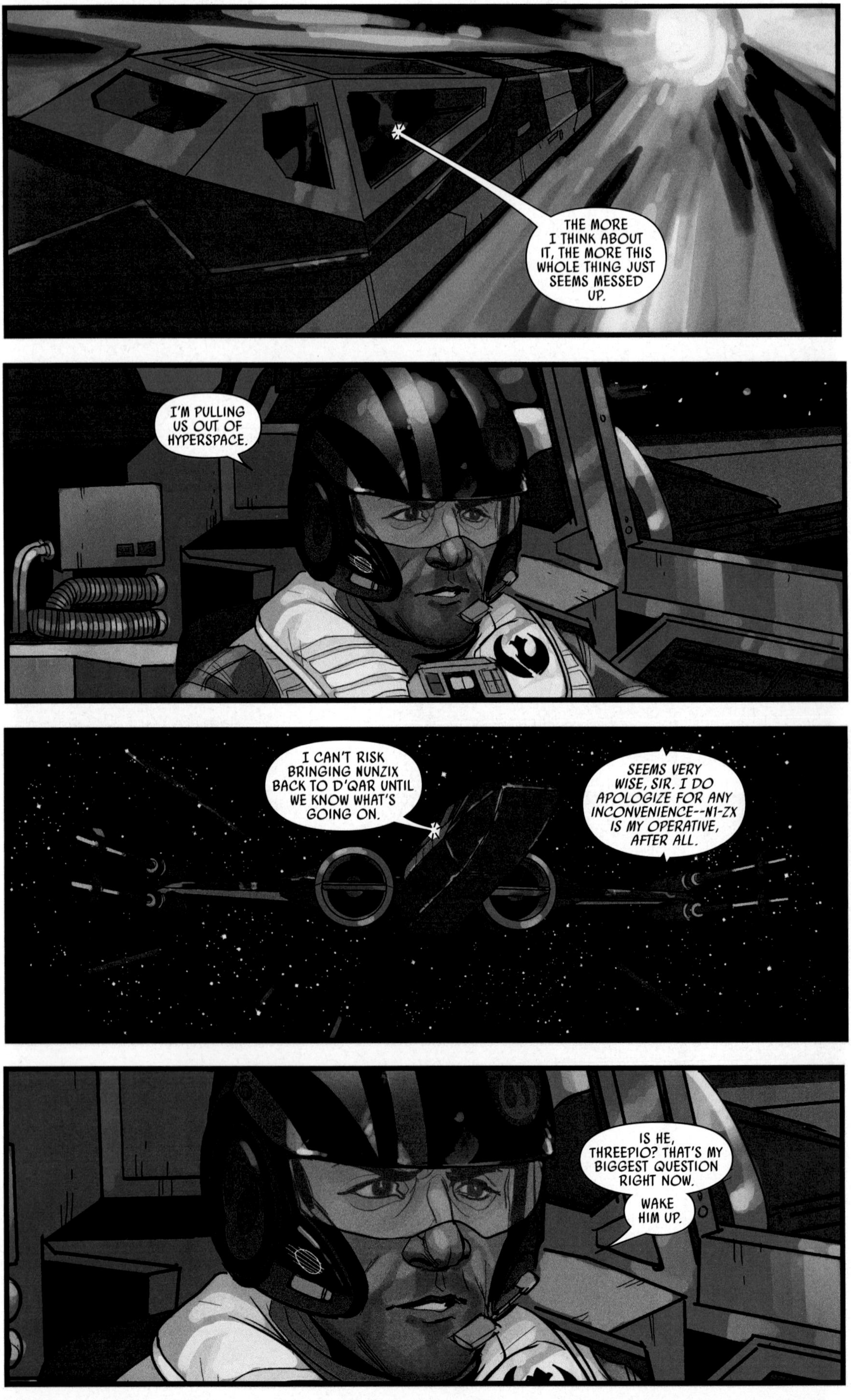
THE MORE I THINK ABOUT IT, THE MORE THIS WHOLE THING JUST SEEMS MESSED UP.
I'M PULLING US OUT OF HYPERSPACE.
I CAN'T RISK BRINGING NUNZIX BACK TO D'QAR UNTIL WE KNOW WHAT'S GOING ON.
SEEMS VERY WISE, SIR. I DO APOLOGIZE FOR ANY INCONVENIENCE--N1-ZX IS MY OPERATIVE, AFTER ALL.
IS HE, THREEPIO? THAT'S MY BIGGEST QUESTION RIGHT NOW.
WAKE HIM UP.

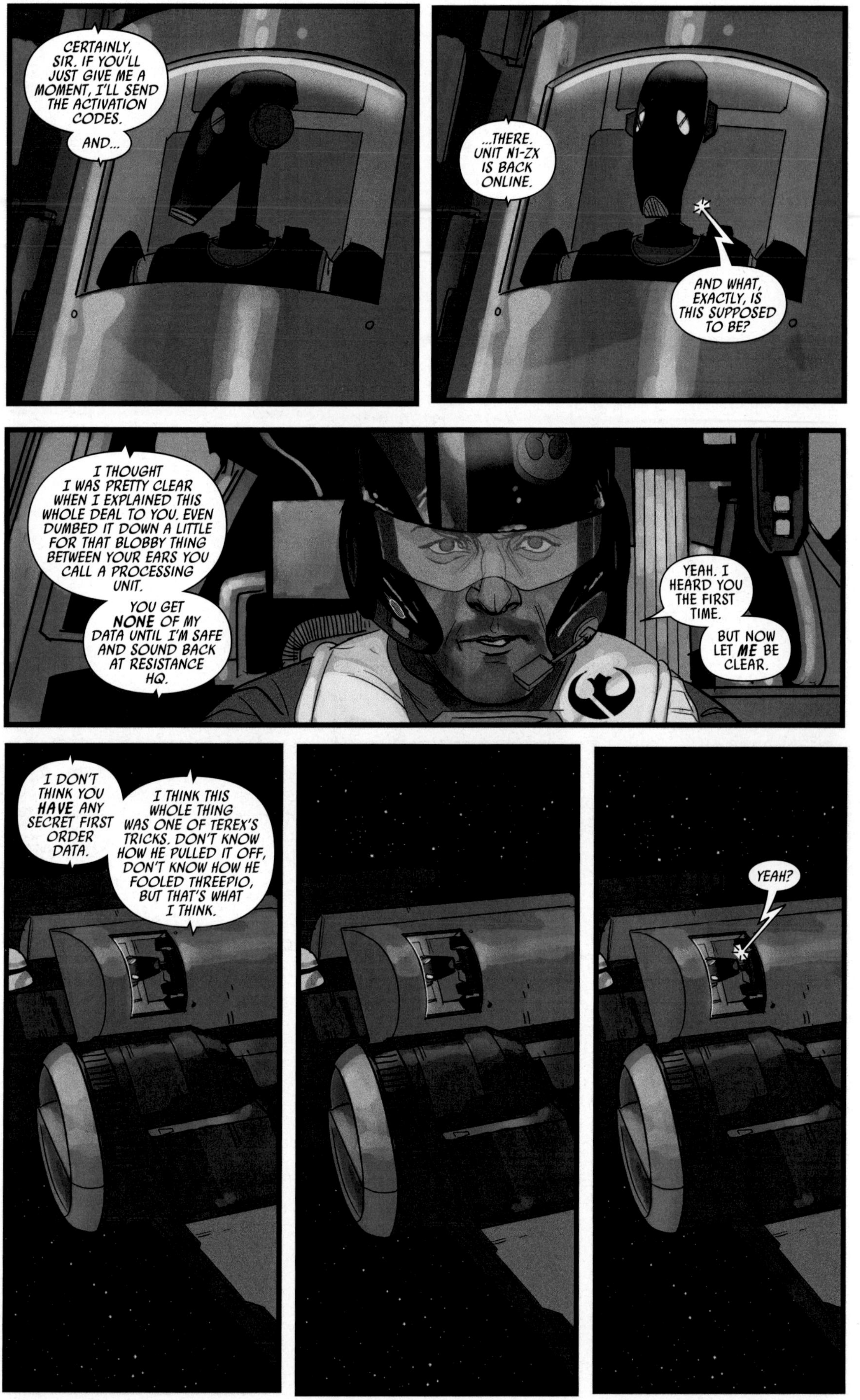
CERTAINLY, SIR. IF YOU'LL JUST GIVE ME A MOMENT, I'LL SEND THE ACTIVATION CODES.
AND...
...THERE. UNIT N1-ZX IS BACK ONLINE.
AND WHAT, EXACTLY, IS THIS SUPPOSED TO BE?
I THOUGHT I WAS PRETTY CLEAR WHEN I EXPLAINED THIS WHOLE DEAL TO YOU. EVEN DUMBED IT DOWN A LITTLE FOR THAT BLOBBY THING BETWEEN YOUR EARS YOU CALL A PROCESSING UNIT.
YOU GET NONE OF MY DATA UNTIL I'M SAFE AND SOUND BACK AT RESISTANCE HQ.
YEAH. I HEARD YOU THE FIRST TIME.
BUT NOW LET ME BE CLEAR.
I DON'T THINK YOU HAVE ANY SECRET FIRST ORDER DATA.
I THINK THIS WHOLE THING WAS ONE OF TEREX'S TRICKS. DON'T KNOW HOW HE PULLED IT OFF, DON'T KNOW HOW HE FOOLED THREEPIO, BUT THAT'S WHAT I THINK.
YEAH?

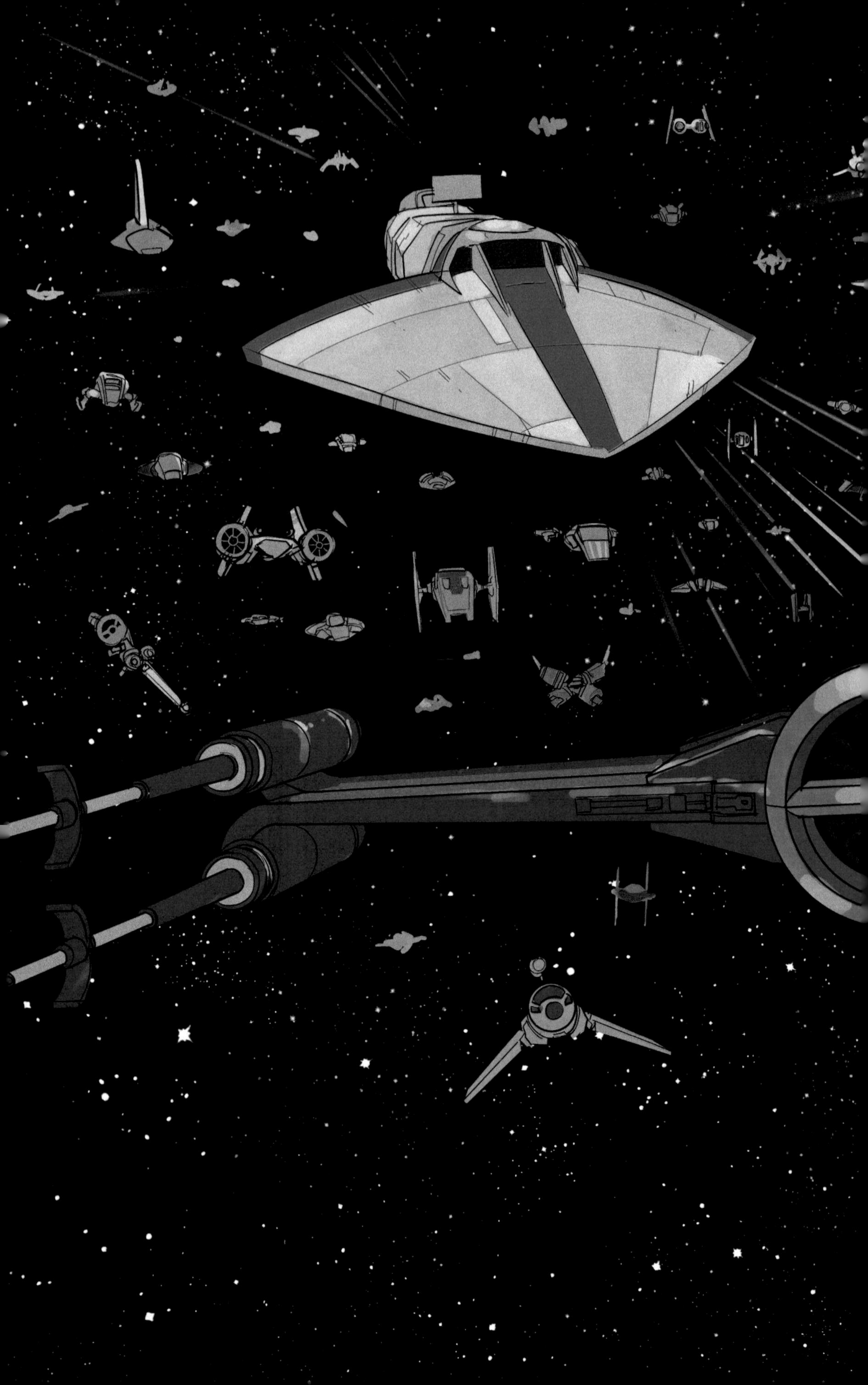

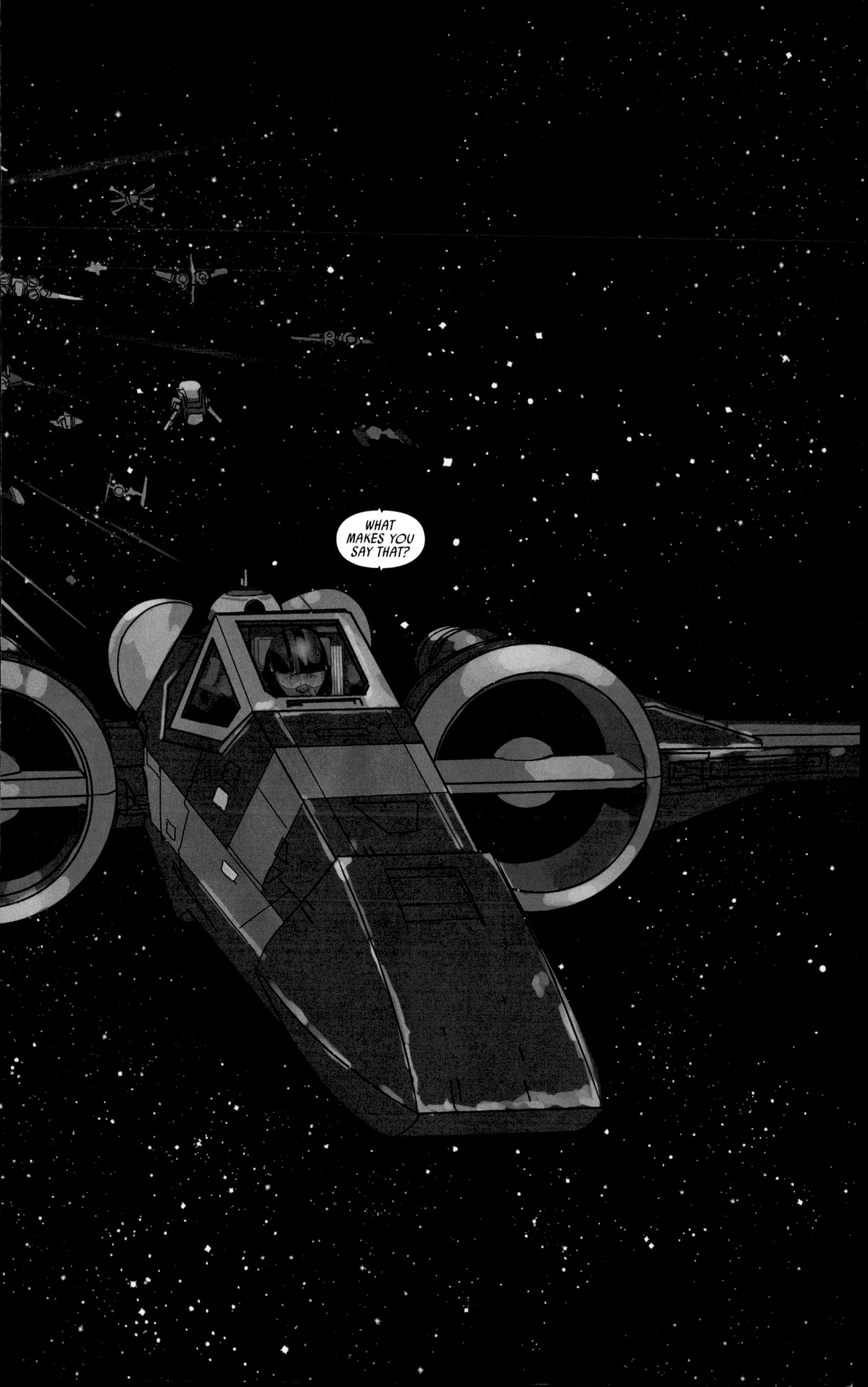
WHAT MAKES YOU SAY THAT?

BLAST! I *KNEW* IT.

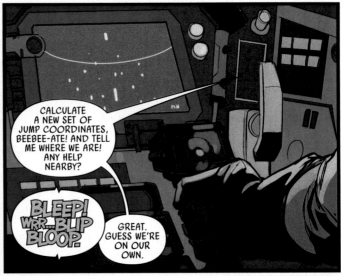

CALCULATE A NEW SET OF JUMP COORDINATES, BEEBEE-ATE! AND TELL ME WHERE WE ARE! ANY HELP NEARBY?

BLEEP! WRR...BLIP BLOOP.

GREAT. GUESS WE'RE ON OUR OWN.

WHERE ARE WE? WE HAVE TO BE CLOSE TO THE RESISTANCE BASE.

LORD TEREX, WE'RE IN THE MIDDLE OF NOWHERE. THERE'S A SYSTEM NOT TOO FAR, BUT WE'RE NOT GETTING ANY READINGS FROM A *BASE.*

WHAT ARE YOU TELLING ME, BRRANG?

I'M SAYING... DAMERON FIGURED OUT WHAT WE WERE DOING AND DROPPED OUT OF LIGHTSPEED.

WE'RE PROBABLY NOWHERE NEAR THE RESISTANCE BASE.

I SEE.

WELL, SO MUCH FOR THAT.

GUESS WE'LL JUST *KILL HIM.*

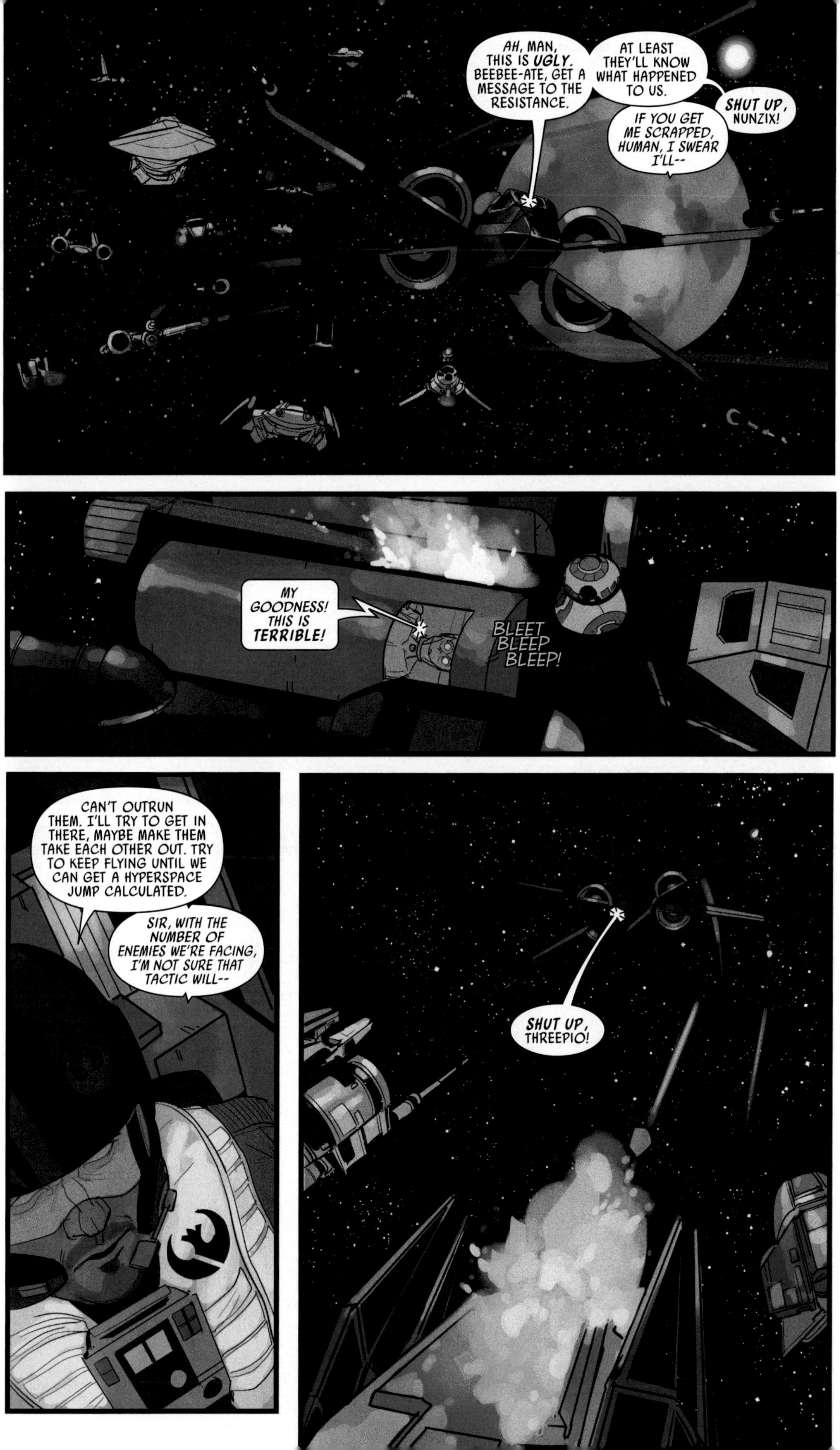
AH, MAN, THIS IS UGLY. BEEBEE-ATE, GET A MESSAGE TO THE RESISTANCE.
AT LEAST THEY'LL KNOW WHAT HAPPENED TO US.
SHUT UP, NUNZIX!
IF YOU GET ME SCRAPPED, HUMAN, I SWEAR I'LL--
MY GOODNESS! THIS IS TERRIBLE!
BLEET BLEEP BLEEP!
CAN'T OUTRUN THEM. I'LL TRY TO GET IN THERE, MAYBE MAKE THEM TAKE EACH OTHER OUT. TRY TO KEEP FLYING UNTIL WE CAN GET A HYPERSPACE JUMP CALCULATED.
SIR, WITH THE NUMBER OF ENEMIES WE'RE FACING, I'M NOT SURE THAT TACTIC WILL--
SHUT UP, THREEPIO!

COME ON...*COME ON!*

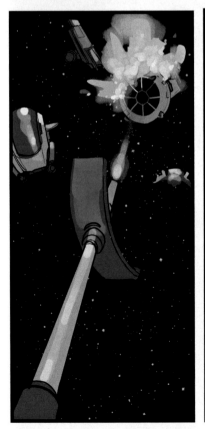

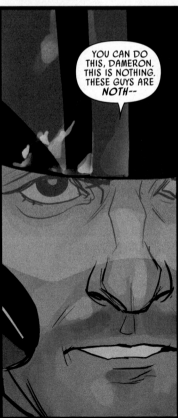

YOU CAN DO THIS, DAMERON. THIS IS NOTHING. THESE GUYS ARE *NOTH--*

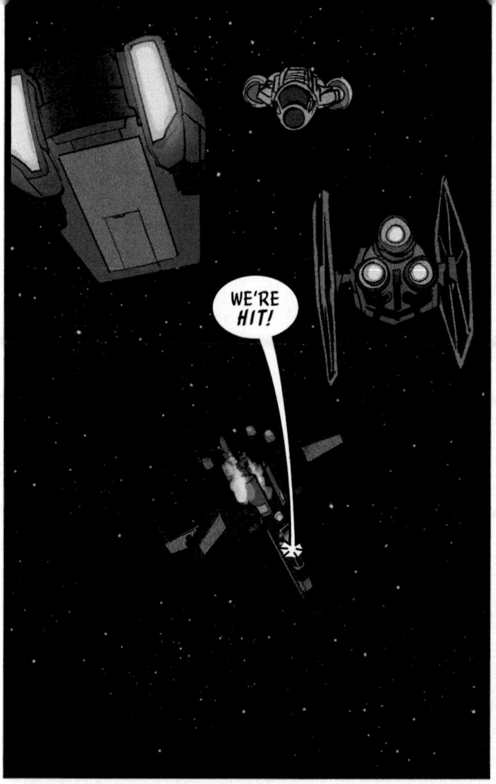
WE'RE HIT!

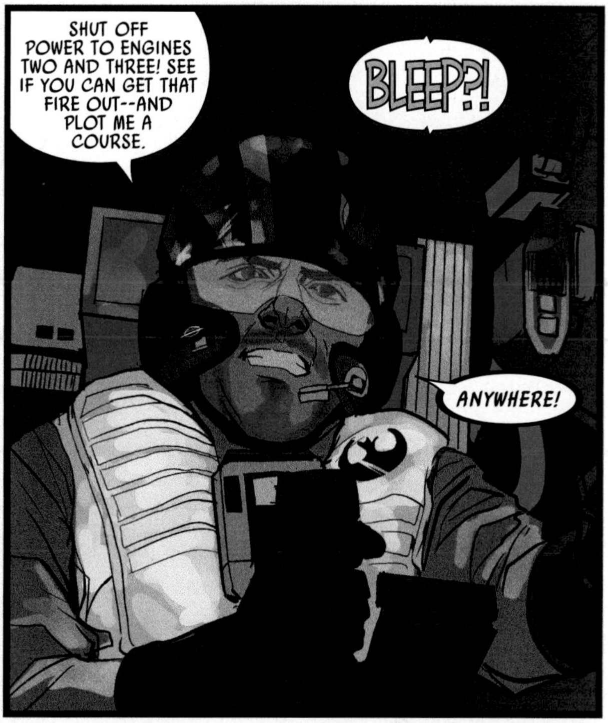
SHUT OFF POWER TO ENGINES TWO AND THREE! SEE IF YOU CAN GET THAT FIRE OUT--AND PLOT ME A COURSE.
BLEEP?!
ANYWHERE!

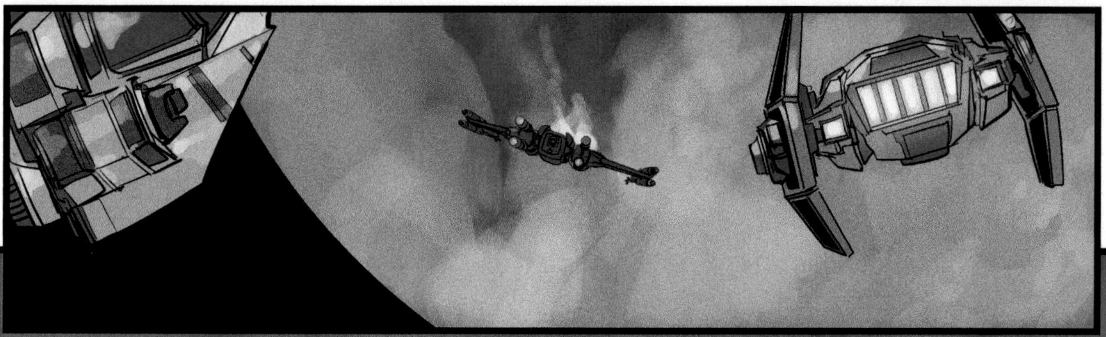

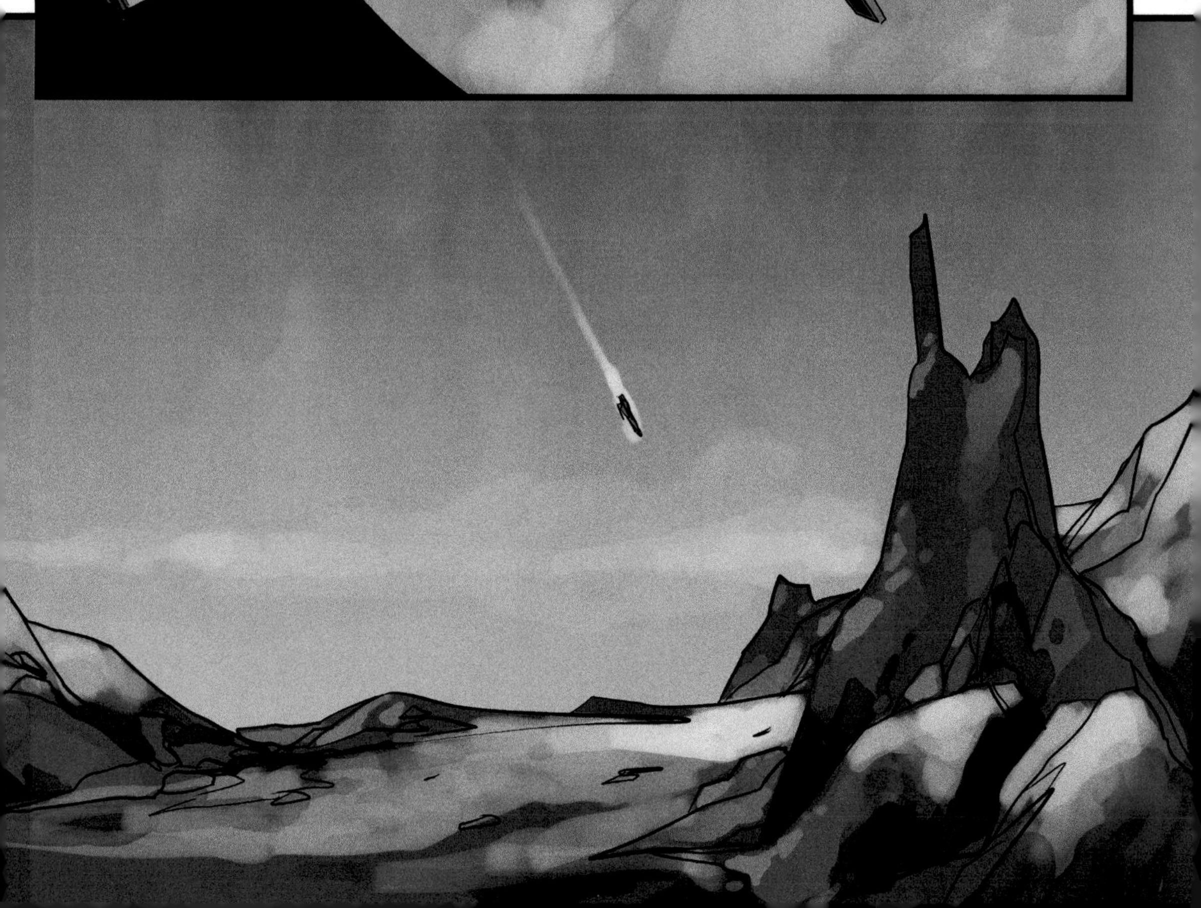

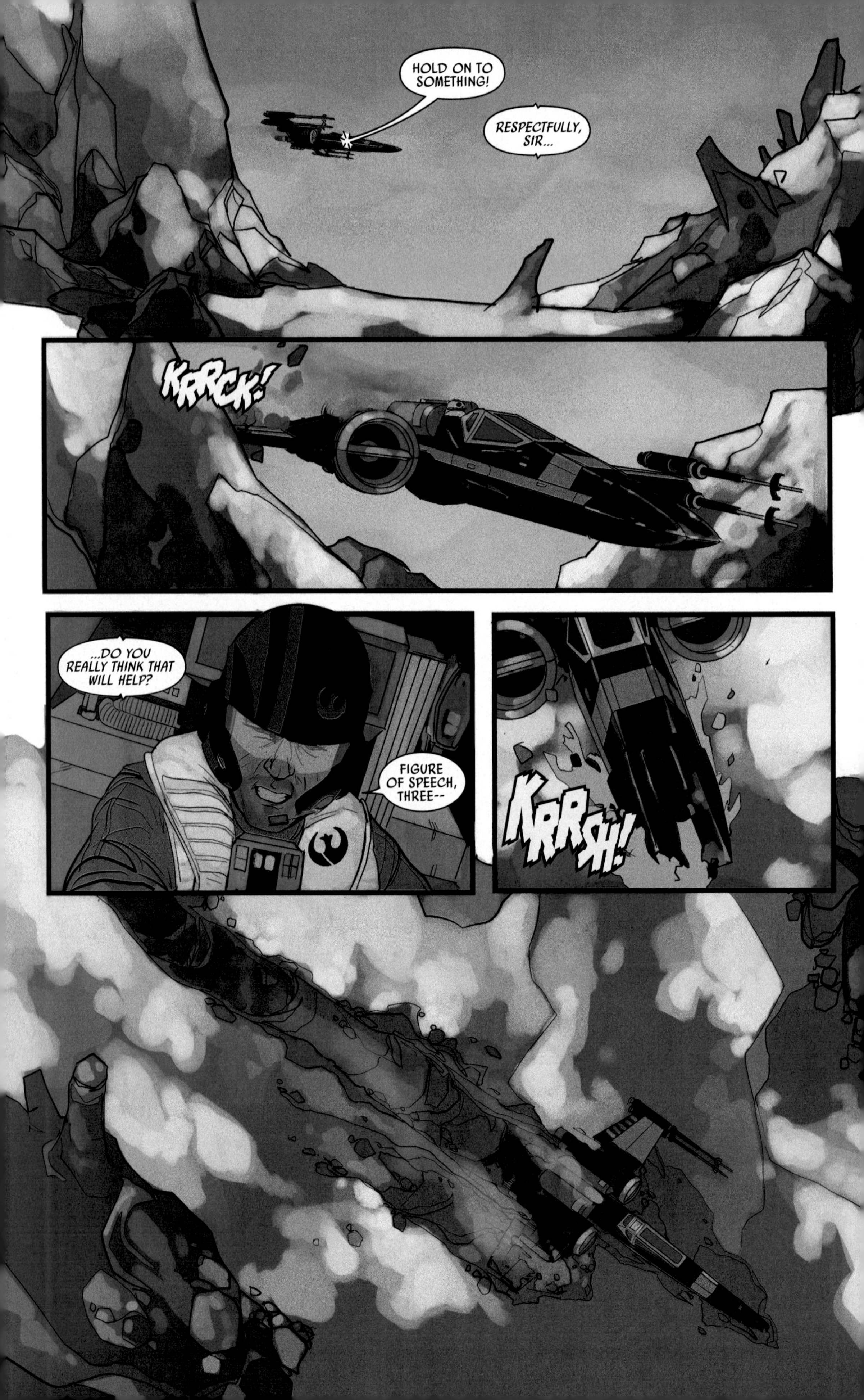
HOLD ON TO SOMETHING!
RESPECTFULLY, SIR...
KRRCK!
...DO YOU REALLY THINK THAT WILL HELP?
FIGURE OF SPEECH, THREE--
KRRSH!

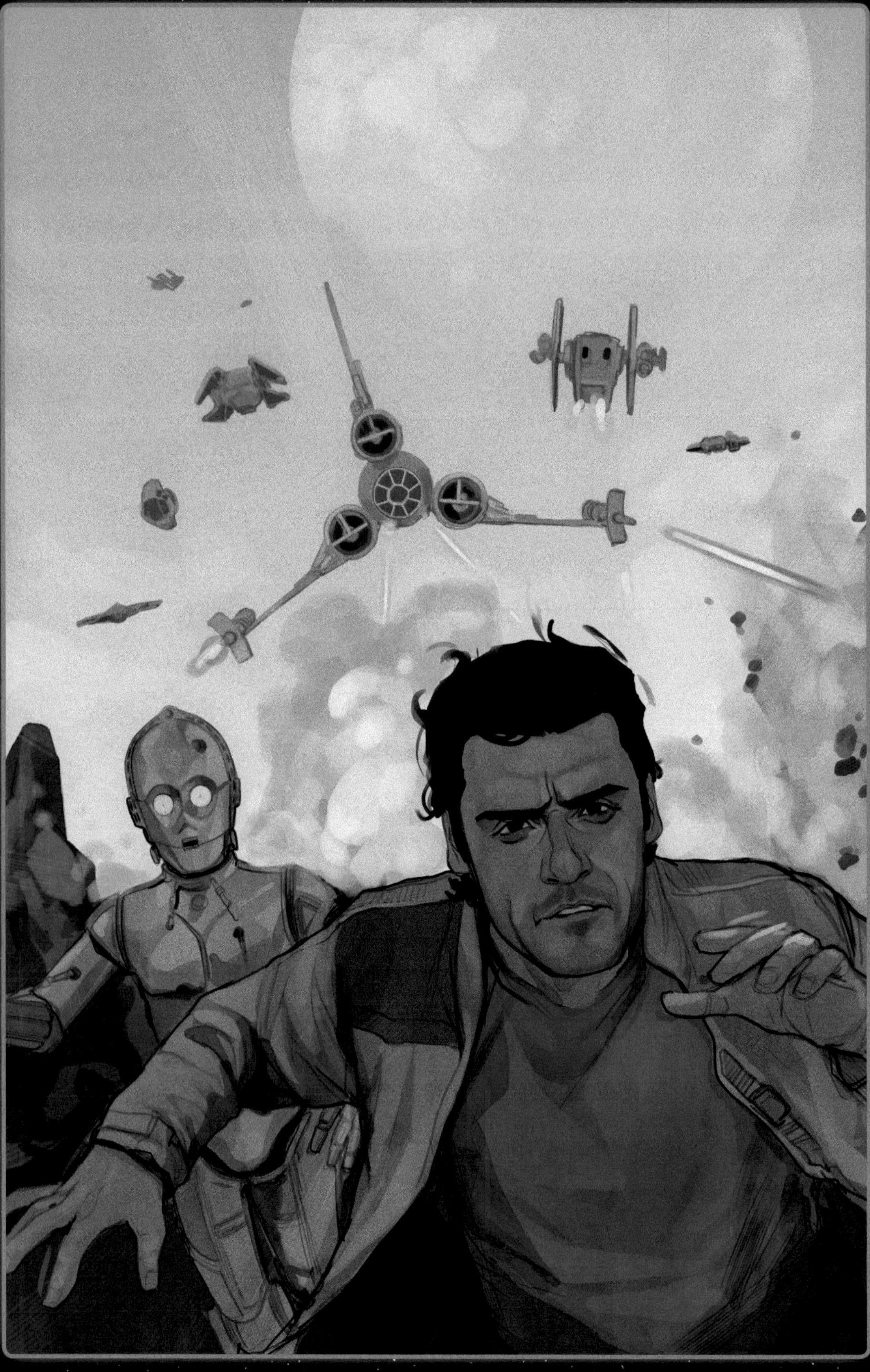

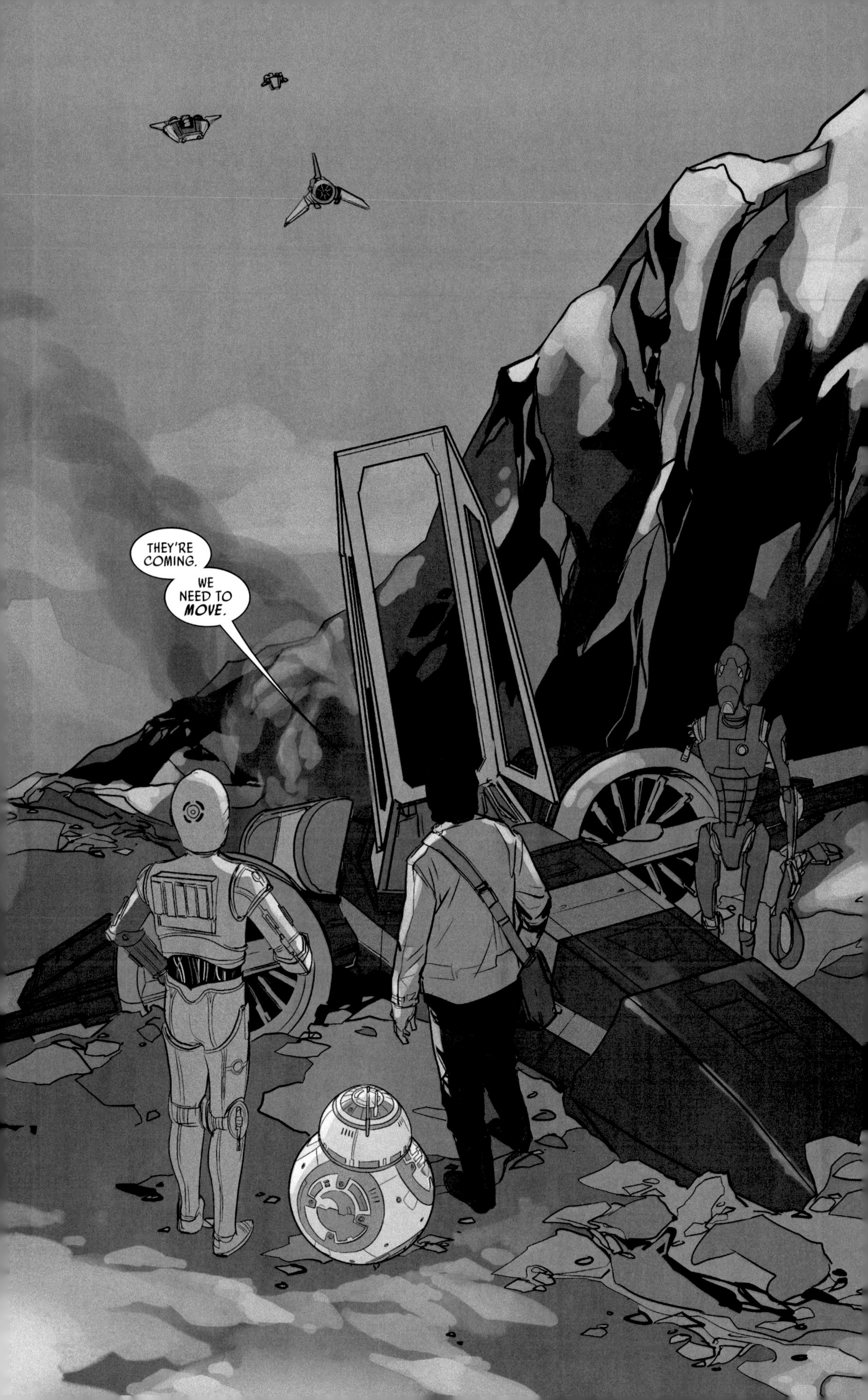
THEY'RE COMING.
WE NEED TO MOVE.

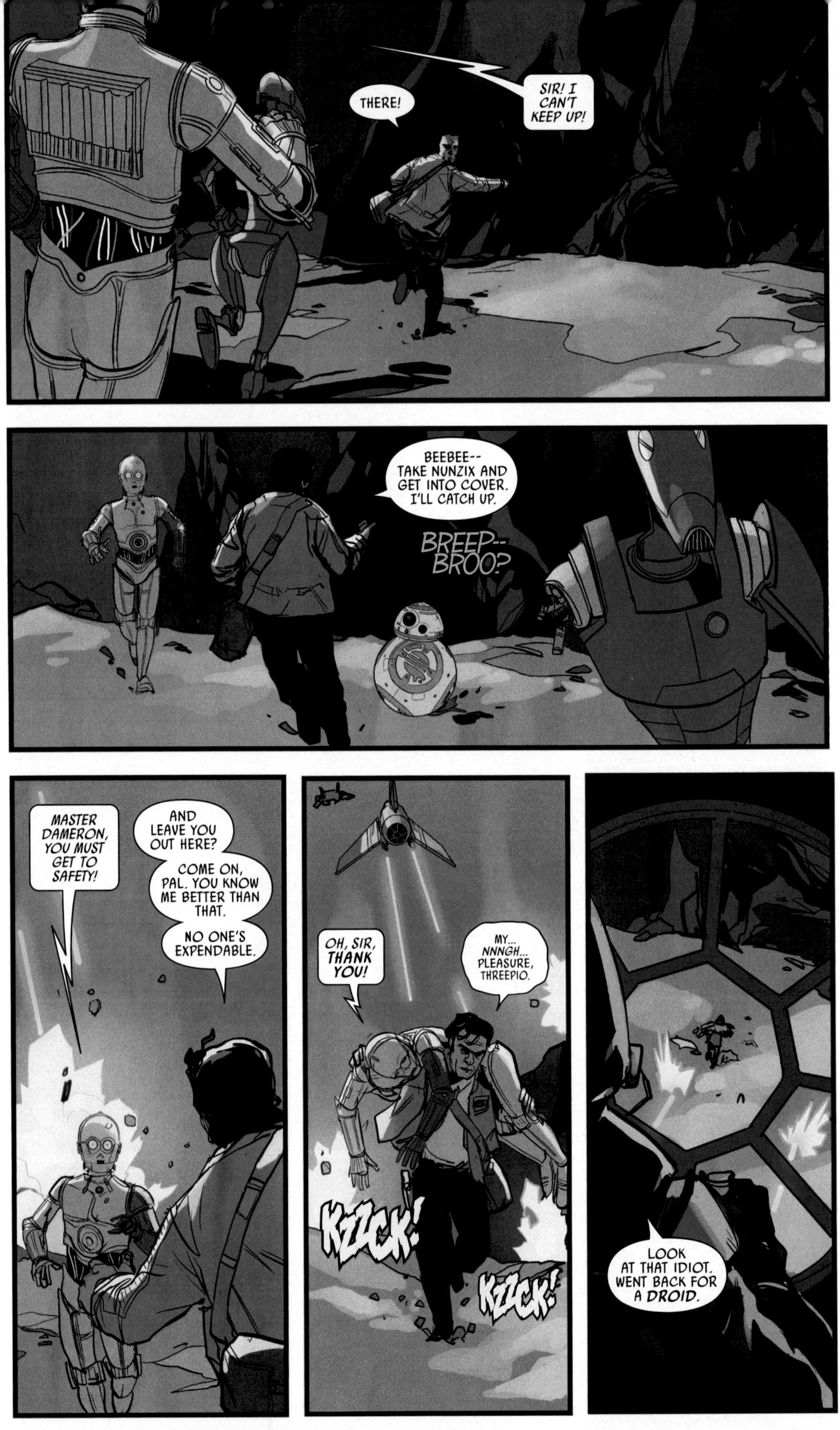
THERE!
SIR! I CAN'T KEEP UP!
BEEBEE-- TAKE NUNZIX AND GET INTO COVER. I'LL CATCH UP.
BREEP-- BROO?
MASTER DAMERON, YOU MUST GET TO SAFETY!
AND LEAVE YOU OUT HERE?
COME ON, PAL. YOU KNOW ME BETTER THAN THAT.
NO ONE'S EXPENDABLE.
OH, SIR, THANK YOU!
MY... NNNGH... PLEASURE, THREEPIO.
KZZCK!
KZZCK!
LOOK AT THAT IDIOT. WENT BACK FOR A DROID.

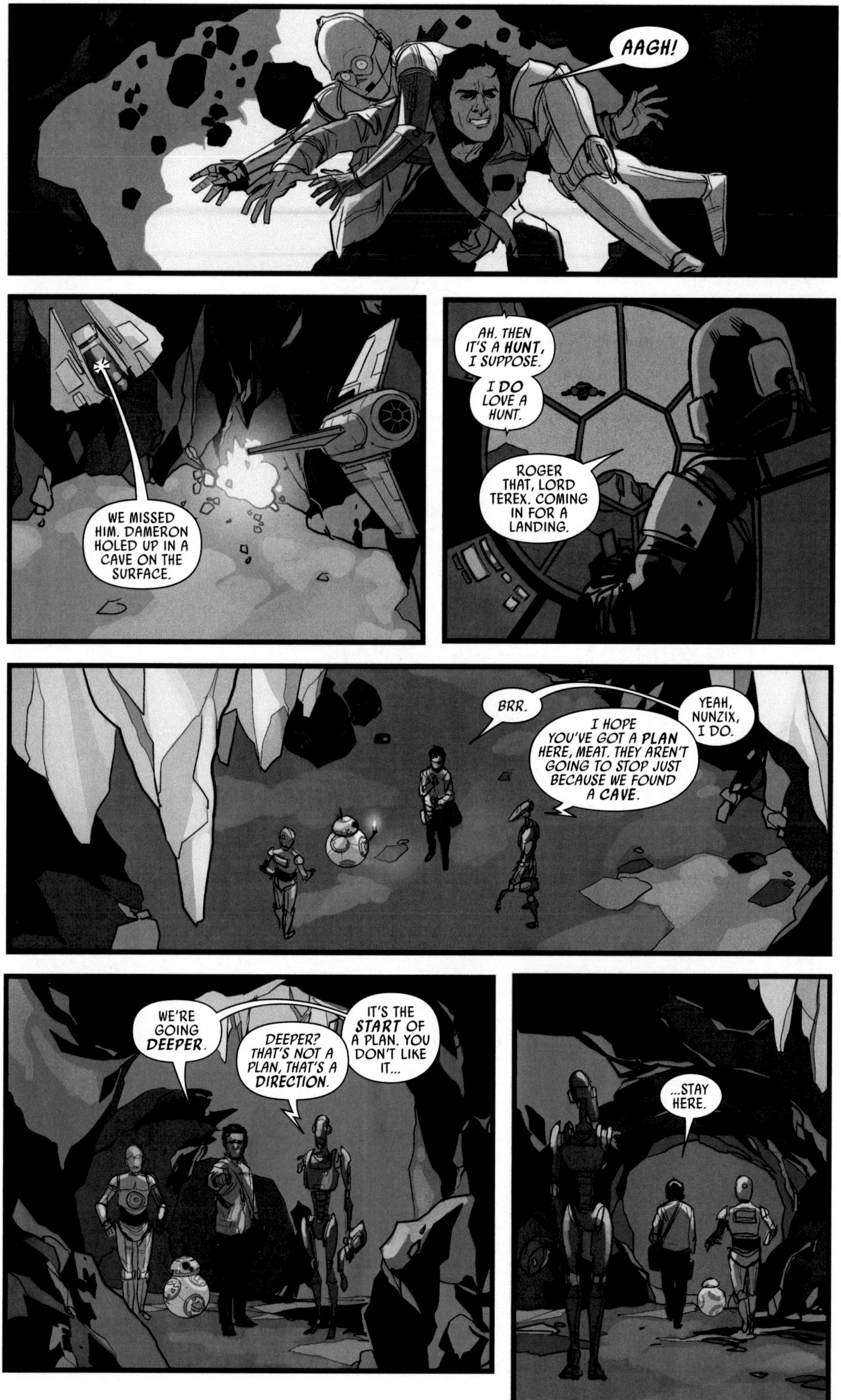
AAGH!
WE MISSED HIM. DAMERON HOLED UP IN A CAVE ON THE SURFACE.
AH. THEN IT'S A HUNT, I SUPPOSE.
I DO LOVE A HUNT.
ROGER THAT, LORD TEREX. COMING IN FOR A LANDING.
BRR.
I HOPE YOU'VE GOT A PLAN HERE, MEAT. THEY AREN'T GOING TO STOP JUST BECAUSE WE FOUND A CAVE.
YEAH, NUNZIX, I DO.
WE'RE GOING DEEPER.
DEEPER? THAT'S NOT A PLAN, THAT'S A DIRECTION.
IT'S THE START OF A PLAN. YOU DON'T LIKE IT...
...STAY HERE.

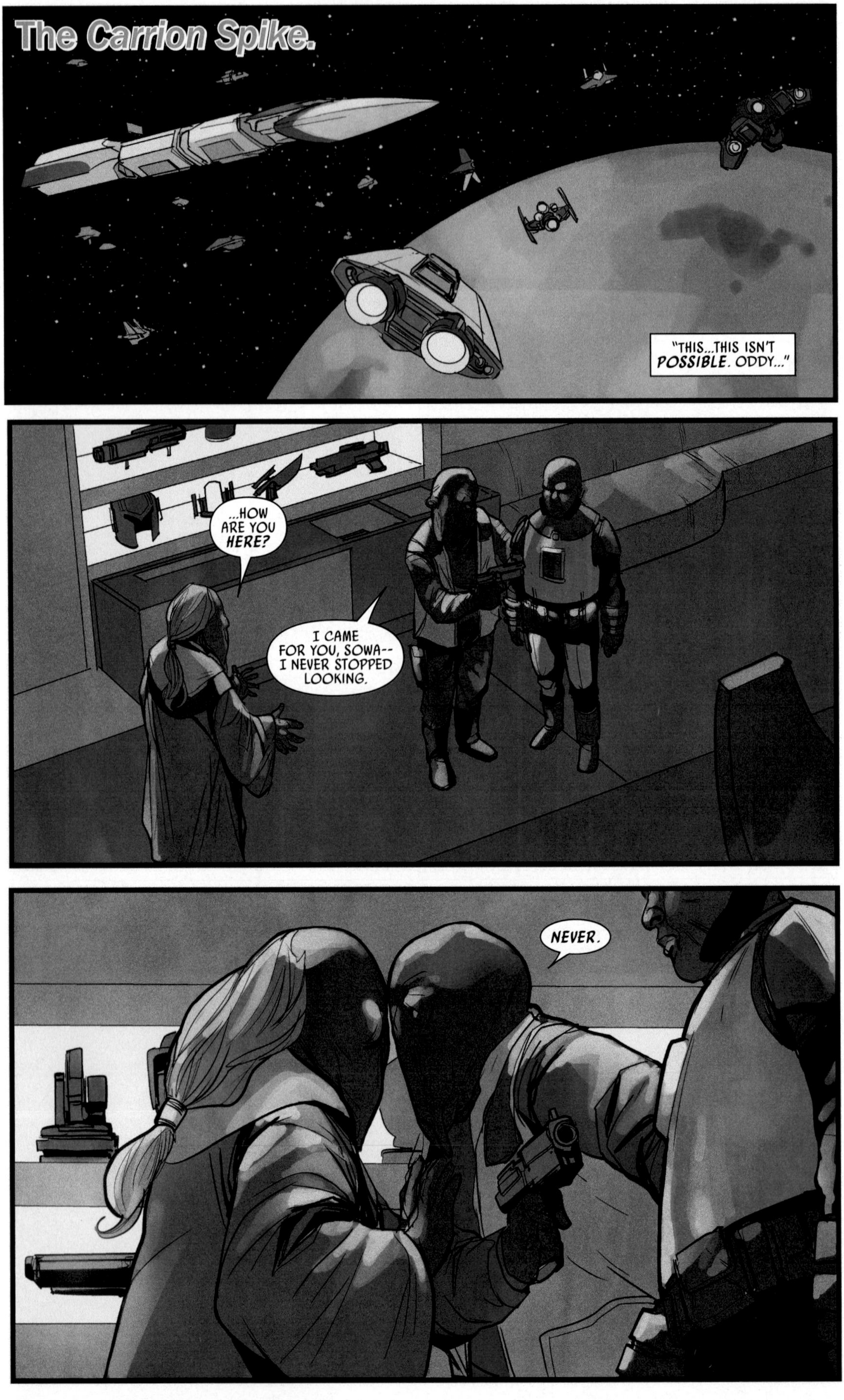
The Carrion Spike.
"THIS...THIS ISN'T POSSIBLE. ODDY..."
...HOW ARE YOU HERE?
I CAME FOR YOU, SOWA-- I NEVER STOPPED LOOKING.
NEVER.

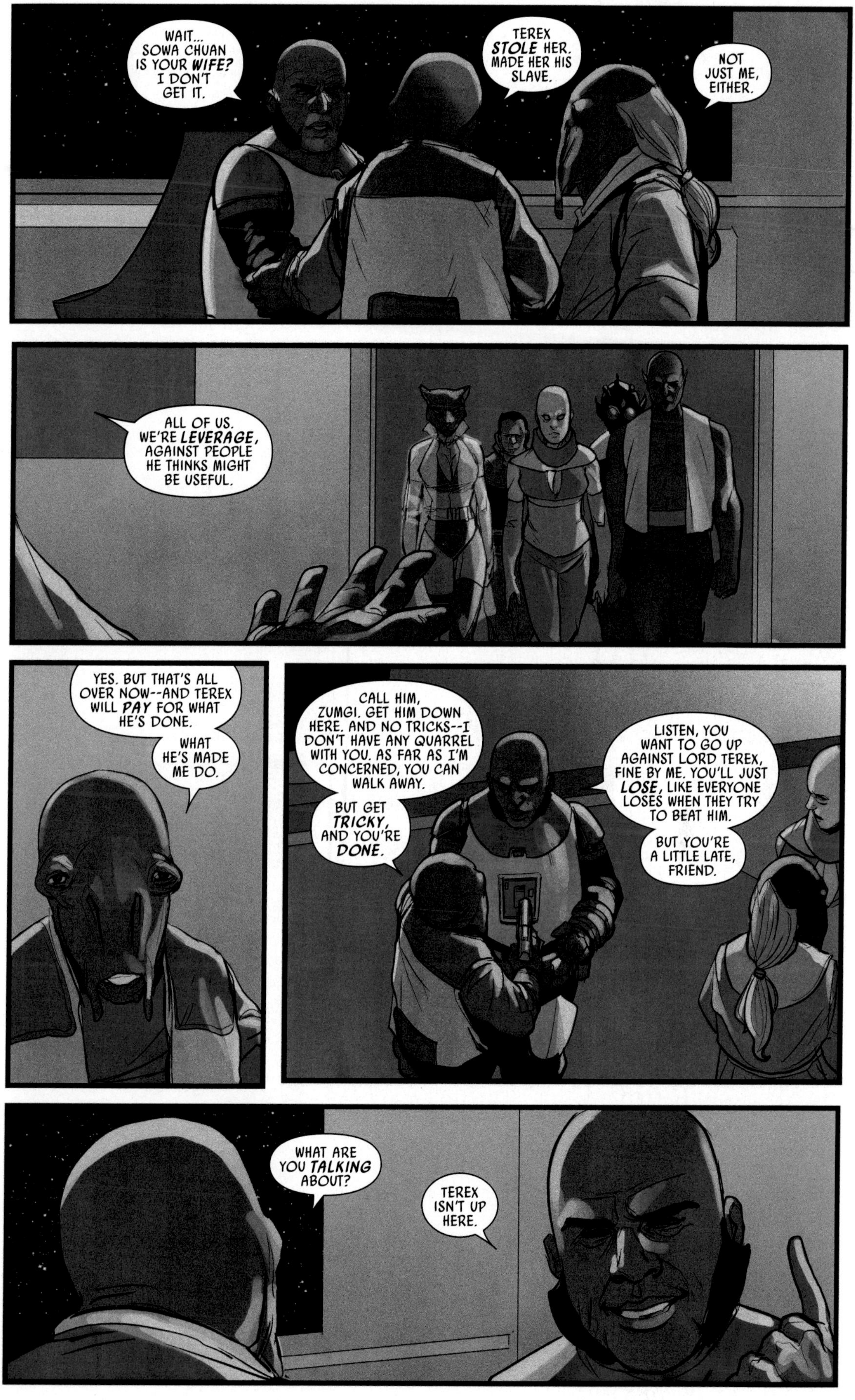
WAIT... SOWA CHUAN IS YOUR WIFE? I DON'T GET IT.
TEREX STOLE HER. MADE HER HIS SLAVE.
NOT JUST ME, EITHER.
ALL OF US. WE'RE LEVERAGE, AGAINST PEOPLE HE THINKS MIGHT BE USEFUL.
YES. BUT THAT'S ALL OVER NOW--AND TEREX WILL PAY FOR WHAT HE'S DONE.
WHAT HE'S MADE ME DO.
CALL HIM, ZUMGI. GET HIM DOWN HERE. AND NO TRICKS--I DON'T HAVE ANY QUARREL WITH YOU. AS FAR AS I'M CONCERNED, YOU CAN WALK AWAY.
BUT GET TRICKY, AND YOU'RE DONE.
LISTEN, YOU WANT TO GO UP AGAINST LORD TEREX, FINE BY ME. YOU'LL JUST LOSE, LIKE EVERYONE LOSES WHEN THEY TRY TO BEAT HIM.
BUT YOU'RE A LITTLE LATE, FRIEND.
WHAT ARE YOU TALKING ABOUT?
TEREX ISN'T UP HERE.

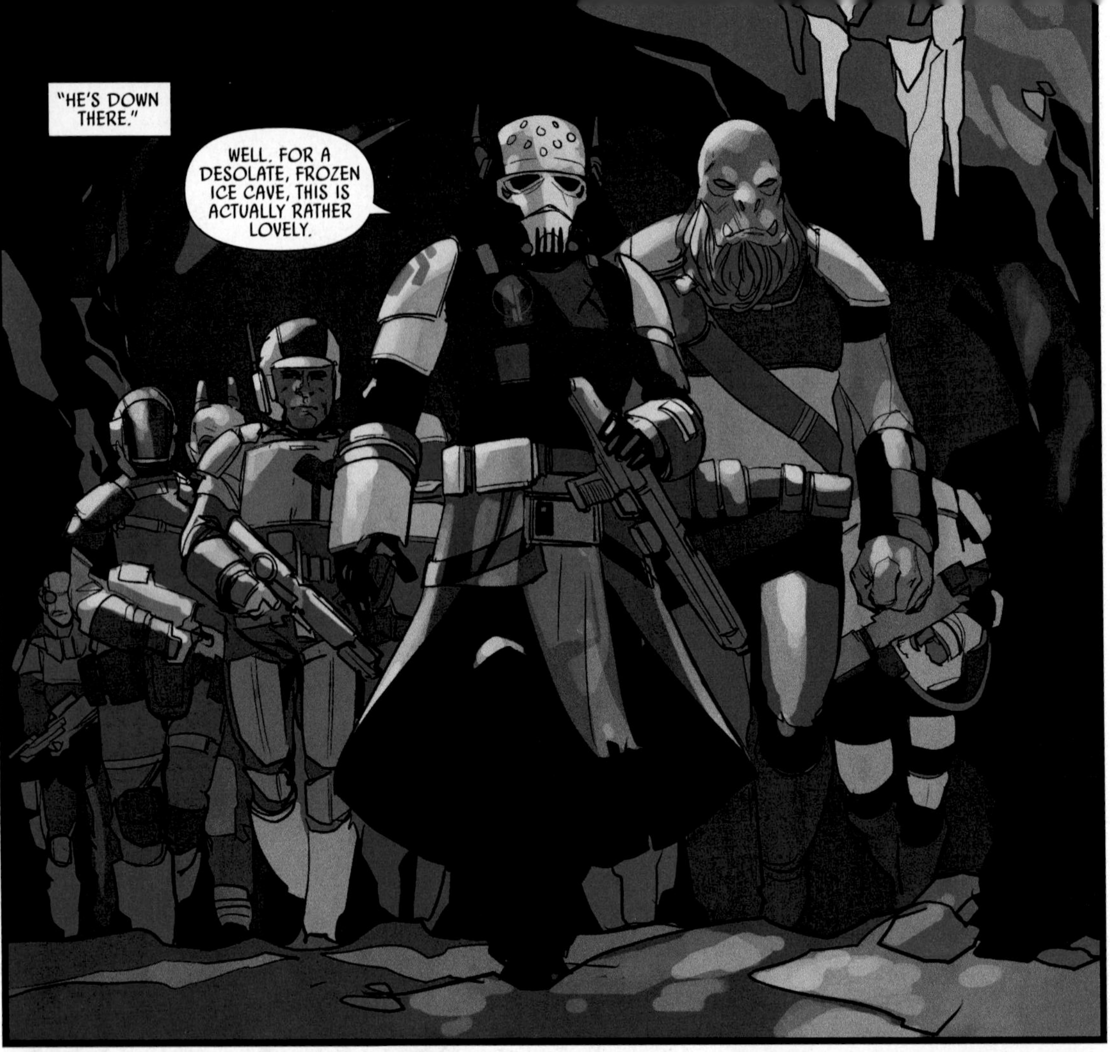
"HE'S DOWN THERE."
WELL. FOR A DESOLATE, FROZEN ICE CAVE, THIS IS ACTUALLY RATHER LOVELY.

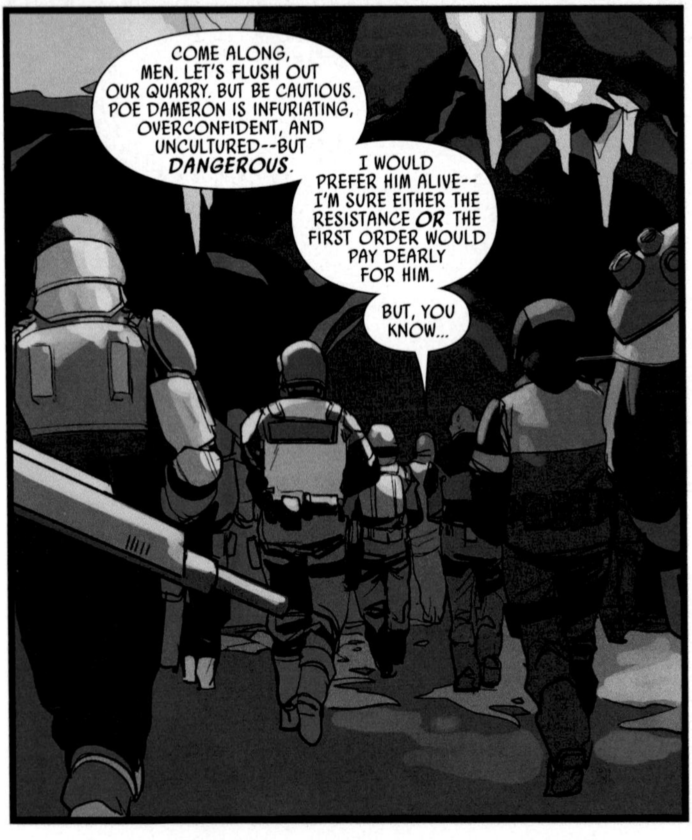
COME ALONG, MEN. LET'S FLUSH OUT OUR QUARRY. BUT BE CAUTIOUS. POE DAMERON IS INFURIATING, OVERCONFIDENT, AND UNCULTURED--BUT *DANGEROUS*.
I WOULD PREFER HIM ALIVE-- I'M SURE EITHER THE RESISTANCE *OR* THE FIRST ORDER WOULD PAY DEARLY FOR HIM.
BUT, YOU KNOW...

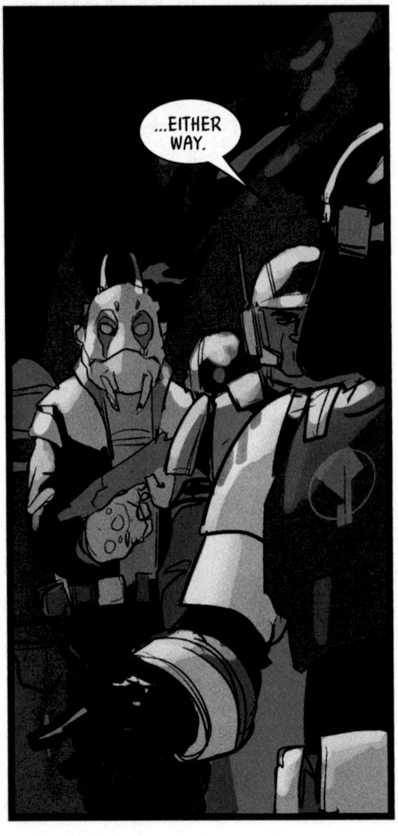
...EITHER WAY.

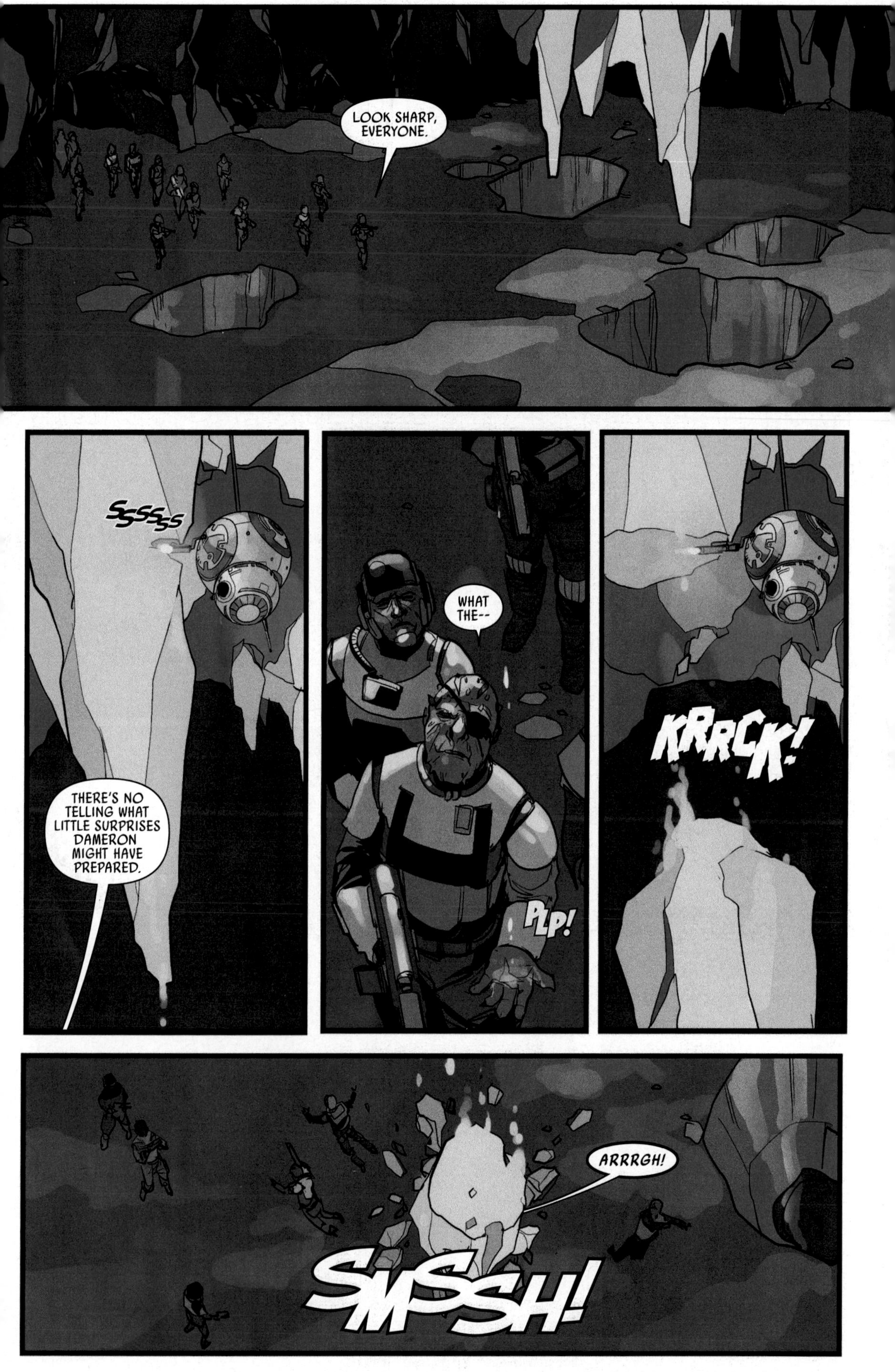
LOOK SHARP, EVERYONE.
SSSSSS
THERE'S NO TELLING WHAT LITTLE SURPRISES DAMERON MIGHT HAVE PREPARED.
WHAT THE--
PLP!
KRRCK!
ARRRGH!
SMSSH!

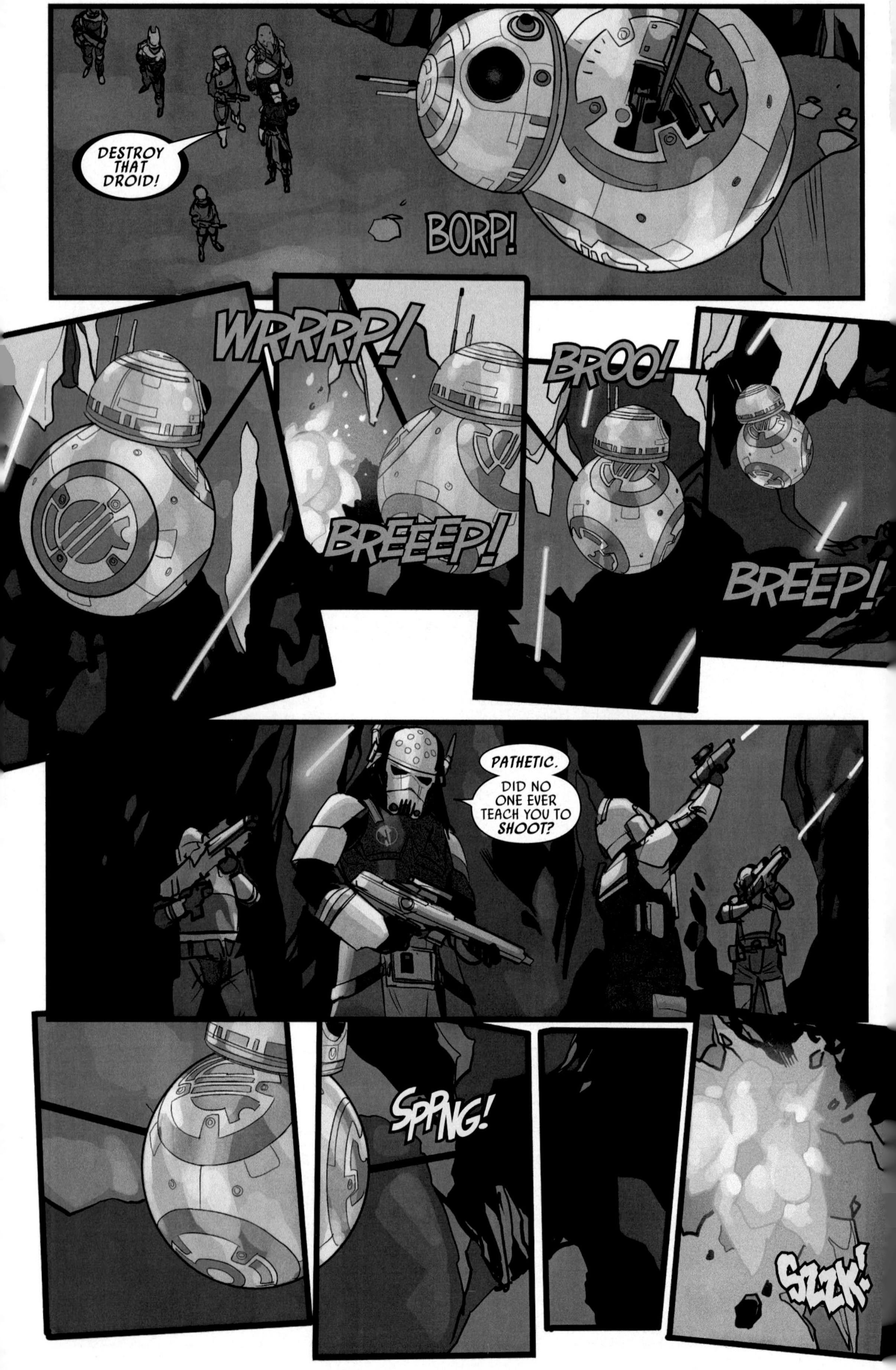
DESTROY THAT DROID!
BORP!
WRRRRP!
BREEEP!
BROO!
BREEP!
PATHETIC.
DID NO ONE EVER TEACH YOU TO SHOOT?
SPPNG!
SZZK!

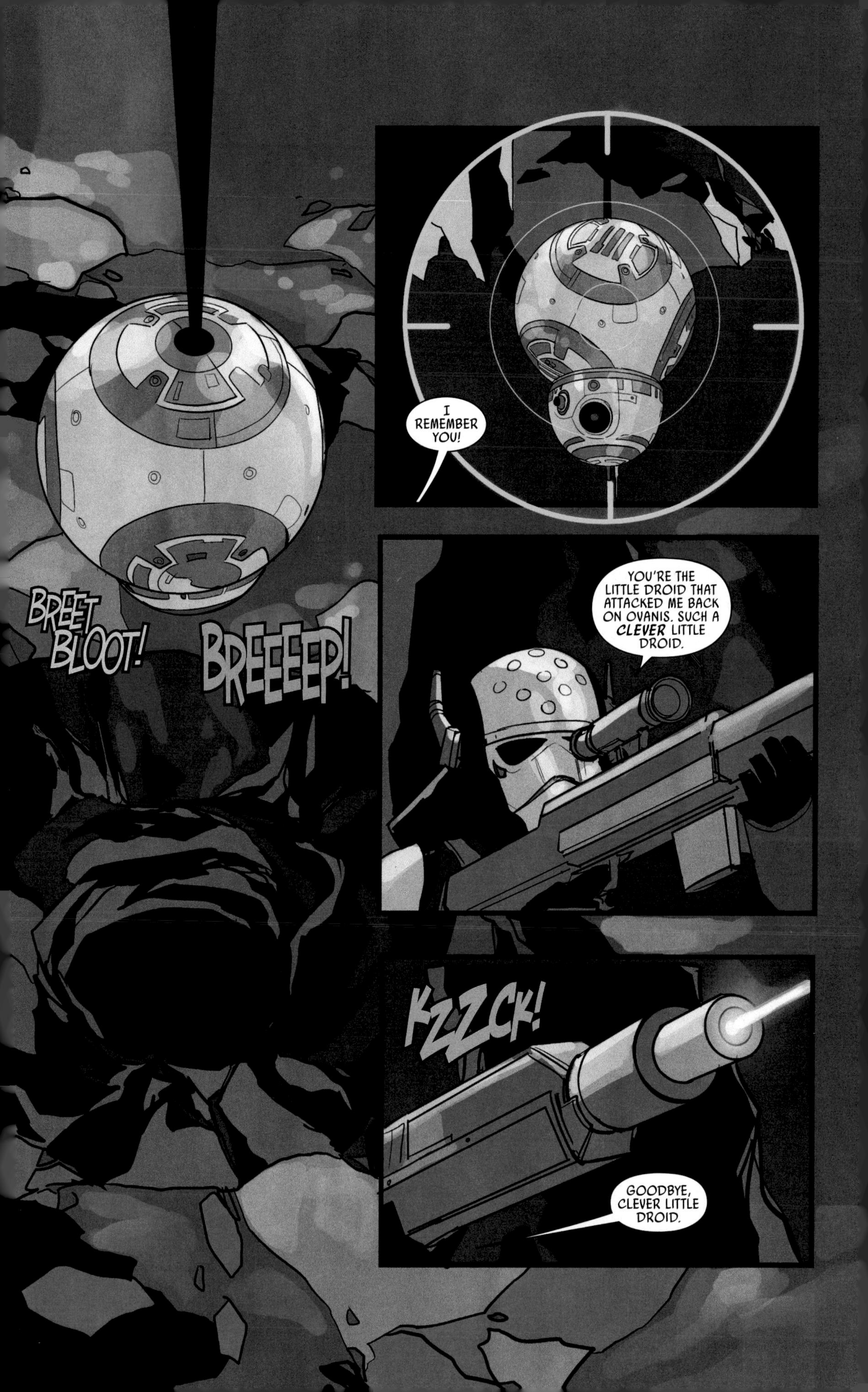
BREET BLOOT!
BREEEEP!
I REMEMBER YOU!
YOU'RE THE LITTLE DROID THAT ATTACKED ME BACK ON OVANIS. SUCH A *CLEVER* LITTLE DROID.
KZZCK!
GOODBYE, CLEVER LITTLE DROID.

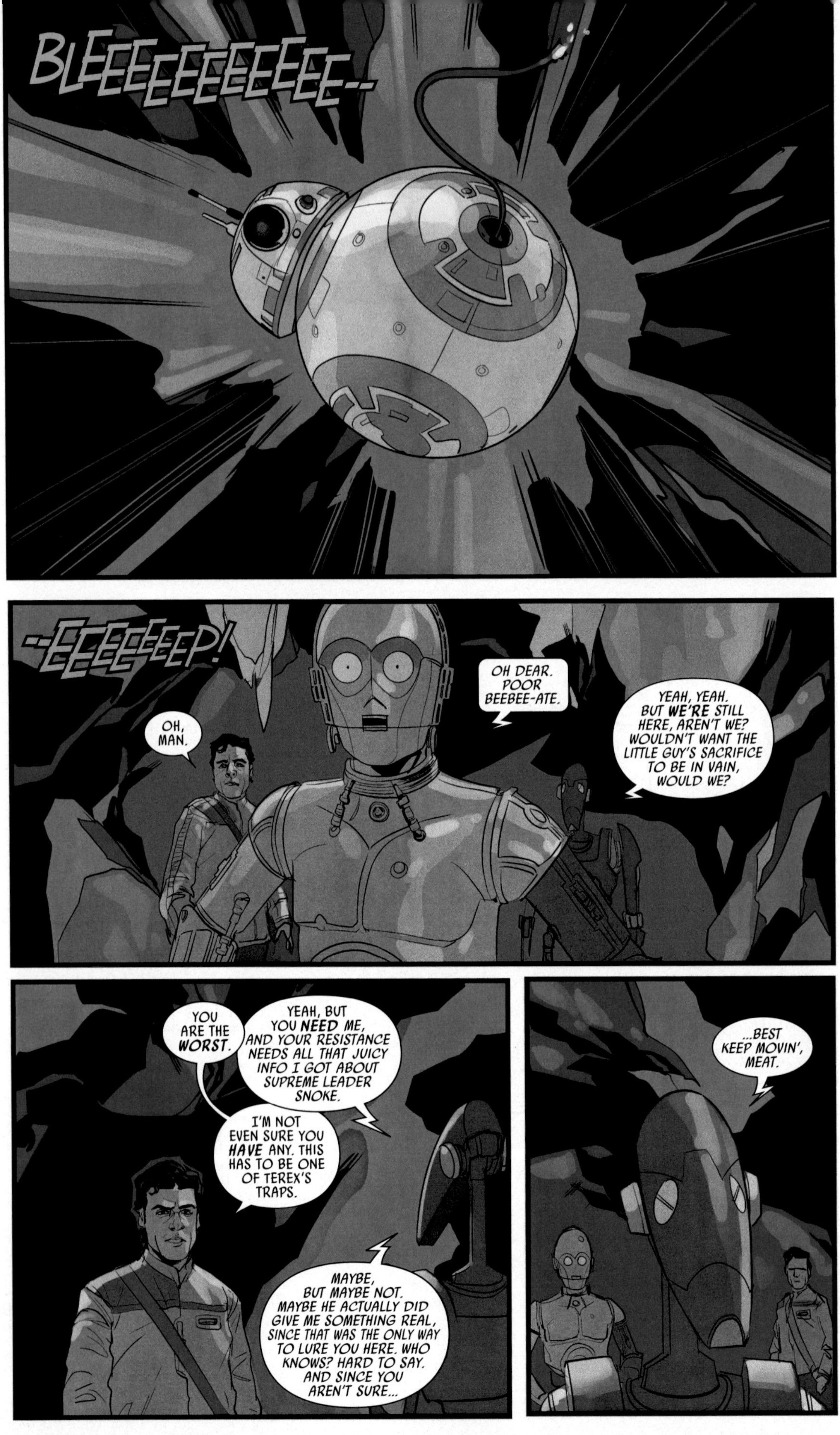

BLEEEEEEEEEEEE--
--EEEEEEEEP!
OH, MAN.
OH DEAR. POOR BEEBEE-ATE.
YEAH, YEAH. BUT WE'RE STILL HERE, AREN'T WE? WOULDN'T WANT THE LITTLE GUY'S SACRIFICE TO BE IN VAIN, WOULD WE?
YOU ARE THE WORST.
YEAH, BUT YOU NEED ME, AND YOUR RESISTANCE NEEDS ALL THAT JUICY INFO I GOT ABOUT SUPREME LEADER SNOKE.
I'M NOT EVEN SURE YOU HAVE ANY. THIS HAS TO BE ONE OF TEREX'S TRAPS.
MAYBE, BUT MAYBE NOT. MAYBE HE ACTUALLY DID GIVE ME SOMETHING REAL, SINCE THAT WAS THE ONLY WAY TO LURE YOU HERE. WHO KNOWS? HARD TO SAY. AND SINCE YOU AREN'T SURE...
...BEST KEEP MOVIN', MEAT.

ANY IDEAS, THREEPIO?

I'M SORRY, SIR. I'M NOT SURE I HAVE MUCH TO OFFER IN A SITUATION LIKE THIS. I'M A *PROTOCOL* DROID.

WE'RE BUILT TO *TALK*, NOT TO FIGHT.

I'VE NOTICED.

IN *DIPLOMACY*, WORDS CAN INDEED BE A VERY POTENT WEAPON, BUT...TEREX DOES NOT SEEM PARTICULARLY...

...DIPLOMATIC. HMM.

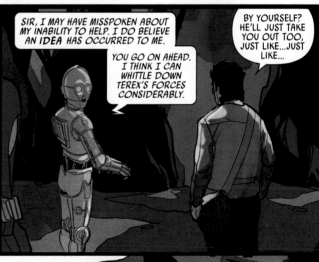

SIR, I MAY HAVE MISSPOKEN ABOUT MY INABILITY TO HELP. I DO BELIEVE AN *IDEA* HAS OCCURRED TO ME.

YOU GO ON AHEAD. I THINK I CAN WHITTLE DOWN TEREX'S FORCES CONSIDERABLY.

BY YOURSELF? HE'LL JUST TAKE YOU OUT TOO, JUST LIKE...JUST LIKE...

IT'S ALL RIGHT, SIR. I'M ONLY A DROID. I *AM* EXPENDABLE. I CAN ALWAYS BE REBUILT.

YOU, HOWEVER, CANNOT.

I DON'T KNOW HOW THINGS GOT TO THIS POINT, THREEPIO...BUT THANK YOU.

OF COURSE, SIR. IT IS MY MOST SINCERE PLEASURE.

BY ALL
THE...WHAT
NOW?

GREETINGS,
LORD TEREX!
MY NAME IS--

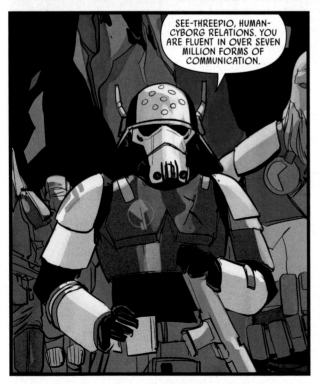

SEE-THREEPIO, HUMAN-
CYBORG RELATIONS. YOU
ARE FLUENT IN OVER SEVEN
MILLION FORMS OF
COMMUNICATION.

ER...YES.
QUITE
RIGHT.

FOR
EXAMPLE...

SQUUUEEEEERRRRGNNNNBKKKKK!*

*ALERT! ALARM! INTRUDERS! THEY HAVE COME FOR THE YOUNGLINGS!

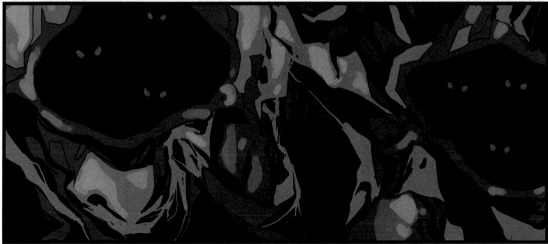

SQUEE! BRRRRKKK! SQUIIIINNNNEEEE!

...THE COMMUNICATION STRATEGIES OF THE FJOR-BATS NATIVE TO THIS SYSTEM.

NOT THE MOST SOPHISTICATED LANGUAGE, OF COURSE, BUT IT'S MOSTLY INFRASONIC.

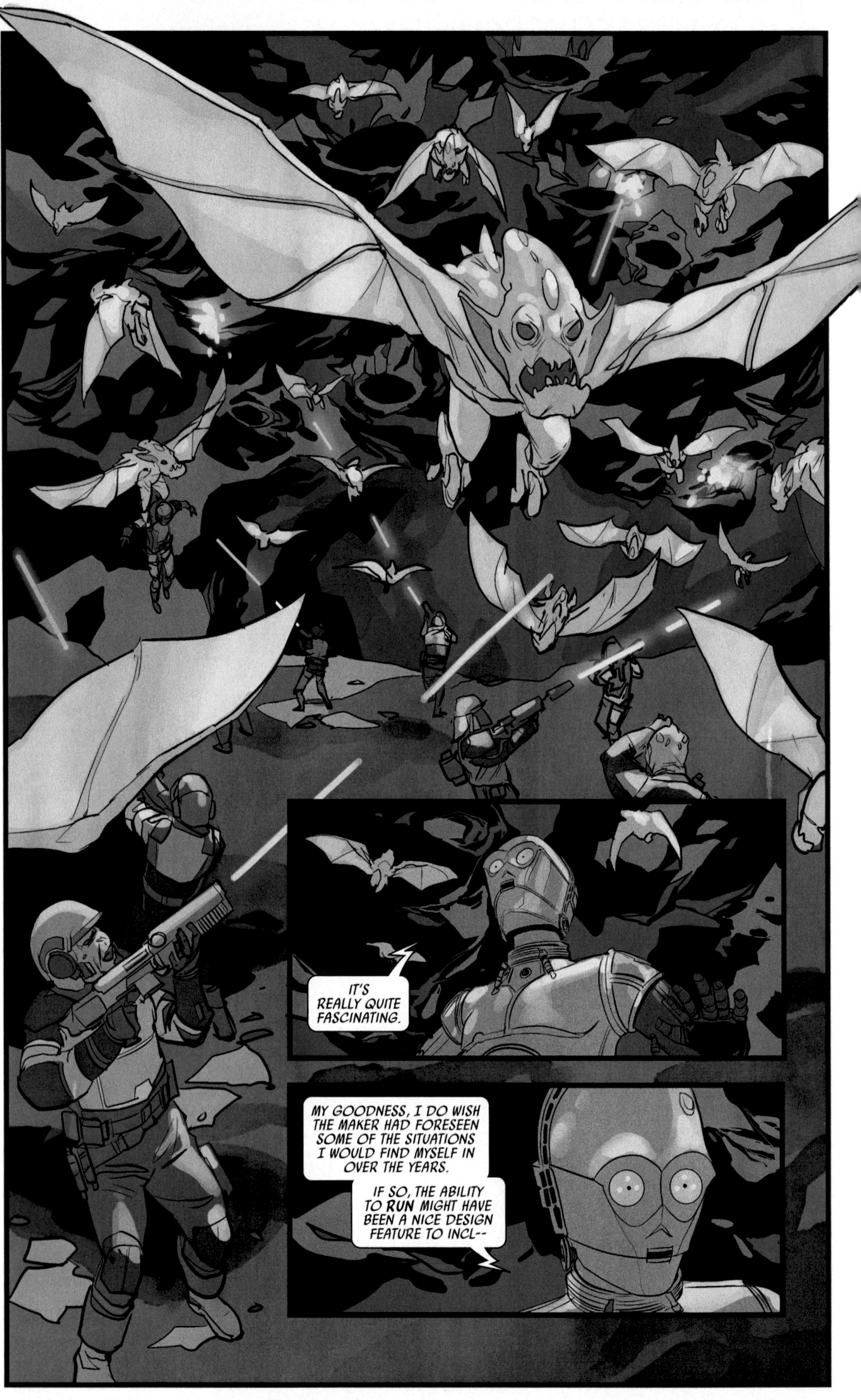
IT'S REALLY QUITE FASCINATING.
MY GOODNESS, I DO WISH THE MAKER HAD FORESEEN SOME OF THE SITUATIONS I WOULD FIND MYSELF IN OVER THE YEARS.
IF SO, THE ABILITY TO **RUN** MIGHT HAVE BEEN A NICE DESIGN FEATURE TO INCL--

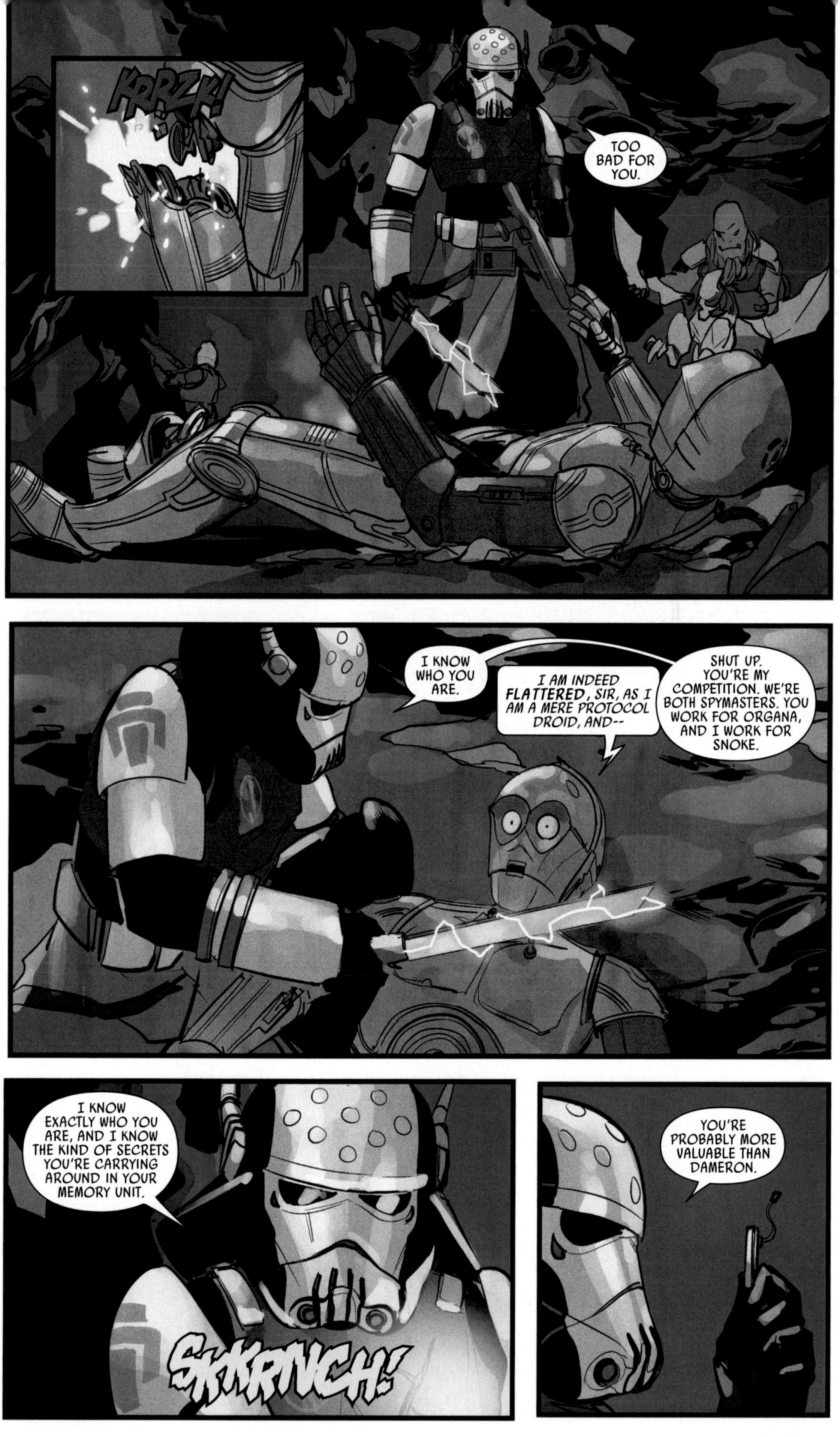
KRRZK!
TOO BAD FOR YOU.
I KNOW WHO YOU ARE.
I AM INDEED **FLATTERED**, SIR, AS I AM A MERE PROTOCOL DROID, AND--
SHUT UP. YOU'RE MY COMPETITION. WE'RE BOTH SPYMASTERS. YOU WORK FOR ORGANA, AND I WORK FOR SNOKE.
I KNOW EXACTLY WHO YOU ARE, AND I KNOW THE KIND OF SECRETS YOU'RE CARRYING AROUND IN YOUR MEMORY UNIT.
SKKRINCH!
YOU'RE PROBABLY MORE VALUABLE THAN DAMERON.

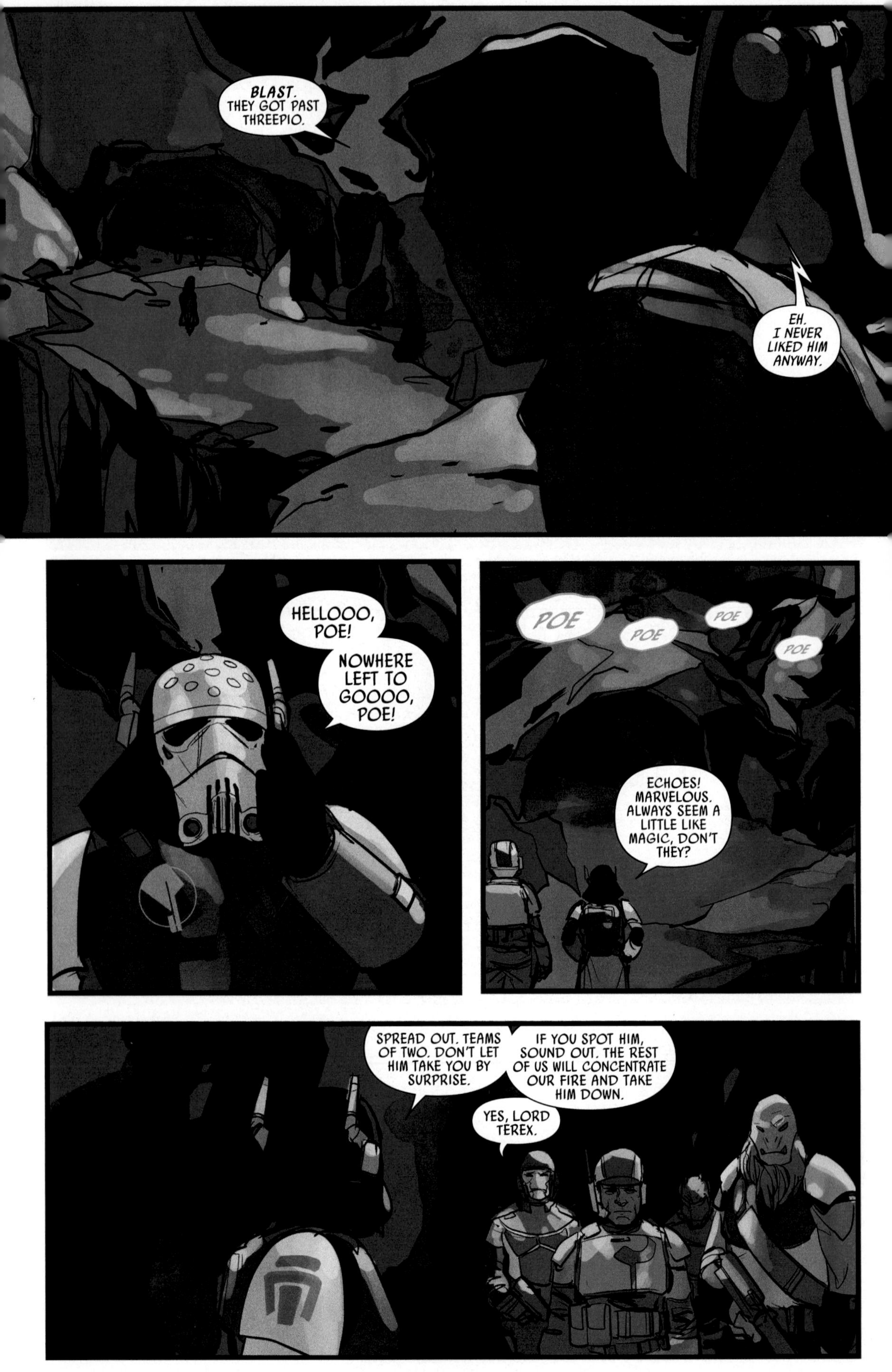
BLAST. THEY GOT PAST THREEPIO.
EH. I NEVER LIKED HIM ANYWAY.
HELLOOO, POE!
NOWHERE LEFT TO GOOOO, POE!
POE
POE
POE
POE
ECHOES! MARVELOUS. ALWAYS SEEM A LITTLE LIKE MAGIC, DON'T THEY?
SPREAD OUT. TEAMS OF TWO. DON'T LET HIM TAKE YOU BY SURPRISE.
IF YOU SPOT HIM, SOUND OUT. THE REST OF US WILL CONCENTRATE OUR FIRE AND TAKE HIM DOWN.
YES, LORD TEREX.

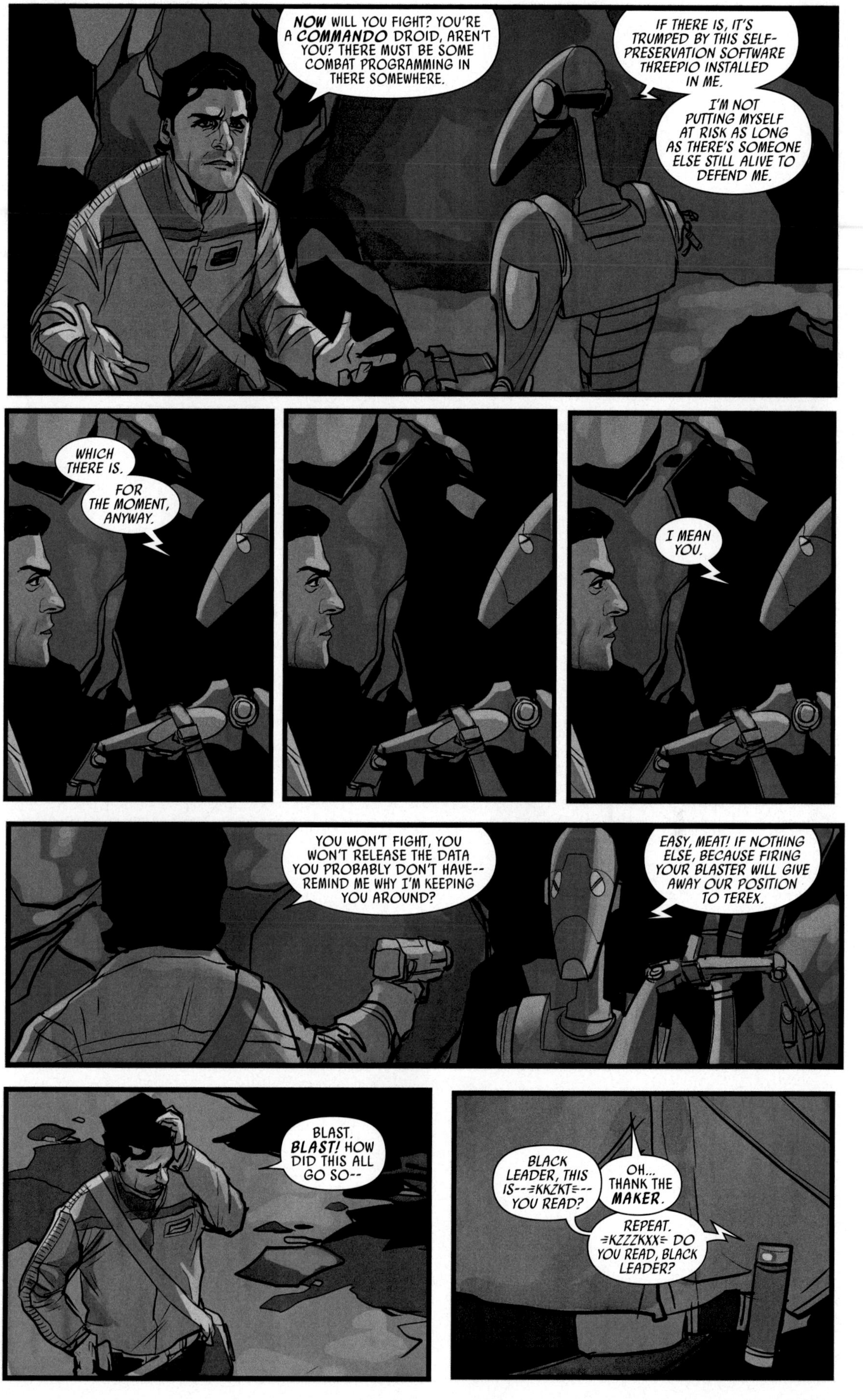
NOW WILL YOU FIGHT? YOU'RE A COMMANDO DROID, AREN'T YOU? THERE MUST BE SOME COMBAT PROGRAMMING IN THERE SOMEWHERE.
IF THERE IS, IT'S TRUMPED BY THIS SELF-PRESERVATION SOFTWARE THREEPIO INSTALLED IN ME.
I'M NOT PUTTING MYSELF AT RISK AS LONG AS THERE'S SOMEONE ELSE STILL ALIVE TO DEFEND ME.
WHICH THERE IS.
FOR THE MOMENT, ANYWAY.
I MEAN YOU.
YOU WON'T FIGHT, YOU WON'T RELEASE THE DATA YOU PROBABLY DON'T HAVE-- REMIND ME WHY I'M KEEPING YOU AROUND?
EASY, MEAT! IF NOTHING ELSE, BECAUSE FIRING YOUR BLASTER WILL GIVE AWAY OUR POSITION TO TEREX.
BLAST. BLAST! HOW DID THIS ALL GO SO--
BLACK LEADER, THIS IS--≠KKZKT≠--YOU READ?
OH... THANK THE MAKER.
REPEAT. ≠KZZZKXX≠ DO YOU READ, BLACK LEADER?

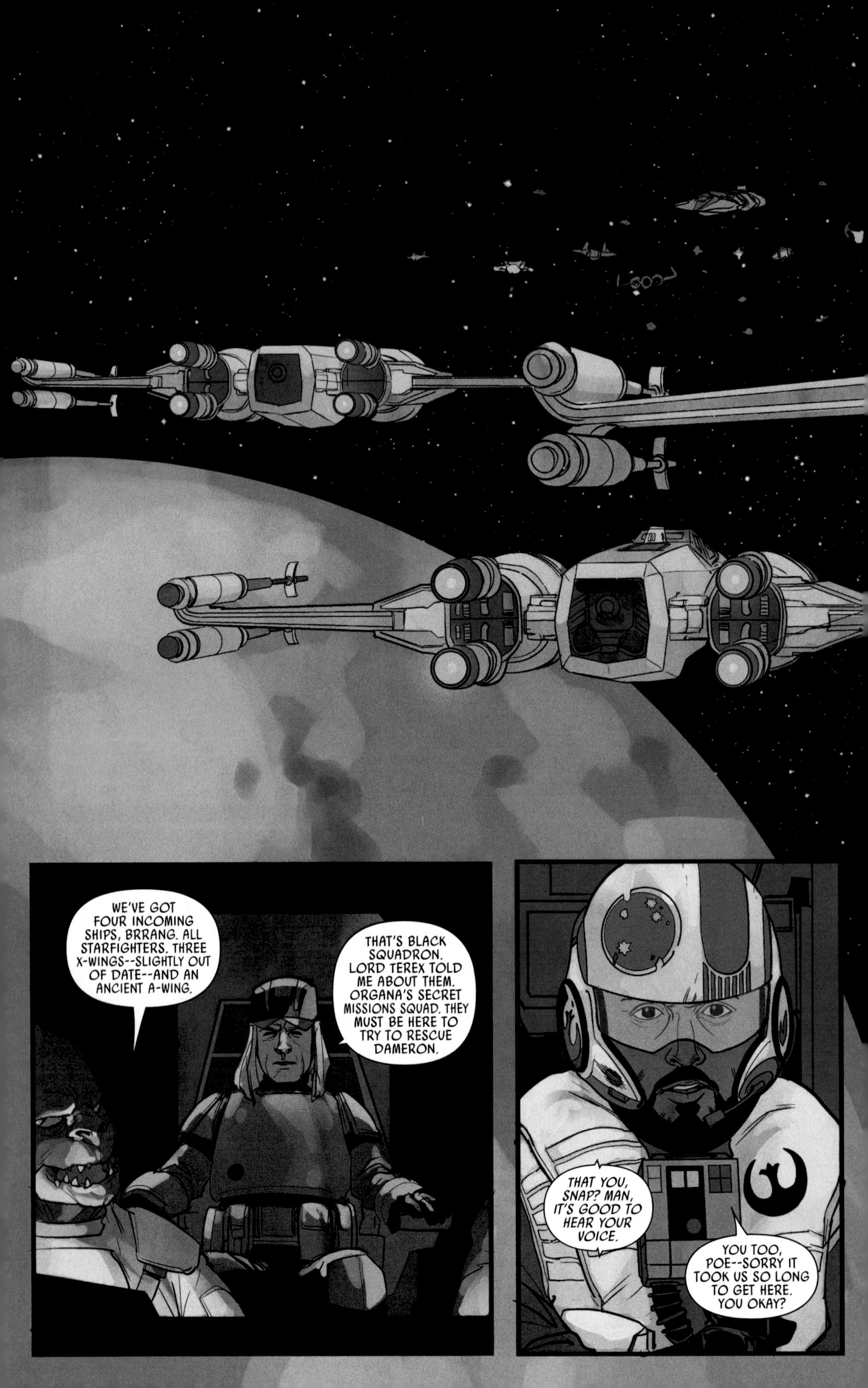
WE'VE GOT FOUR INCOMING SHIPS, BRRANG. ALL STARFIGHTERS. THREE X-WINGS--SLIGHTLY OUT OF DATE--AND AN ANCIENT A-WING.
THAT'S BLACK SQUADRON. LORD TEREX TOLD ME ABOUT THEM. ORGANA'S SECRET MISSIONS SQUAD. THEY MUST BE HERE TO TRY TO RESCUE DAMERON.
THAT YOU, SNAP? MAN, IT'S GOOD TO HEAR YOUR VOICE.
YOU TOO, POE--SORRY IT TOOK US SO LONG TO GET HERE. YOU OKAY?

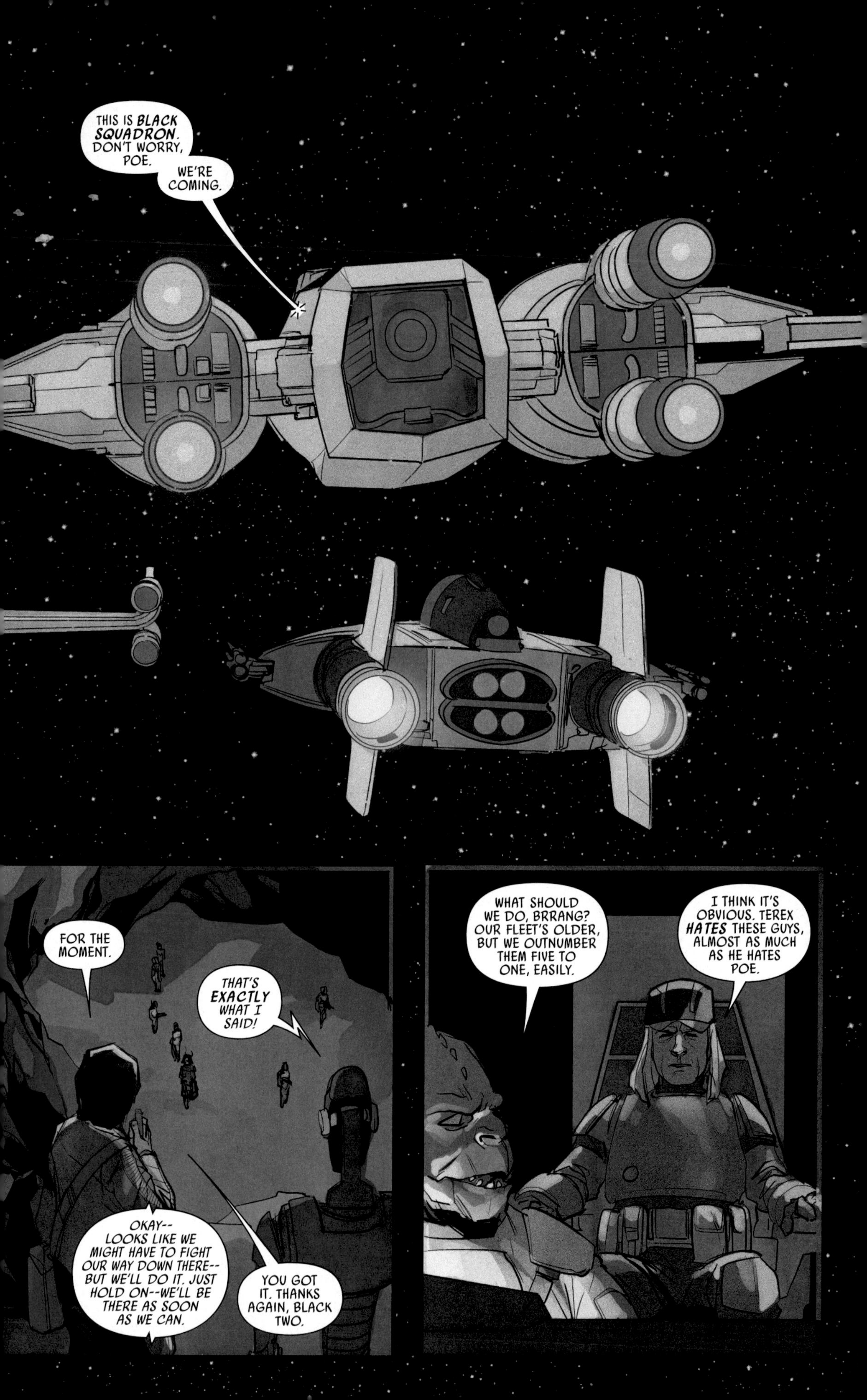
THIS IS BLACK SQUADRON. DON'T WORRY, POE.
WE'RE COMING.
FOR THE MOMENT.
THAT'S EXACTLY WHAT I SAID!
OKAY-- LOOKS LIKE WE MIGHT HAVE TO FIGHT OUR WAY DOWN THERE-- BUT WE'LL DO IT. JUST HOLD ON--WE'LL BE THERE AS SOON AS WE CAN.
YOU GOT IT. THANKS AGAIN, BLACK TWO.
WHAT SHOULD WE DO, BRRANG? OUR FLEET'S OLDER, BUT WE OUTNUMBER THEM FIVE TO ONE, EASILY.
I THINK IT'S OBVIOUS. TEREX HATES THESE GUYS, ALMOST AS MUCH AS HE HATES POE.

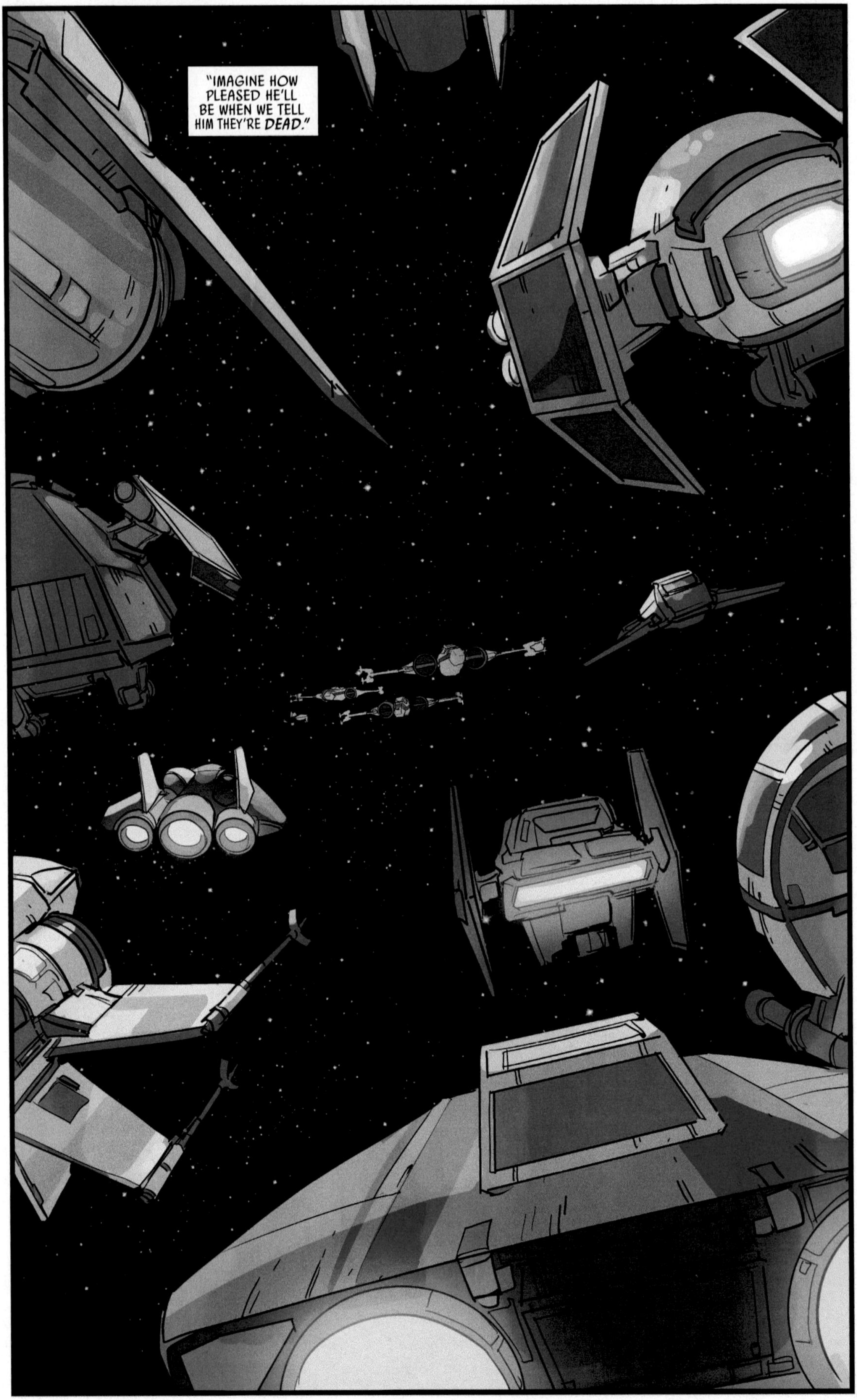
"IMAGINE HOW PLEASED HE'LL BE WHEN WE TELL HIM THEY'RE *DEAD*."

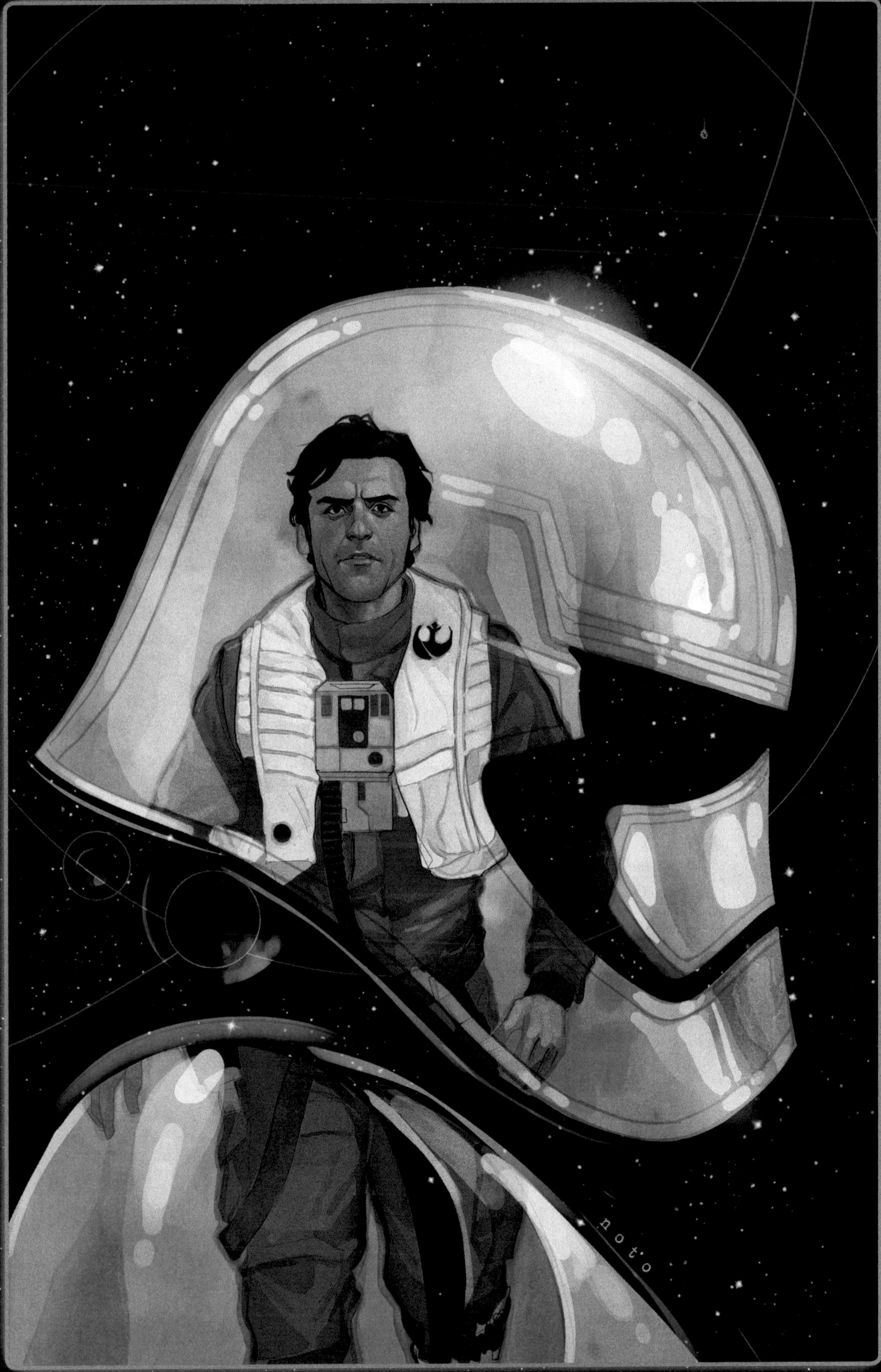
noto

13

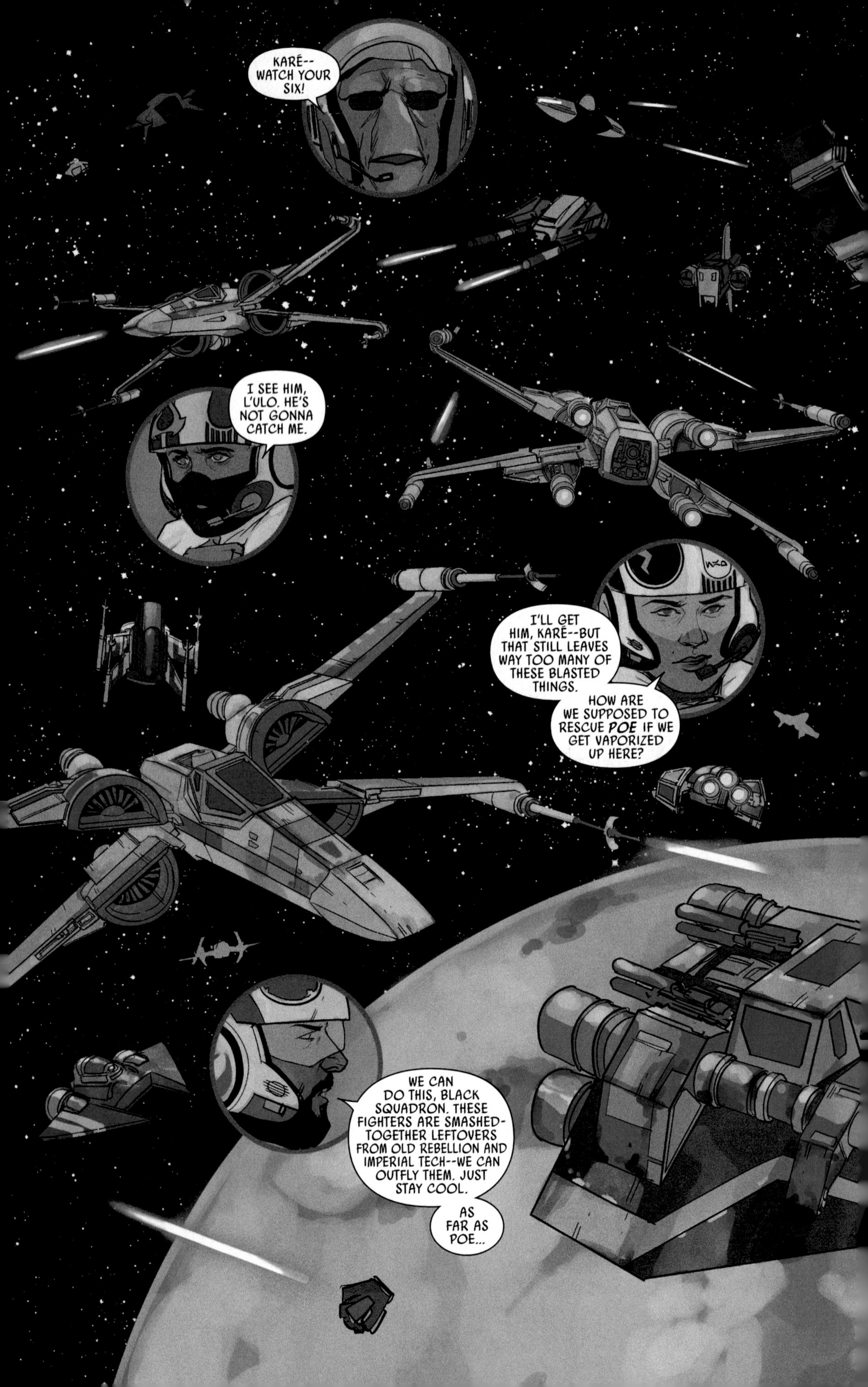
KARÉ-- WATCH YOUR SIX!
I SEE HIM, L'ULO. HE'S NOT GONNA CATCH ME.
I'LL GET HIM, KARÉ--BUT THAT STILL LEAVES WAY TOO MANY OF THESE BLASTED THINGS.
HOW ARE WE SUPPOSED TO RESCUE POE IF WE GET VAPORIZED UP HERE?
WE CAN DO THIS, BLACK SQUADRON. THESE FIGHTERS ARE SMASHED-TOGETHER LEFTOVERS FROM OLD REBELLION AND IMPERIAL TECH--WE CAN OUTFLY THEM. JUST STAY COOL.
AS FAR AS POE...

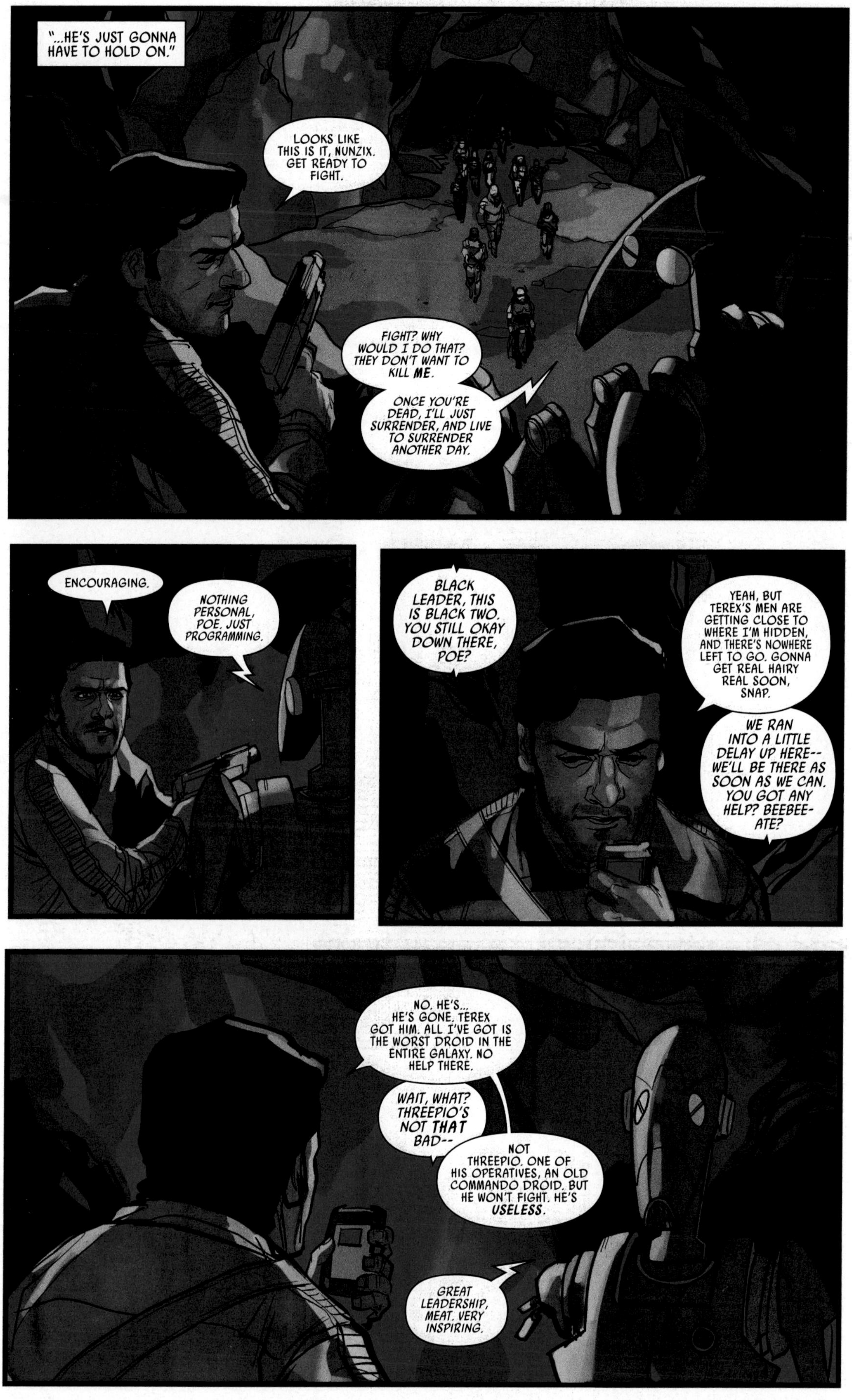
"...HE'S JUST GONNA HAVE TO HOLD ON."
LOOKS LIKE THIS IS IT, NUNZIX. GET READY TO FIGHT.
FIGHT? WHY WOULD I DO THAT? THEY DON'T WANT TO KILL ME.
ONCE YOU'RE DEAD, I'LL JUST SURRENDER, AND LIVE TO SURRENDER ANOTHER DAY.
ENCOURAGING.
NOTHING PERSONAL, POE. JUST PROGRAMMING.
BLACK LEADER, THIS IS BLACK TWO. YOU STILL OKAY DOWN THERE, POE?
YEAH, BUT TEREX'S MEN ARE GETTING CLOSE TO WHERE I'M HIDDEN, AND THERE'S NOWHERE LEFT TO GO. GONNA GET REAL HAIRY REAL SOON, SNAP.
WE RAN INTO A LITTLE DELAY UP HERE-- WE'LL BE THERE AS SOON AS WE CAN. YOU GOT ANY HELP? BEEBEE-ATE?
NO. HE'S... HE'S GONE. TEREX GOT HIM. ALL I'VE GOT IS THE WORST DROID IN THE ENTIRE GALAXY. NO HELP THERE.
WAIT, WHAT? THREEPIO'S NOT THAT BAD--
NOT THREEPIO. ONE OF HIS OPERATIVES, AN OLD COMMANDO DROID. BUT HE WON'T FIGHT. HE'S USELESS.
GREAT LEADERSHIP, MEAT. VERY INSPIRING.

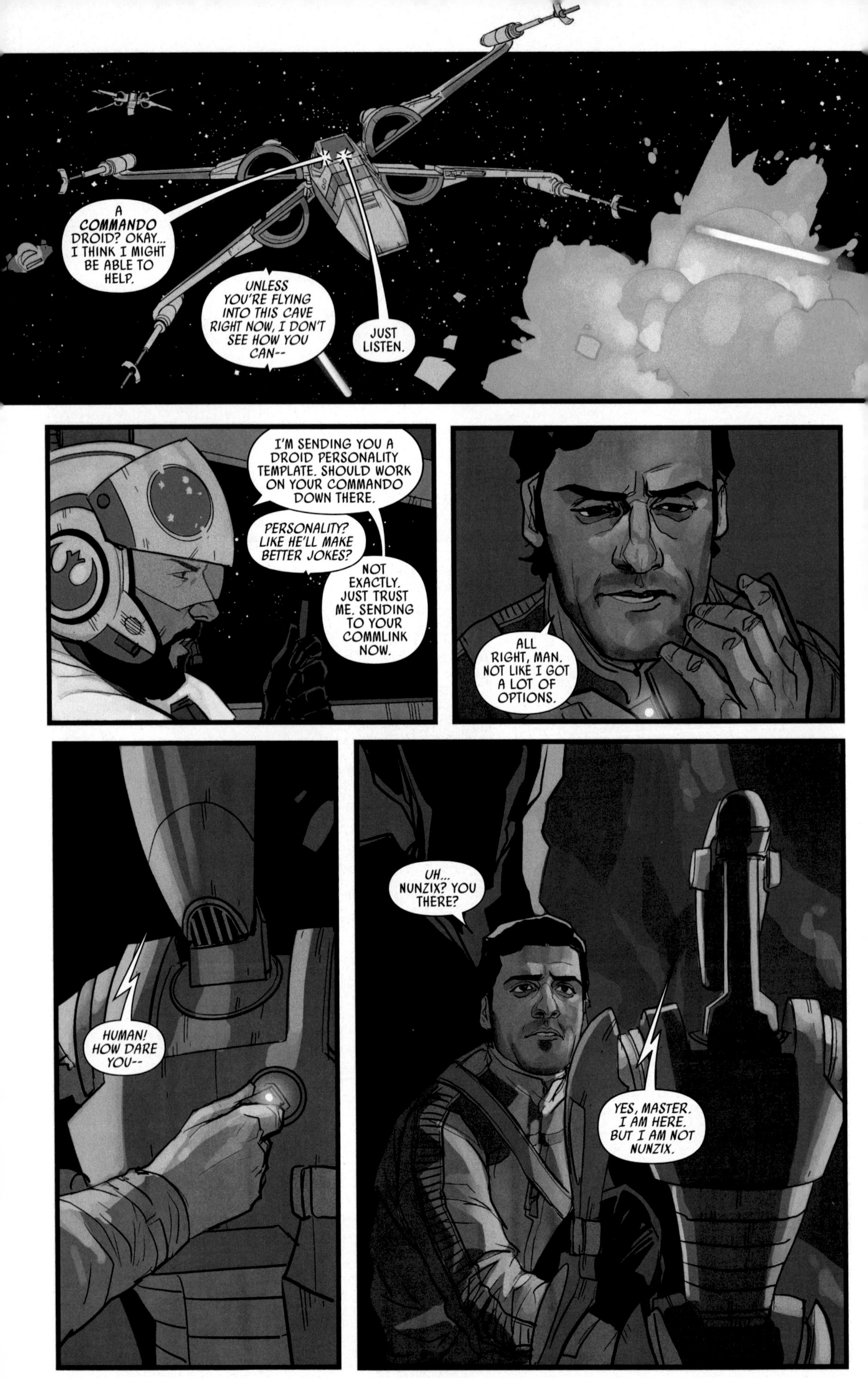
A COMMANDO DROID? OKAY... I THINK I MIGHT BE ABLE TO HELP.
UNLESS YOU'RE FLYING INTO THIS CAVE RIGHT NOW, I DON'T SEE HOW YOU CAN--
JUST LISTEN.
I'M SENDING YOU A DROID PERSONALITY TEMPLATE. SHOULD WORK ON YOUR COMMANDO DOWN THERE.
PERSONALITY? LIKE HE'LL MAKE BETTER JOKES?
NOT EXACTLY. JUST TRUST ME. SENDING TO YOUR COMMLINK NOW.
ALL RIGHT, MAN. NOT LIKE I GOT A LOT OF OPTIONS.
HUMAN! HOW DARE YOU--
UH... NUNZIX? YOU THERE?
YES, MASTER. I AM HERE. BUT I AM NOT NUNZIX.

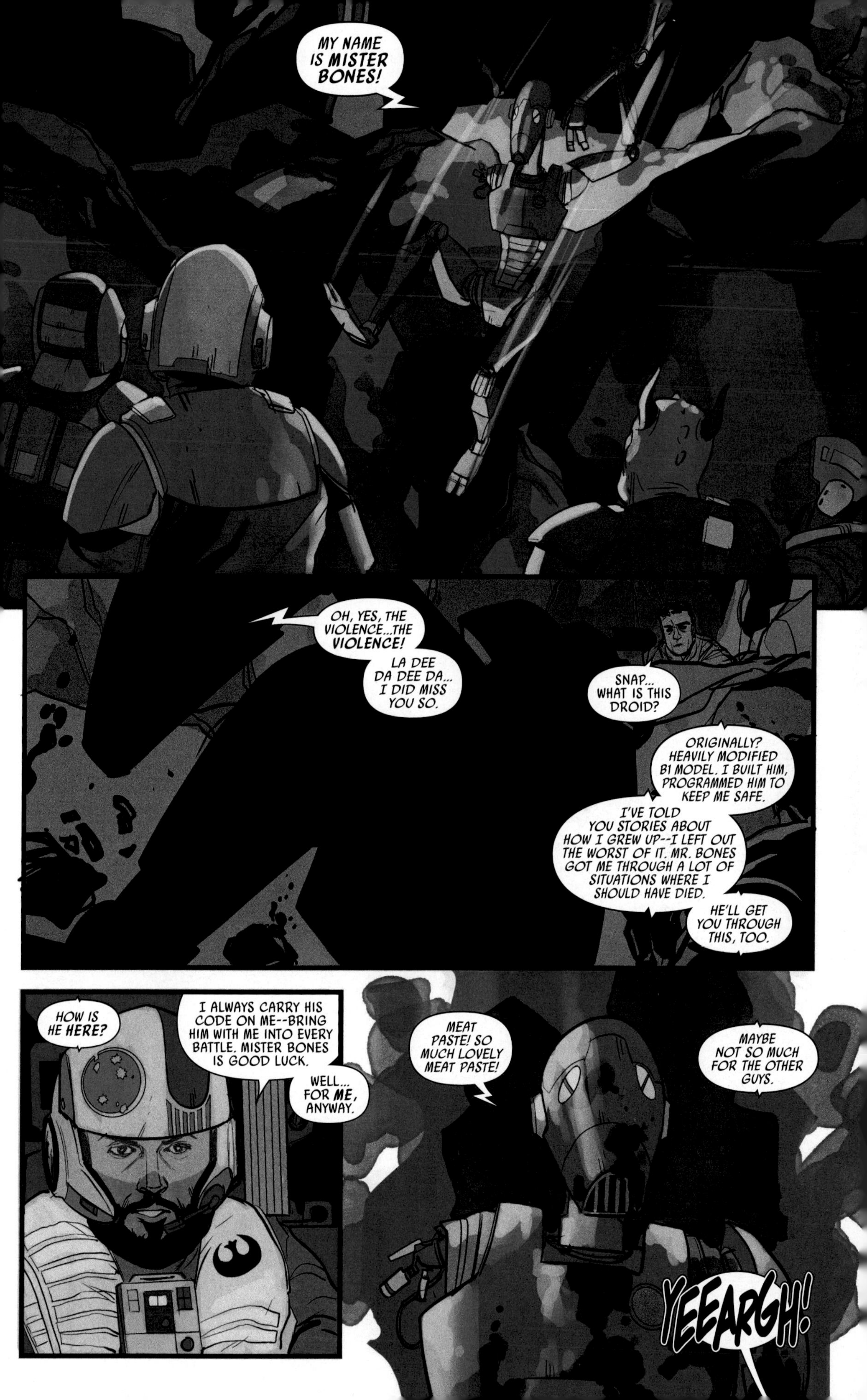
MY NAME IS MISTER BONES!
OH, YES, THE VIOLENCE...THE VIOLENCE!
LA DEE DA DEE DA... I DID MISS YOU SO.
SNAP... WHAT IS THIS DROID?
ORIGINALLY? HEAVILY MODIFIED B1 MODEL. I BUILT HIM, PROGRAMMED HIM TO KEEP ME SAFE.
I'VE TOLD YOU STORIES ABOUT HOW I GREW UP--I LEFT OUT THE WORST OF IT. MR. BONES GOT ME THROUGH A LOT OF SITUATIONS WHERE I SHOULD HAVE DIED.
HE'LL GET YOU THROUGH THIS, TOO.
HOW IS HE HERE?
I ALWAYS CARRY HIS CODE ON ME--BRING HIM WITH ME INTO EVERY BATTLE. MISTER BONES IS GOOD LUCK.
WELL... FOR ME, ANYWAY.
MEAT PASTE! SO MUCH LOVELY MEAT PASTE!
MAYBE NOT SO MUCH FOR THE OTHER GUYS.
YEEARGH!

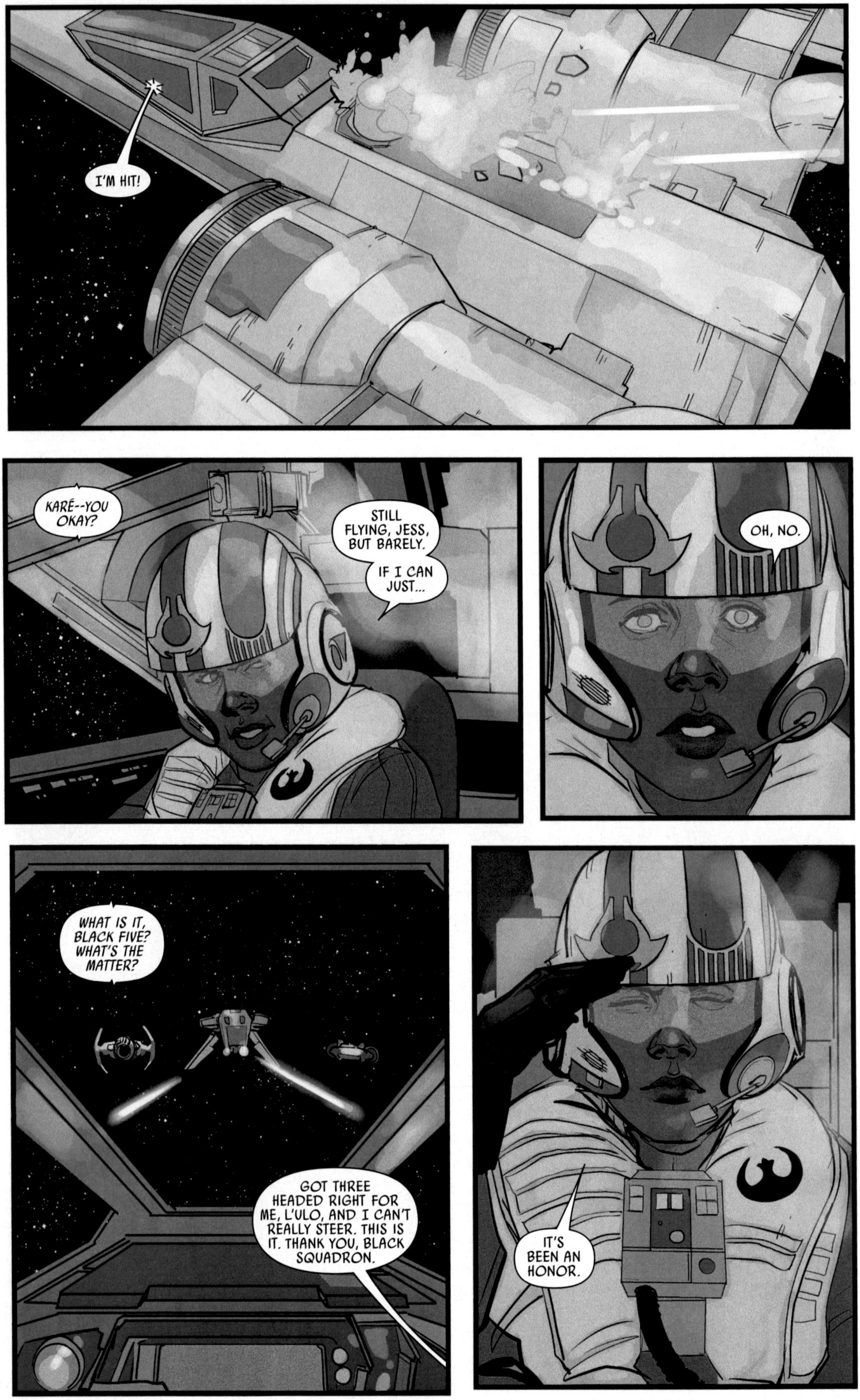
I'M HIT!
KARÉ--YOU OKAY?
STILL FLYING, JESS, BUT BARELY.
IF I CAN JUST...
OH, NO.
WHAT IS IT, BLACK FIVE? WHAT'S THE MATTER?
GOT THREE HEADED RIGHT FOR ME, L'ULO, AND I CAN'T REALLY STEER. THIS IS IT. THANK YOU, BLACK SQUADRON.
IT'S BEEN AN HONOR.

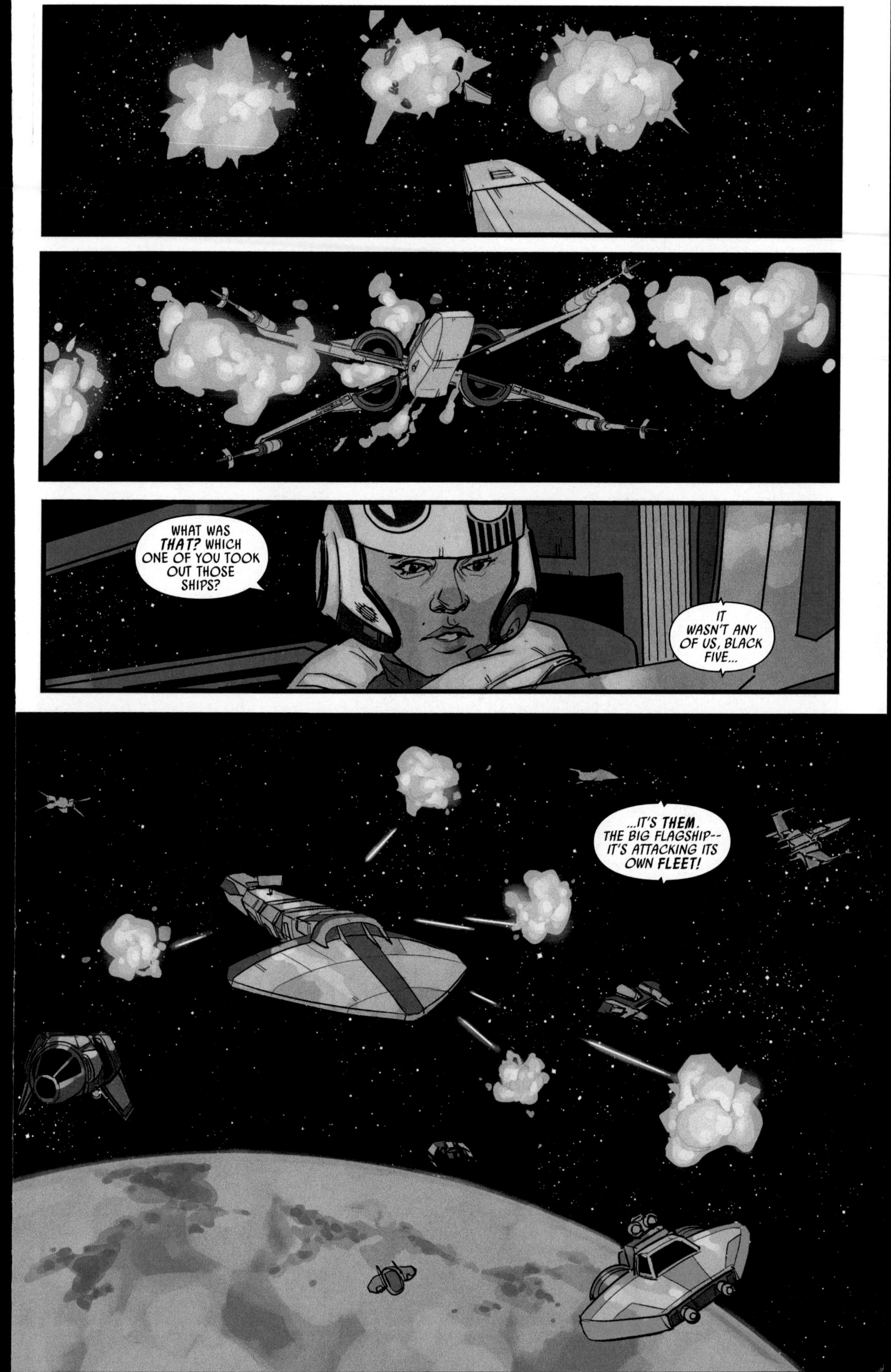
WHAT WAS THAT? WHICH ONE OF YOU TOOK OUT THOSE SHIPS?
IT WASN'T ANY OF US, BLACK FIVE...
...IT'S THEM. THE BIG FLAGSHIP-- IT'S ATTACKING ITS OWN FLEET!

WHAT IS *HAPPENING?* WHY ARE WE ATTACKING OUR OWN *SHIPS?*

WE'RE NOT DOING IT, BRRANG. WE'RE LOCKED OUT OF THE CONTROL SYSTEMS. THE *CARRION SPIKE* IS TARGETING OUR FLEET ON ITS OWN!

THAT'S NOT ALL--A BUNCH OF ESCAPE PODS JUST LAUNCHED.

ESCAPE PODS? WHO IN ALL THE BLASTED HELLS IS *ESCAPING?*

BLACK SQUADRON-- COME IN BLACK SQUADRON. DO YOU READ?

WHAT THE... IS THAT *ODDY MUVA?* HOW ARE YOU--

JUST LISTEN, KARÉ! I SABOTAGED THE CARRION SPIKE'S BATTLE COMPUTERS TO AUTO-TARGET ANYTHING WITHOUT A RESISTANCE TRANSPONDER. SHOULD BUY US SOME TIME.

TEREX WAS KEEPING *SLAVES* ON HIS SHIP--I GOT THEM OUT. WE'RE IN *ESCAPE PODS*--FILLED UP EVERY LAST ONE THE SPIKE HAD.

BUT...THESE PODS DON'T HAVE *WEAPONS.* WE'LL TRY TO REACH THE SURFACE OF THAT PLANET, BUT WITH ALL THOSE RANC FIGHTERS OUT THERE...

UNDERSTOOD, ODDY. WE'LL KEEP YOU SAFE.

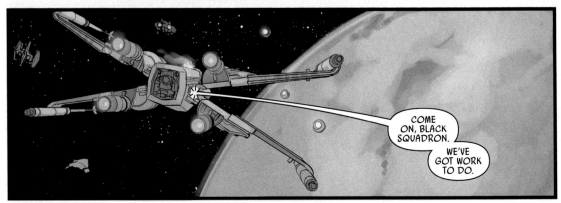

COME ON, BLACK SQUADRON.

WE'VE GOT WORK TO DO.

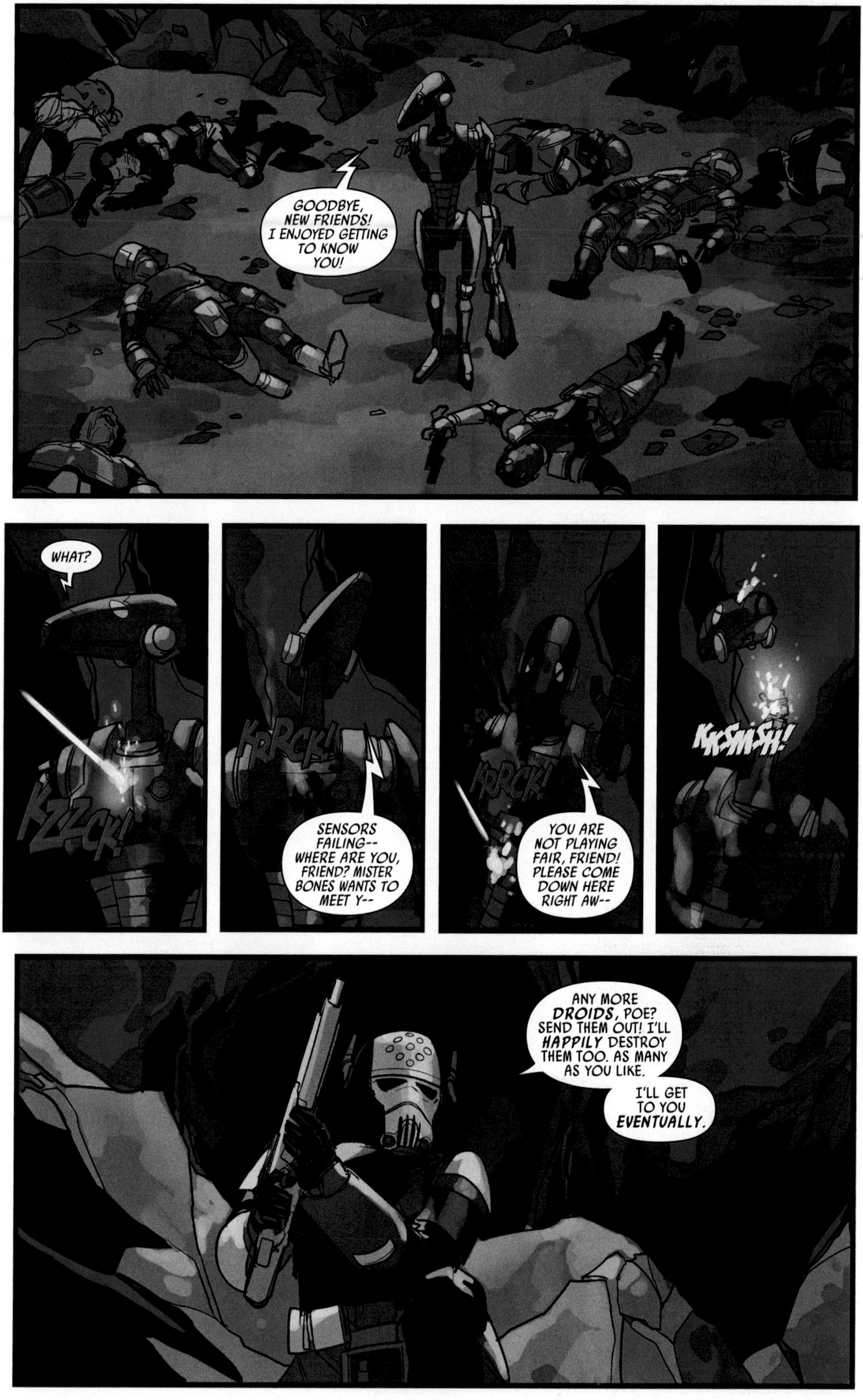
GOODBYE, NEW FRIENDS! I ENJOYED GETTING TO KNOW YOU!
WHAT?
KZZCK!
KRRCK!
SENSORS FAILING-- WHERE ARE YOU, FRIEND? MISTER BONES WANTS TO MEET Y--
KRRCK!
YOU ARE NOT PLAYING FAIR, FRIEND! PLEASE COME DOWN HERE RIGHT AW--
KKSMSH!
ANY MORE DROIDS, POE? SEND THEM OUT! I'LL HAPPILY DESTROY THEM TOO. AS MANY AS YOU LIKE.
I'LL GET TO YOU EVENTUALLY.

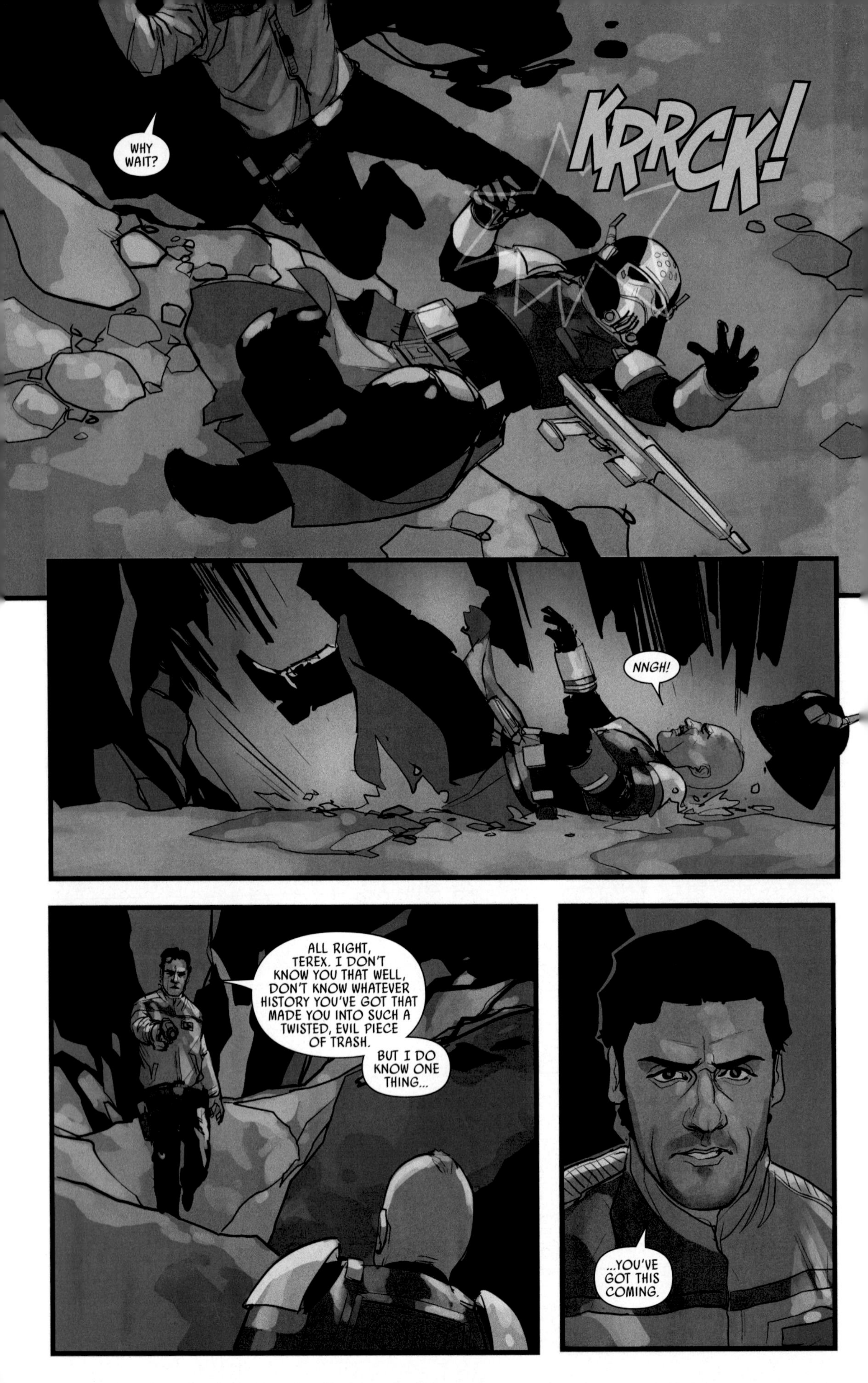
WHY WAIT?
KRRCK!
NNGH!
ALL RIGHT, TEREX. I DON'T KNOW YOU THAT WELL, DON'T KNOW WHATEVER HISTORY YOU'VE GOT THAT MADE YOU INTO SUCH A TWISTED, EVIL PIECE OF TRASH.
BUT I DO KNOW ONE THING...
...YOU'VE GOT THIS COMING.

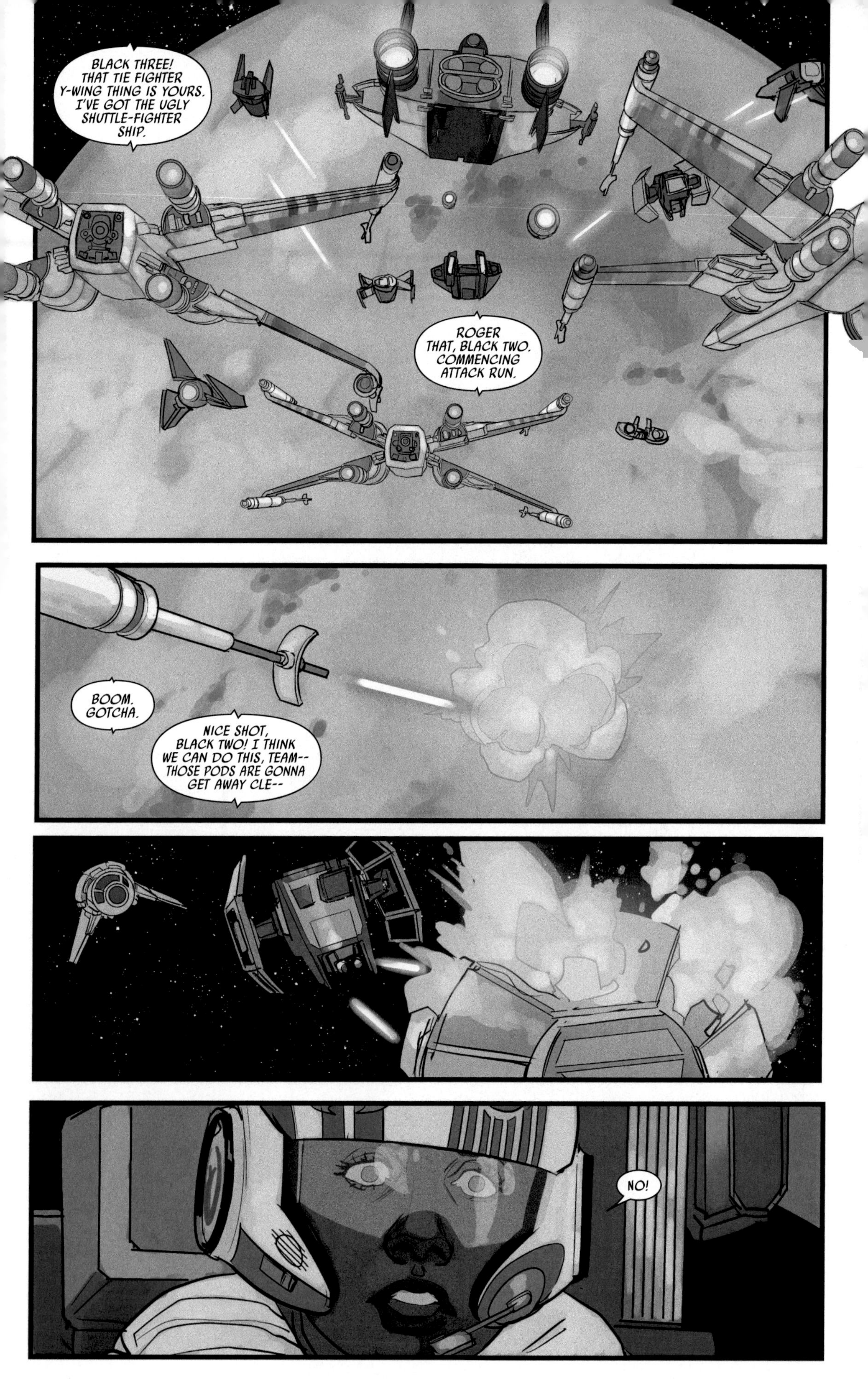
BLACK THREE! THAT TIE FIGHTER Y-WING THING IS YOURS. I'VE GOT THE UGLY SHUTTLE-FIGHTER SHIP.
ROGER THAT, BLACK TWO. COMMENCING ATTACK RUN.
BOOM. GOTCHA.
NICE SHOT, BLACK TWO! I THINK WE CAN DO THIS, TEAM-- THOSE PODS ARE GONNA GET AWAY CLE--
NO!

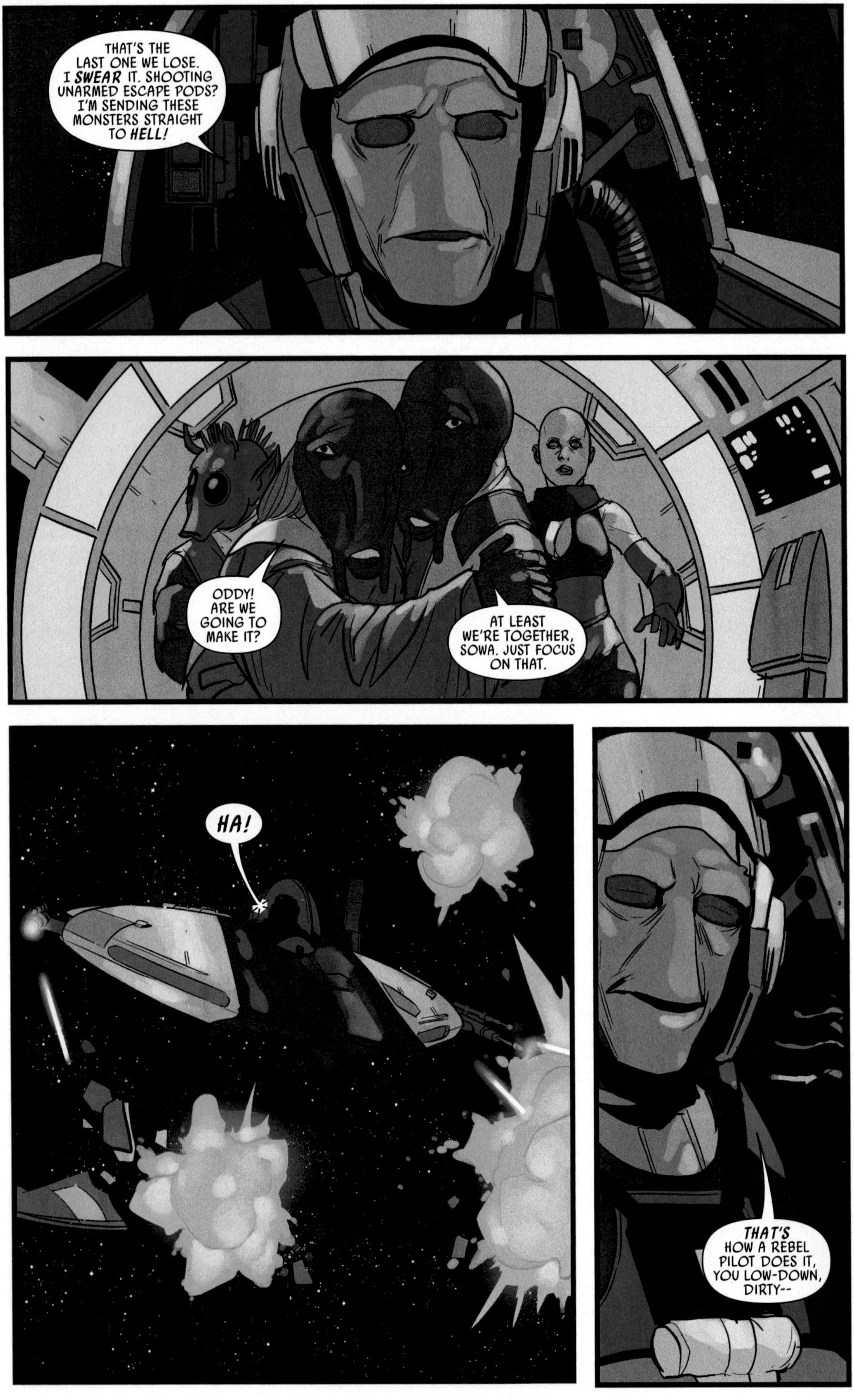
THAT'S THE LAST ONE WE LOSE. I SWEAR IT. SHOOTING UNARMED ESCAPE PODS? I'M SENDING THESE MONSTERS STRAIGHT TO HELL!
ODDY! ARE WE GOING TO MAKE IT?
AT LEAST WE'RE TOGETHER, SOWA. JUST FOCUS ON THAT.
HA!
THAT'S HOW A REBEL PILOT DOES IT, YOU LOW-DOWN, DIRTY--

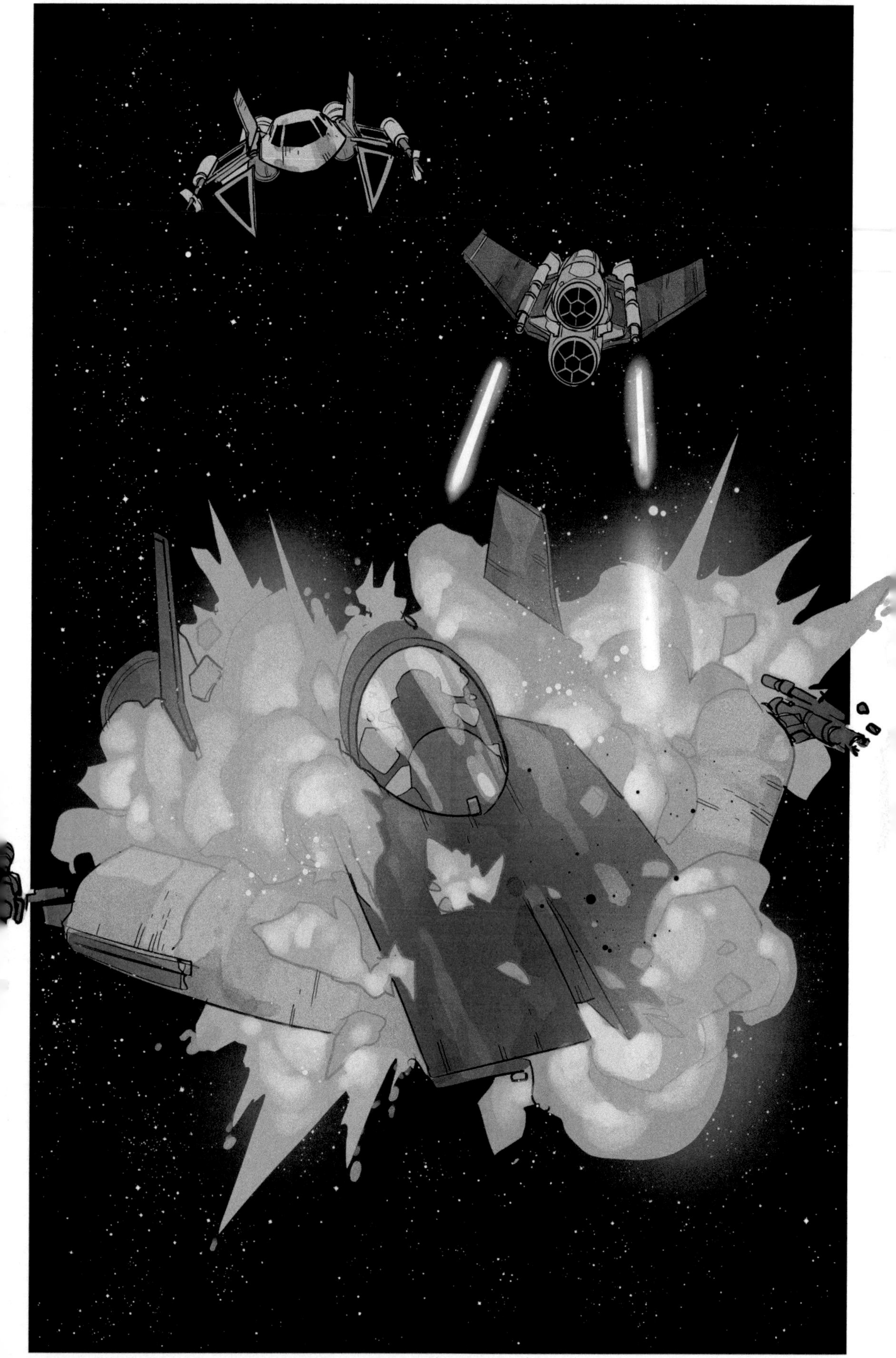

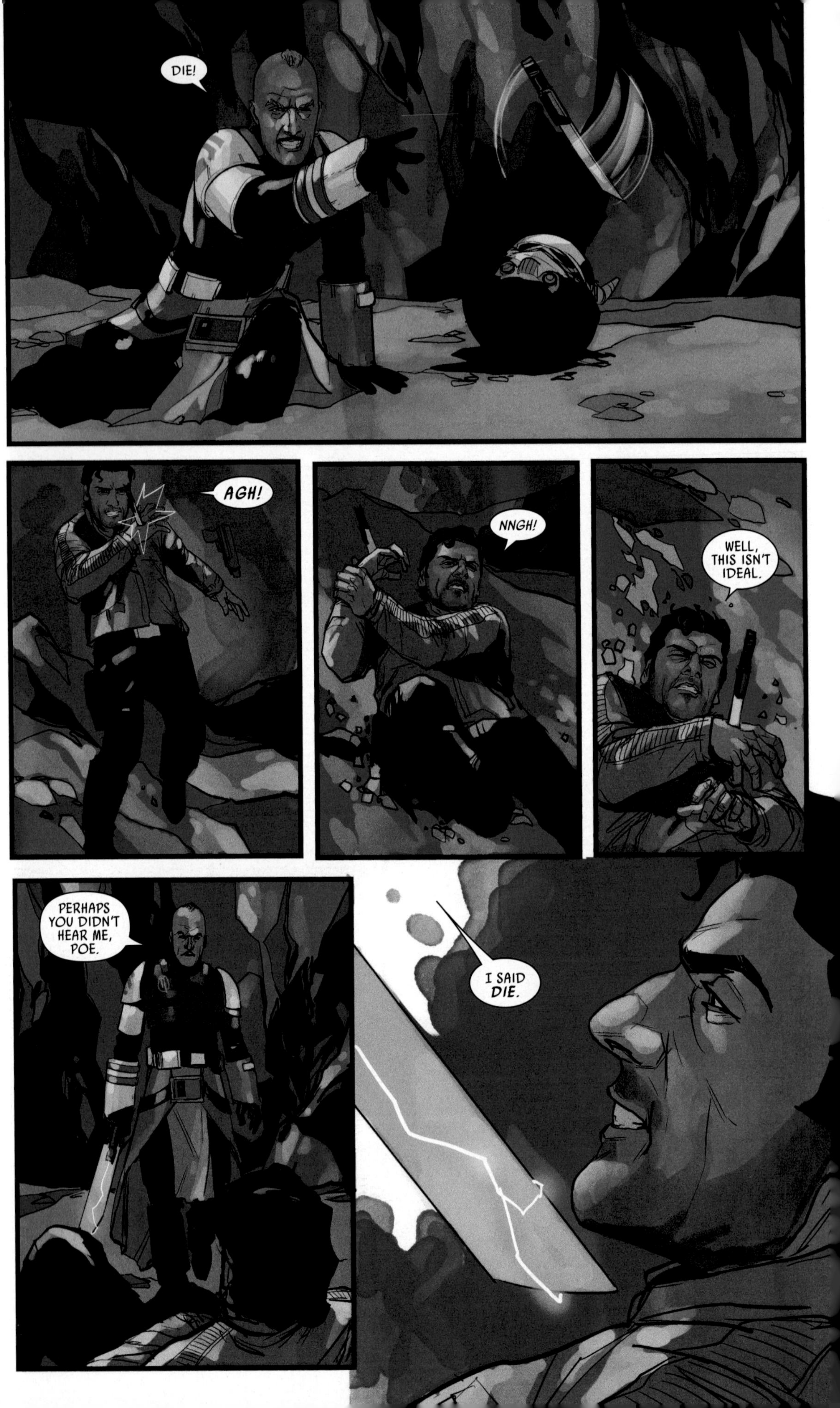
DIE!
AGH!
NNGH!
WELL, THIS ISN'T IDEAL.
PERHAPS YOU DIDN'T HEAR ME, POE.
I SAID DIE.

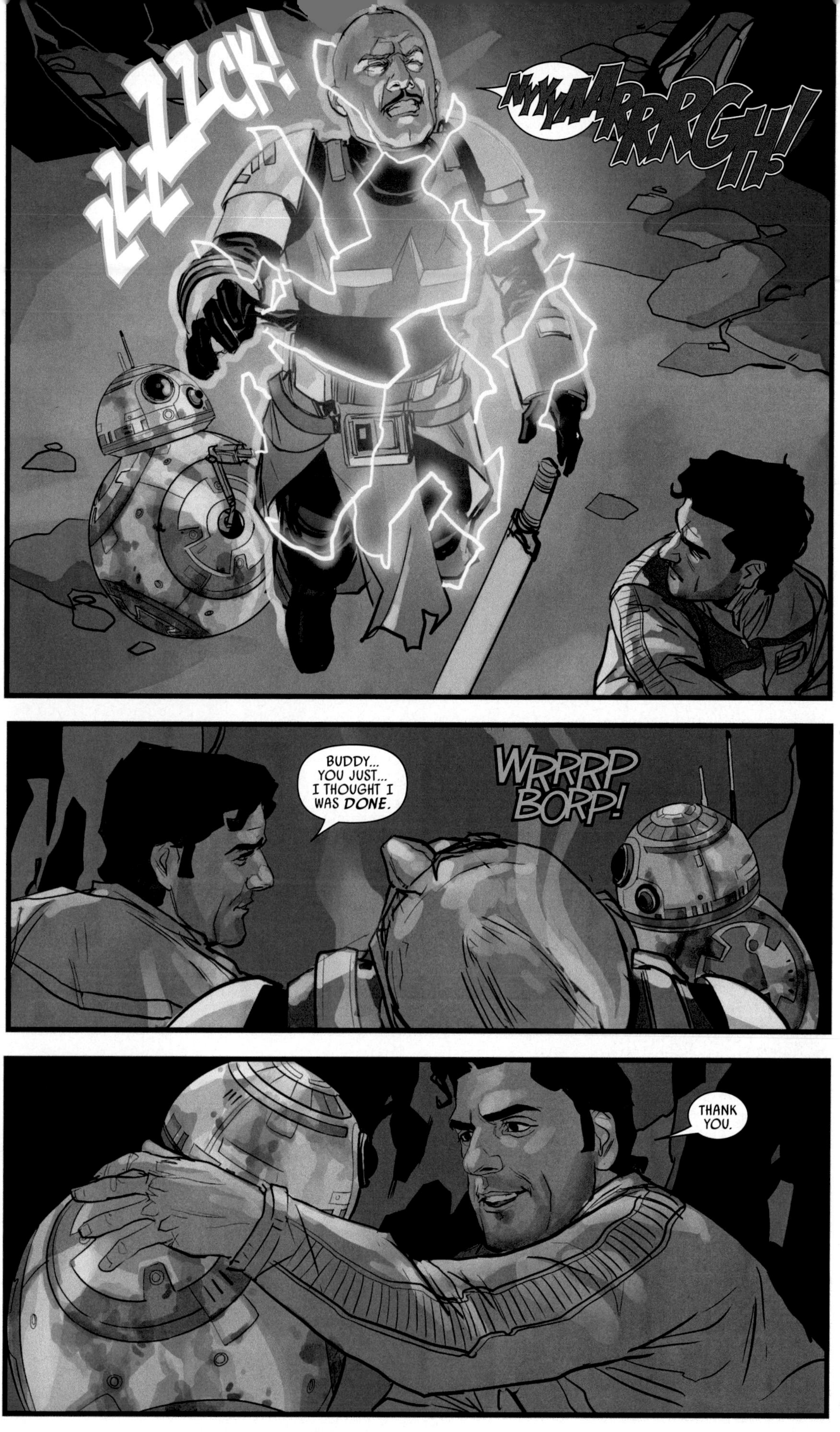
ZZZZCK!
NYYAARRRGH!
BUDDY... YOU JUST... I THOUGHT I WAS DONE.
WRRRP BORP!
THANK YOU.

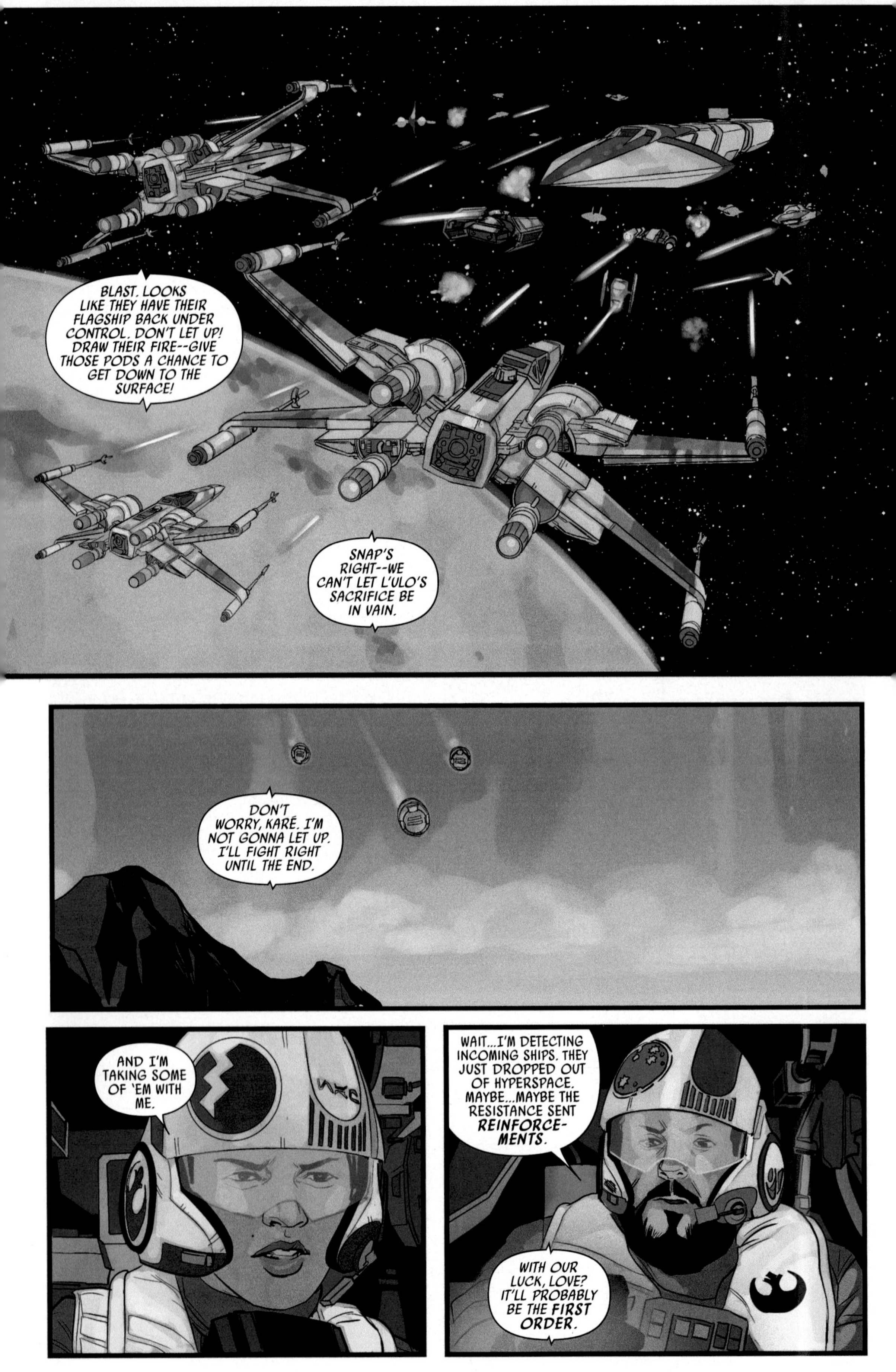
BLAST. LOOKS LIKE THEY HAVE THEIR FLAGSHIP BACK UNDER CONTROL. DON'T LET UP! DRAW THEIR FIRE--GIVE THOSE PODS A CHANCE TO GET DOWN TO THE SURFACE!
SNAP'S RIGHT--WE CAN'T LET L'ULO'S SACRIFICE BE IN VAIN.
DON'T WORRY, KARÉ. I'M NOT GONNA LET UP. I'LL FIGHT RIGHT UNTIL THE END.
AND I'M TAKING SOME OF 'EM WITH ME.
WAIT...I'M DETECTING INCOMING SHIPS. THEY JUST DROPPED OUT OF HYPERSPACE. MAYBE...MAYBE THE RESISTANCE SENT REINFORCE-MENTS.
WITH OUR LUCK, LOVE? IT'LL PROBABLY BE THE FIRST ORDER.

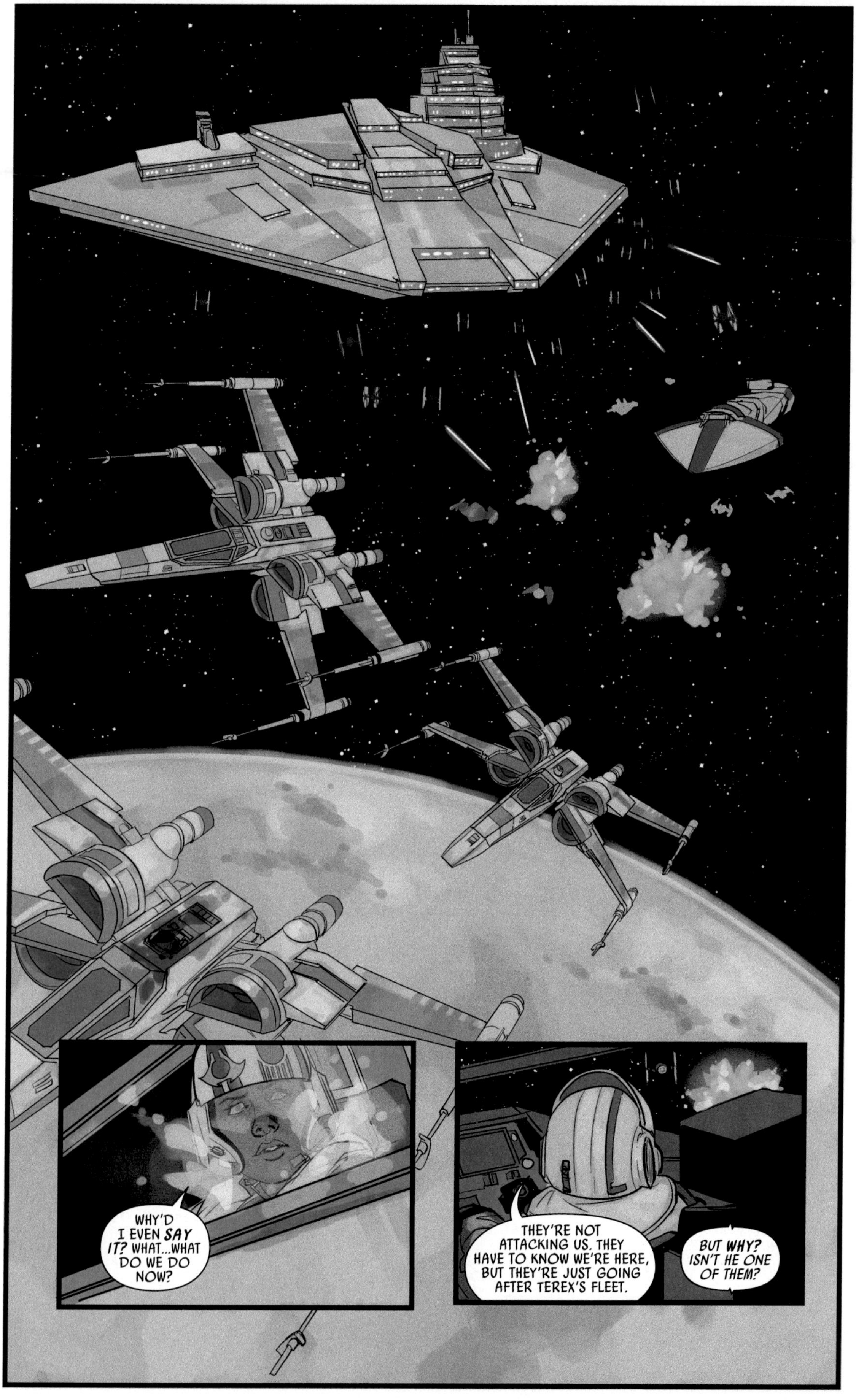

WHY'D I EVEN SAY IT? WHAT...WHAT DO WE DO NOW?
THEY'RE NOT ATTACKING US. THEY HAVE TO KNOW WE'RE HERE, BUT THEY'RE JUST GOING AFTER TEREX'S FLEET.
BUT WHY? ISN'T HE ONE OF THEM?

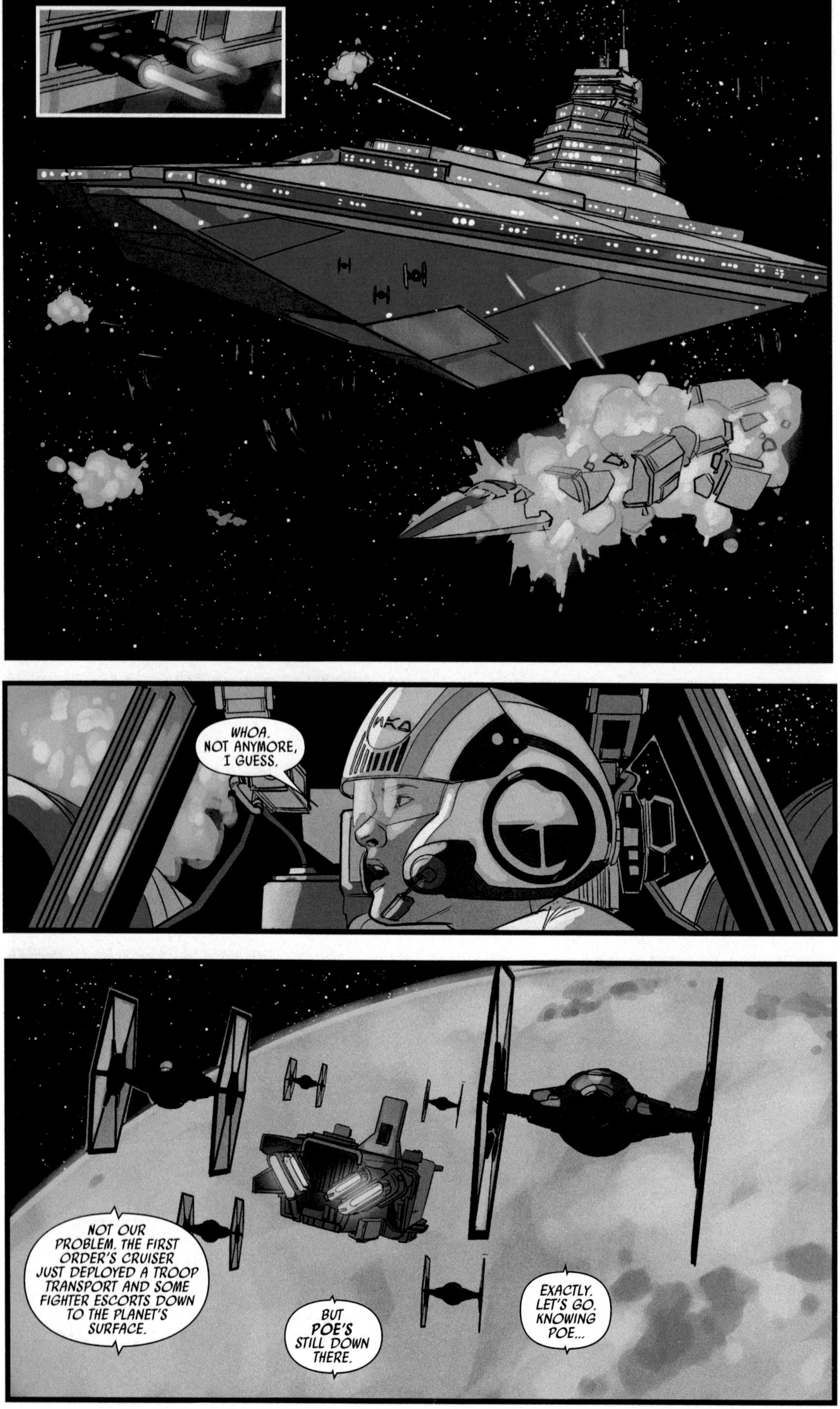
WHOA. NOT ANYMORE, I GUESS.
NOT OUR PROBLEM. THE FIRST ORDER'S CRUISER JUST DEPLOYED A TROOP TRANSPORT AND SOME FIGHTER ESCORTS DOWN TO THE PLANET'S SURFACE.
BUT POE'S STILL DOWN THERE.
EXACTLY. LET'S GO. KNOWING POE...

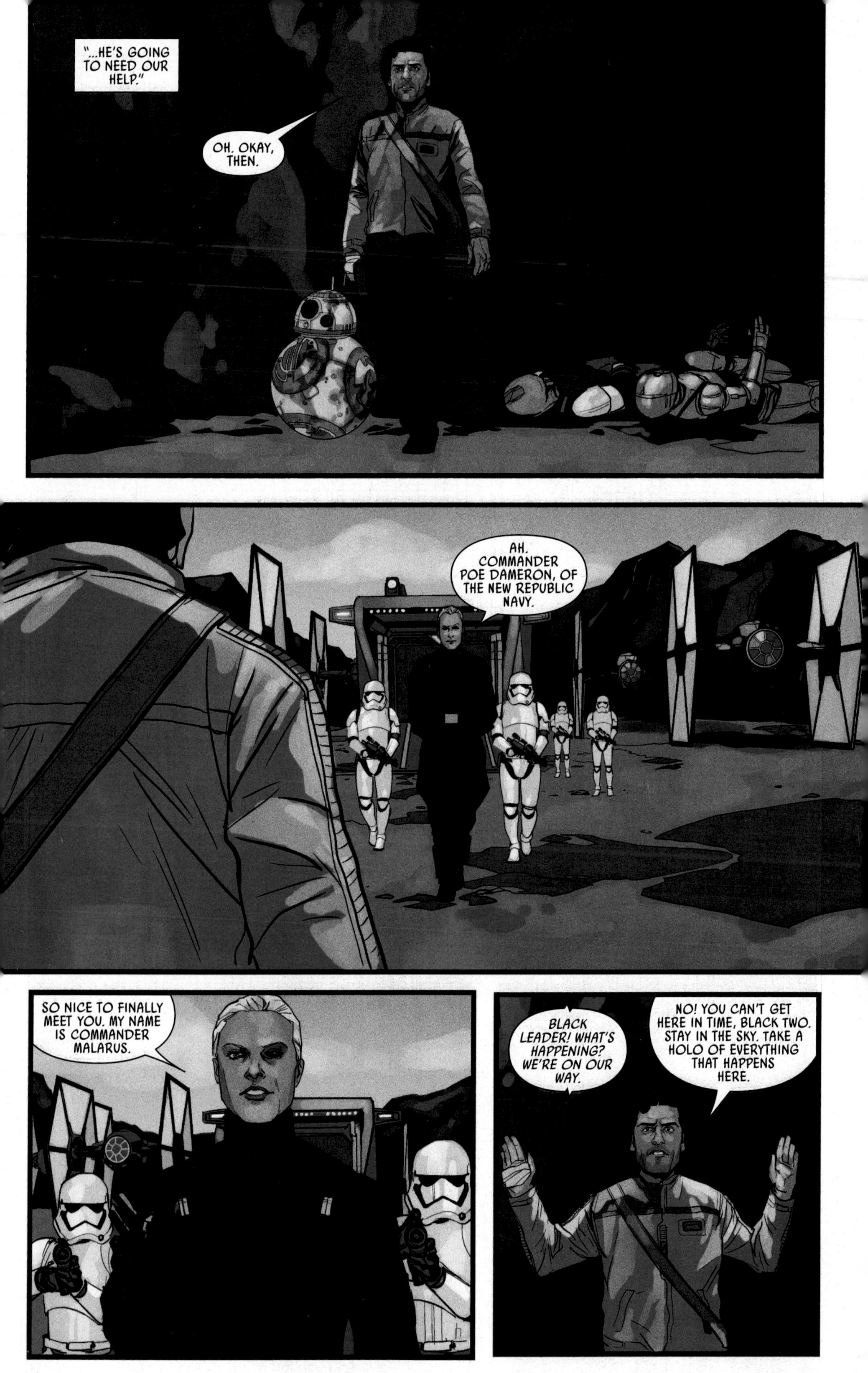
"...HE'S GOING TO NEED OUR HELP."
OH. OKAY, THEN.
AH. COMMANDER POE DAMERON, OF THE NEW REPUBLIC NAVY.
SO NICE TO FINALLY MEET YOU. MY NAME IS COMMANDER MALARUS.
BLACK LEADER! WHAT'S HAPPENING? WE'RE ON OUR WAY.
NO! YOU CAN'T GET HERE IN TIME, BLACK TWO. STAY IN THE SKY. TAKE A HOLO OF EVERYTHING THAT HAPPENS HERE.

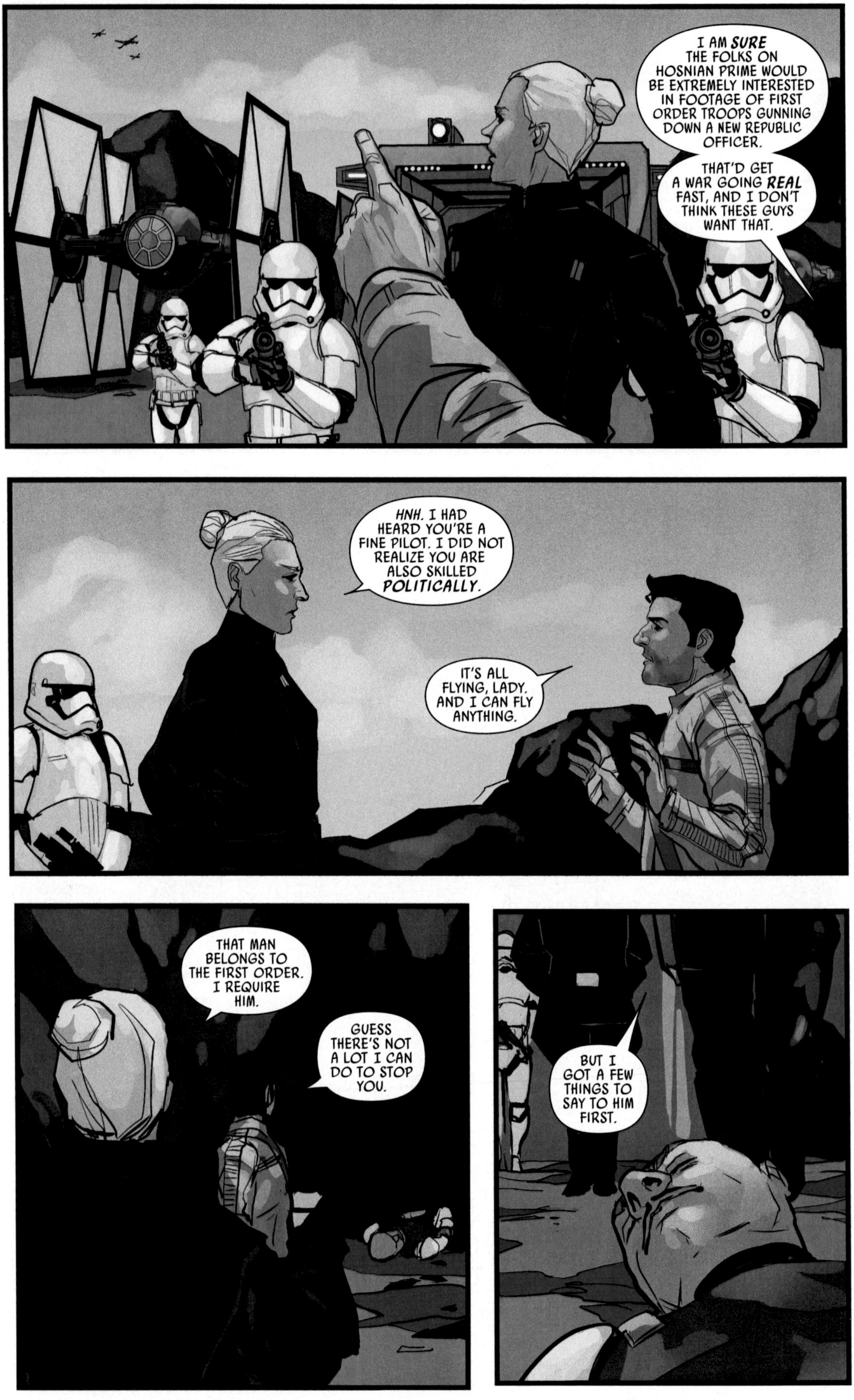
I AM SURE THE FOLKS ON HOSNIAN PRIME WOULD BE EXTREMELY INTERESTED IN FOOTAGE OF FIRST ORDER TROOPS GUNNING DOWN A NEW REPUBLIC OFFICER.
THAT'D GET A WAR GOING REAL FAST, AND I DON'T THINK THESE GUYS WANT THAT.
HNH. I HAD HEARD YOU'RE A FINE PILOT. I DID NOT REALIZE YOU ARE ALSO SKILLED POLITICALLY.
IT'S ALL FLYING, LADY. AND I CAN FLY ANYTHING.
THAT MAN BELONGS TO THE FIRST ORDER. I REQUIRE HIM.
GUESS THERE'S NOT A LOT I CAN DO TO STOP YOU.
BUT I GOT A FEW THINGS TO SAY TO HIM FIRST.

BLACK TWO, IF YOU'RE HERE, IT MEANS YOU GOT PAST TEREX'S FLEET, RIGHT?

TEREX'S FLEET IS *GONE*. EVERY SHIP. WE DID OUR PART, BUT THEN THE FIRST ORDER SHOWED UP AND FINISHED THEM OFF.

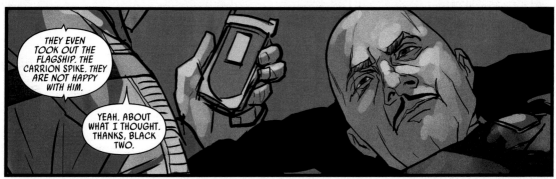

THEY EVEN TOOK OUT THE FLAGSHIP. THE *CARRION SPIKE*. THEY ARE NOT HAPPY WITH HIM.

YEAH. ABOUT WHAT I THOUGHT. THANKS, BLACK TWO.

I CAN SEE ONLY *THREE* FIGHTERS IN THE AIR, DAMERON, WHEN THERE SHOULD BE FOUR. YOU *LOST* SOMEONE TODAY.

YEAH. SAW THAT, TOO. I THINK IT WAS MY FRIEND L'ULO. STILL PROCESSING THAT. YOU AND I BOTH LOST, TEREX. NO DOUBT IN MY MIND.

BUT THERE'S A DIFFERENCE BETWEEN US. I LOST A FRIEND, BUT YOU LOST PRETTY MUCH *EVERYTHING*. AND WHEN I GIVE YOU TO THE FIRST ORDER, I BET THEY'LL TAKE THE REST.

YOUR FIGHT IS *OVER*.

MINE'S JUST GETTING STARTED.

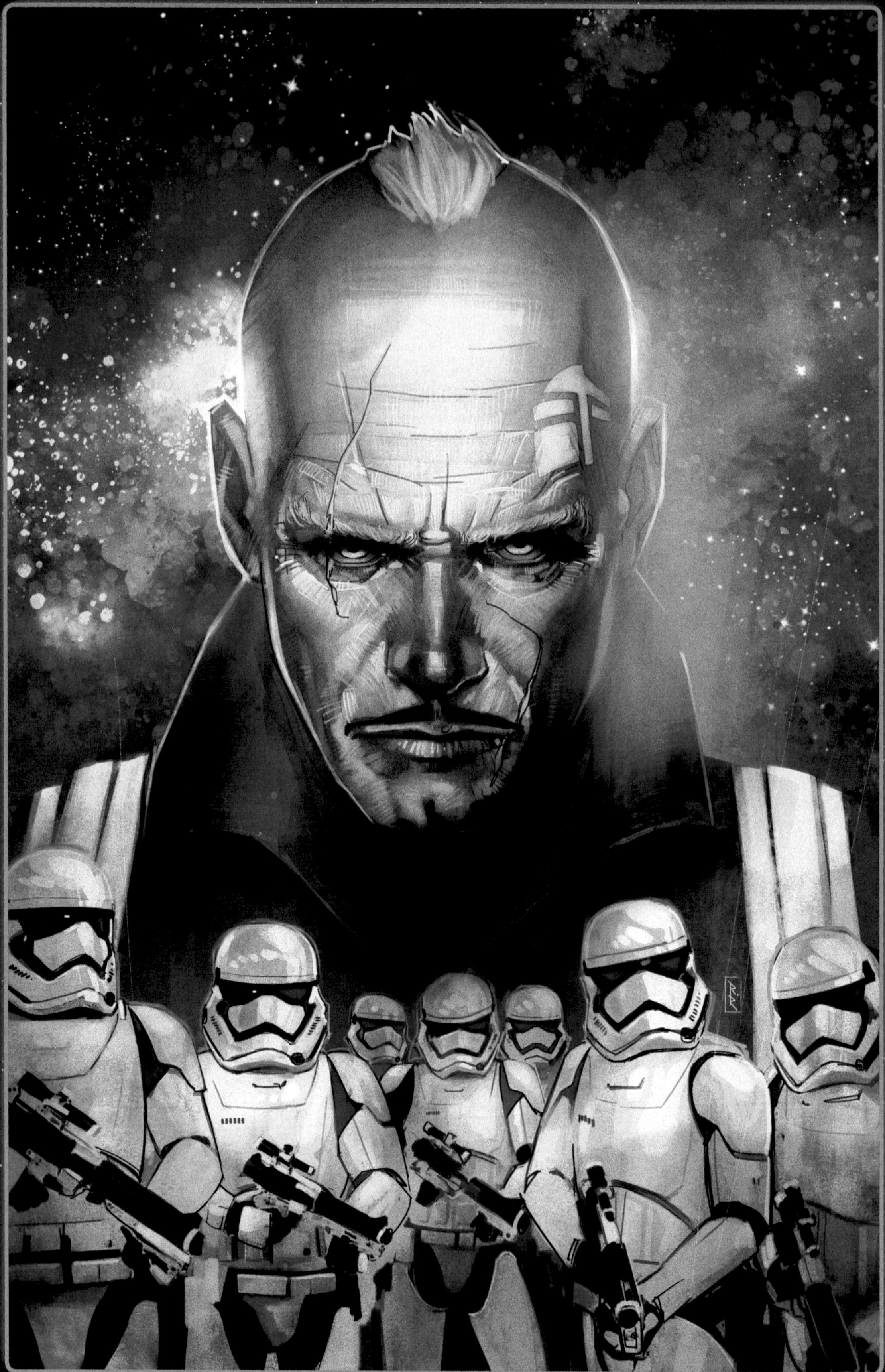

STAR WARS: POE DAMERON 8
VARIANT BY ROD REIS

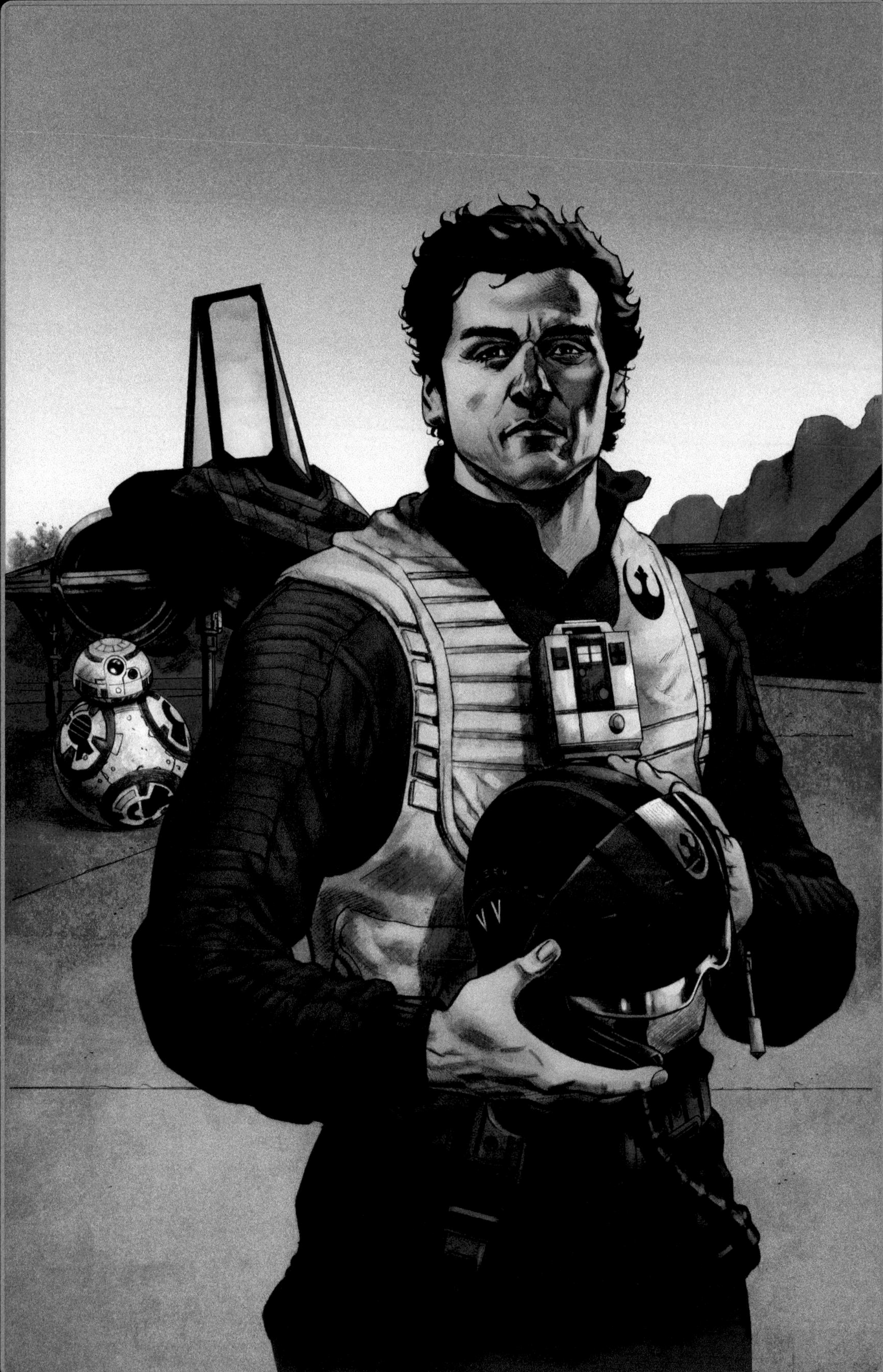

STAR WARS: POE DAMERON 9
VARIANT BY MIKE HAWTHORNE

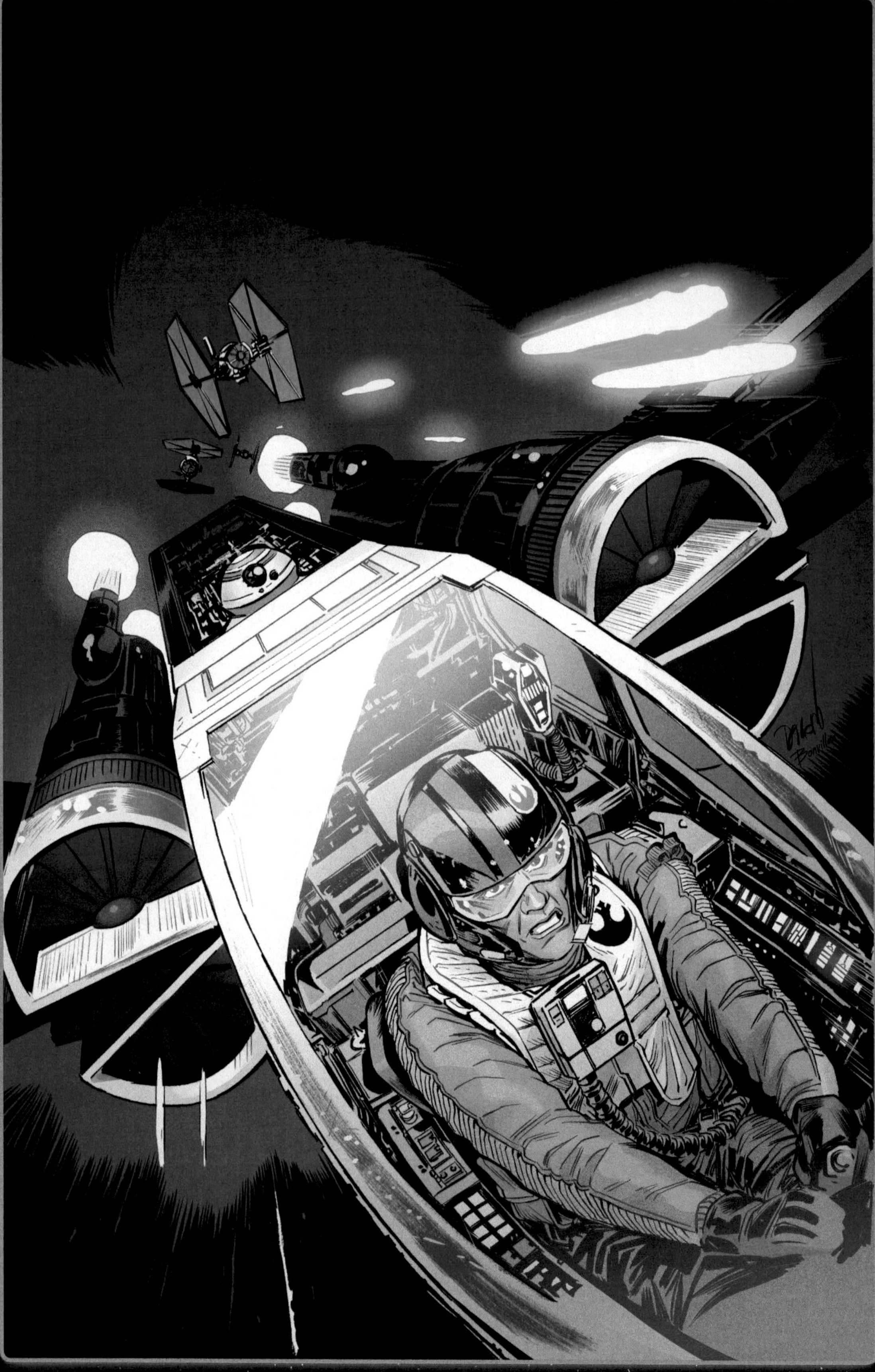

STAR WARS: POE DAMERON 10
VARIANT BY DANILO BEYRUTH & TAMRA BONVILLAIN

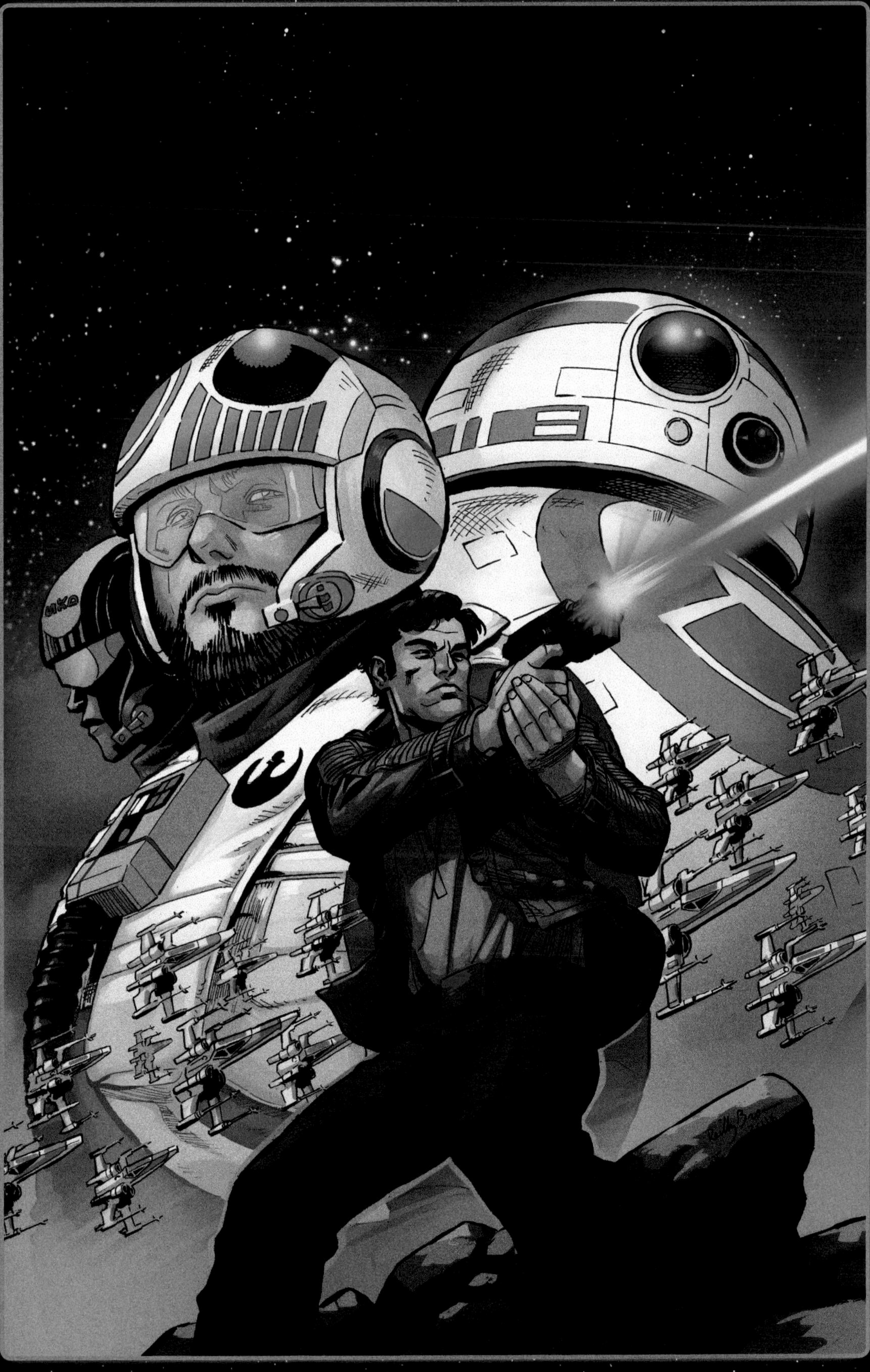

STAR WARS: POE DAMERON 11
VARIANT BY REILLY BROWN & JIM CHARALAMPIDIS

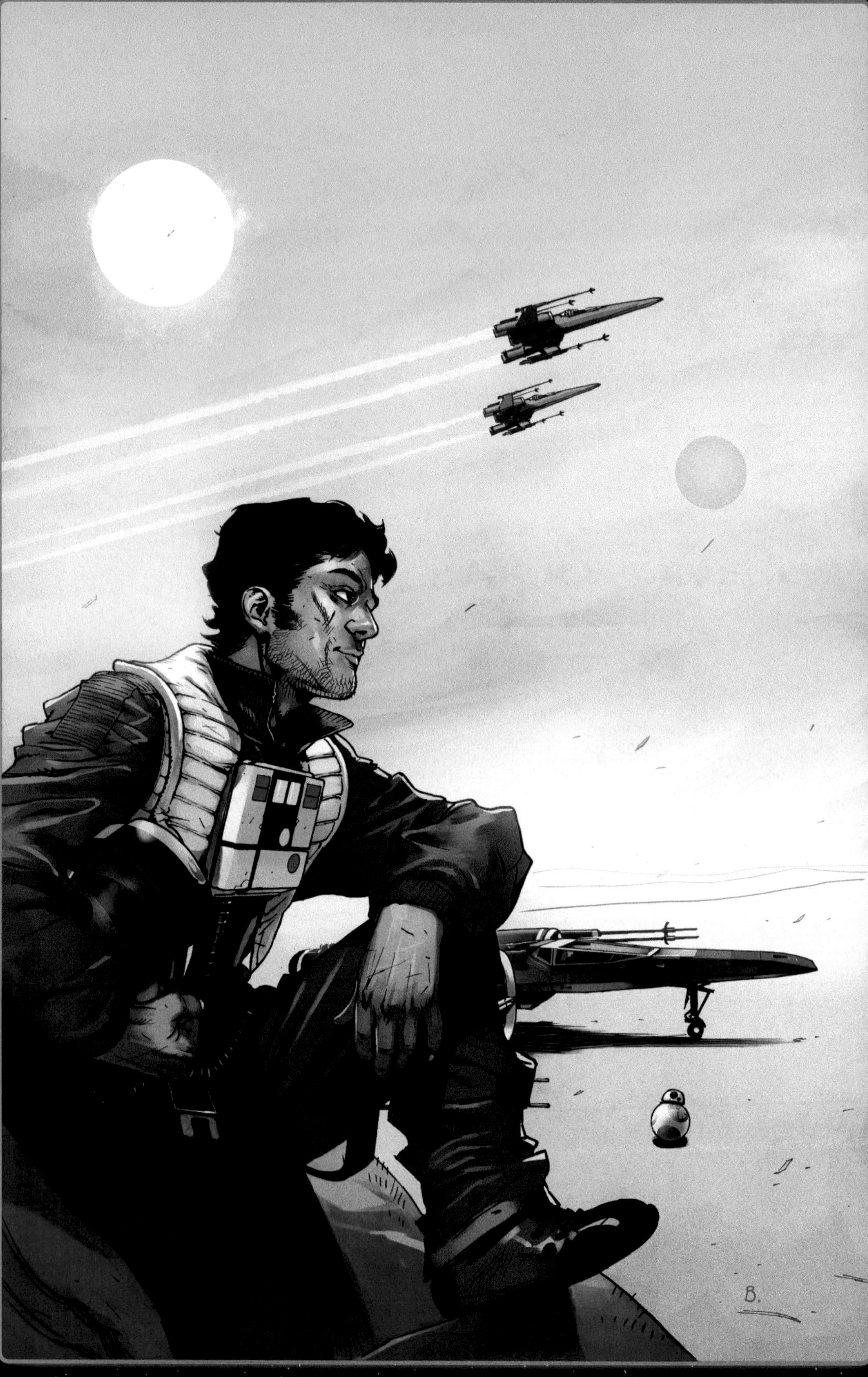
B.

STAR WARS: POE DAMERON 12
VARIANT BY BENGAL

WHAT IS A PRINCESS WITHOUT A WORLD?

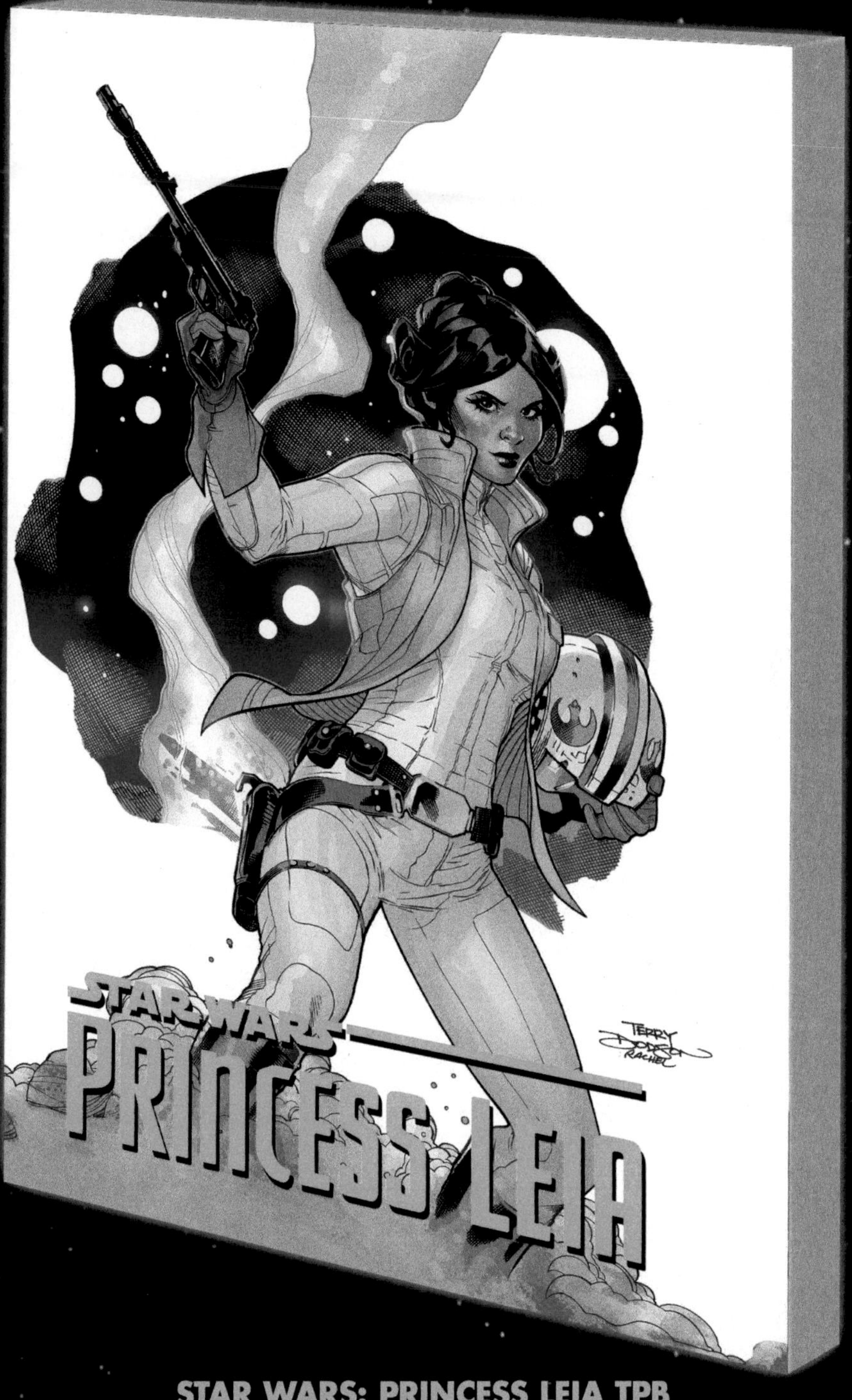

STAR WARS
PRINCESS LEIA
TERRY DODSON RACHEL

STAR WARS: PRINCESS LEIA TPB

978-0-7851-9317-3

ON SALE NOW!

MARVEL Disney LUCASFILM

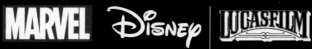

CHARACTERS YOU KNOW.
STORIES YOU DON'T.

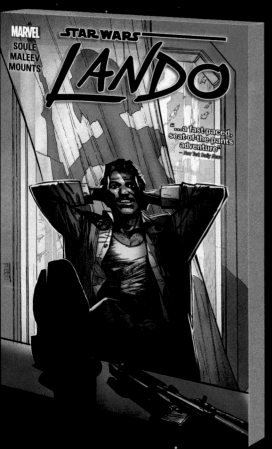
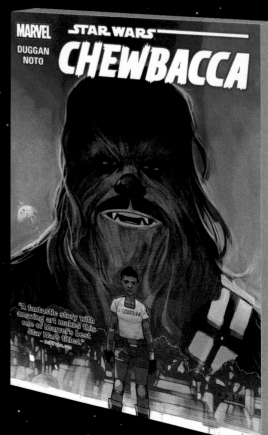

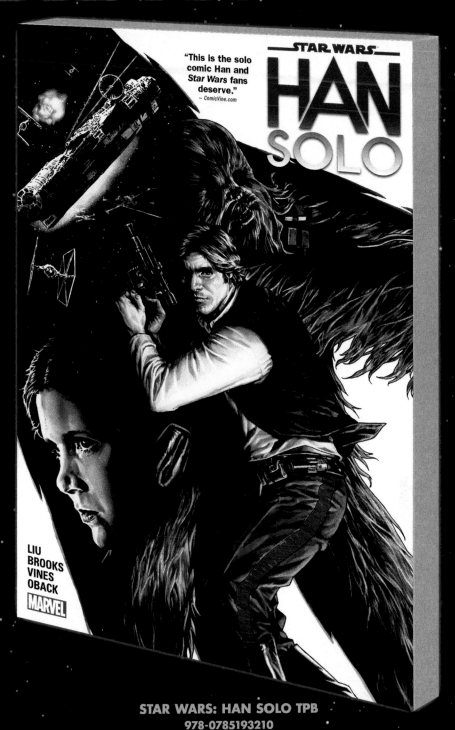

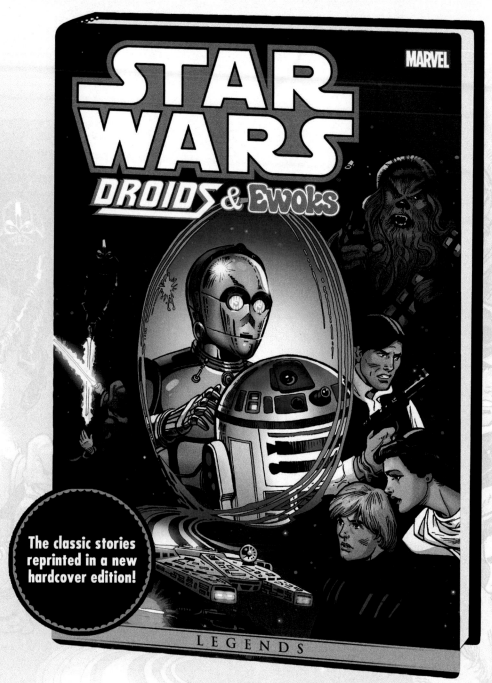

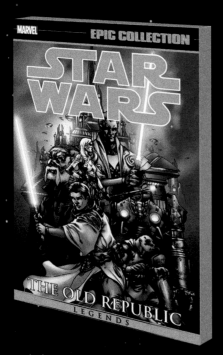
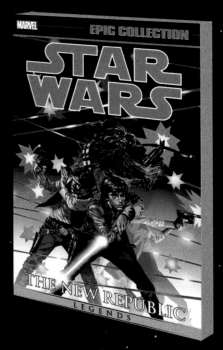
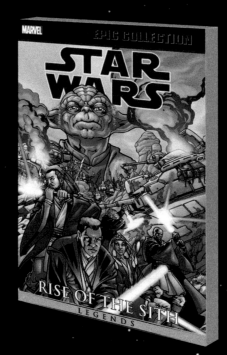

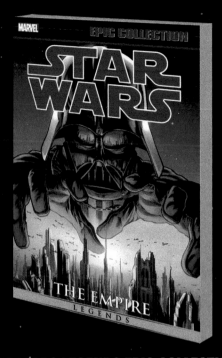

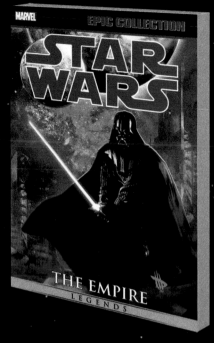

**STAR WARS LEGENDS EPIC COLLECTION:
THE EMPIRE VOL. 1 TPB**

JAN150884 • $34.99

**STAR WARS LEGENDS EPIC COLLECTION:
THE EMPIRE VOL. 2 TPB**

AUG150914 • $39.99

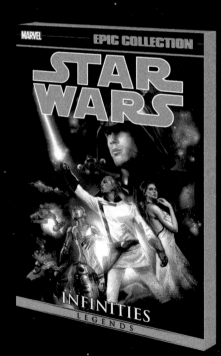

**STAR WARS LEGENDS EPIC COLLECTION:
INFINITIES TPB**

SEP150880 • $39.99

RETURN TO THE ORIGINAL MARVEL YEARS WITH THESE DELUXE CLASSIC COLLECTIONS!

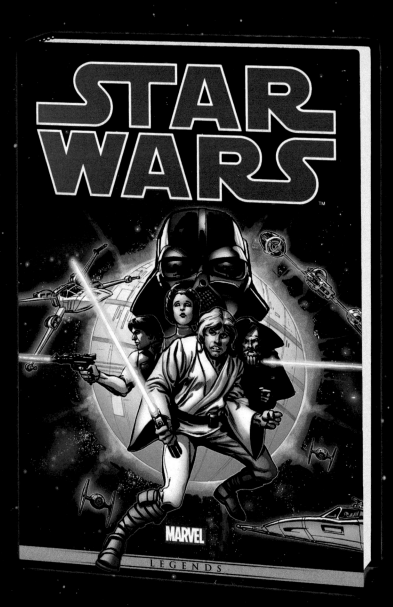

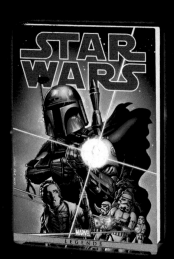

**STAR WARS:
THE ORIGINAL MARVEL YEARS
OMNIBUS VOL. 2
978-0-7851-9342-5**

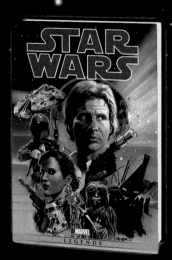

**STAR WARS: THE ORIGINAL MARVEL YEARS
OMNIBUS VOL. 1
978-0-7851-9106-3**

**STAR WARS:
THE ORIGINAL MARVEL YEARS
OMNIBUS VOL. 3
978-0-7851-9346-3**

AVAILABLE NOW WHEREVER BOOKS ARE SOLD